T0259911

Web Programming with PHP and MySQL

Max Bramer

Web Programming with PHP and MySQL

A Practical Guide

Max Bramer
School of Computing
University of Portsmouth
Portsmouth, UK

ISBN 978-3-319-22658-3 ISBN 978-3-319-22659-0 (eBook)
DOI 10.1007/978-3-319-22659-0

Library of Congress Control Number: 2015954953

Springer Cham Heidelberg New York Dordrecht London

Printed on acid-free paper

Springer International Publishing AG Switzerland is part of Springer Science+Business Media (www.springer.com)

Contents

Chapter 1
Introduction

Chapter Aims

After reading this chapter you should be able to:

- understand the value of using the PHP language to enable non-static information to be included on webpages, especially information retrieved from a relational database using the popular database query language MySQL
- understand how a web browser processes an HTML file and how PHP files are processed
- check that your web server is able to run PHP scripts
- understand how a valuable improvement to a webpage can sometimes be made using only a single line of PHP.

PHP is a programming language designed for the age of the World Wide Web. Originally all web pages were written using HTML (HyperText Markup Language). HTML was (and is) a language that enables information to be displayed over the Internet by a standard piece of software, known as a web browser, in a very flexible way. It was developed by the British scientist Tim Berners-Lee in the early 1990s and the rest is very well-known history.

Freely available web browsers and web page authoring tools combined with broadband telephone connections in most offices and many homes, the availability of WiFi wireless internet connections, high-powered search engines, etc. has made the WWW one of the most influential (although almost entirely unpredicted) developments of the late twentieth and early twenty-first centuries, providing information at zero or minimal cost worldwide to businesses, individuals in the home and travellers using mobile devices. Increasingly the web is used as the medium of choice for buying (or often just downloading free of charge) music, books and films as well as for booking holidays and buying goods.

M. Bramer, *Web Programming with PHP and MySQL*,
DOI 10.1007/978-3-319-22659-0_1

The Erewhon Society

Welcome to our home page

Today is Tuesday

Our next meeting is on December 12th at the usual venue

Fig. 1.1 A simple webpage

The range of applications is too wide and too well-known to need labouring here and will in any case expand yet further as time goes by. However for many applications basic HTML is not enough.

Figure 1.1 illustrates the problem. It is a very short and simple text-based page, but typical of many millions of others. It shows the (very simple) home page for an imaginary organisation, the Erewhon Society.[1]

The problem with such a webpage is that it is the same every time it is seen and for all possible users. The millionth time it is viewed it will look just the same as the first time (we will ignore possible slight incompatibilities between different web browsers). Every detail of its content and layout is as specified by the writer of the HTML file. We will call this a *static webpage*.

We have to admit that for a very large number of webpages none of this is a problem at all. However, there are at least three reasons why for some purposes it may not be satisfactory.

(1) We may wish to include information that varies from one viewing of a web page to another, e.g. the current date and time.
(2) The user may wish to provide information for a web page to use, e.g. he or she may wish to specify a location and a range of prices for which a list of holidays should be displayed or the name of an author for which a list of available books should be displayed.
(3) We may wish to include information that varies from one user to another, e.g. details of holidays or aeroplane flights booked or a household account with an energy provider, or that changes frequently, such as the prices of shares owned by an investor in a stock market.

Requirements (1) and (2) cannot be met by HTML alone. Requirement (3) could be met provided the writer of the HTML file could be persuaded to update it with new share prices, perhaps several hundred or even several thousand times a day. It would obviously be far more convenient if the file could be left unaltered but information such as current prices could somehow be extracted automatically from a database and inserted in the right place when the corresponding webpage was displayed.

[1] To be more accurate, it is meant to be an imaginary organisation. If it turns out to be a real one, not yet known to our search engine, we apologise in advance for any misrepresentation.

This can certainly be done and is done every day by the well-known e-commerce websites and many others, but it cannot be done using HTML alone. It needs augmenting with facilities to create, maintain and search databases and to customise the pages displayed to the needs of individual users. PHP is one of a number of programming languages that have been developed to work with HTML to give this considerably enhanced functionality. Compared with many other computer programming languages it is easy to use and makes building even quite elaborate applications straightforward to do.

Using PHP extends the facilities available in HTML considerably, especially when used in conjunction with a database query language such as MySQL. Web pages are still written in HTML but parts of the HTML are created automatically from PHP 'insertions' in the HTML code by a special program known as the PHP 'interpreter'. This is located on the web server, which is why PHP is called a *server-side* programming language. The PHP programmer needs no special software on his or her PC. The user of a page written with PHP needs just a standard web browser and will generally be entirely unaware that a page was not originally written in HTML – except that it will often be possible to do more with it.

As an example, a travel company may wish to advertise 500 different holiday locations. It could do this by writing 500 different web pages, one per location, but this would be very tedious to do and the pages would inevitably all have common features, such as the name of the company, a hyperlink to a booking form, etc. Alternatively the company could write one 'generic' web page, giving its name, address, etc., which displays the information about one of 500 locations taken from a database depending on options selected by the user. This latter option is clearly far more attractive to the company and storing the information in a database will probably make it far easier to provide the user with good search facilities.

This book is about using PHP to enhance the functionality of webpages, especially but not exclusively by providing facilities to create, maintain and interrogate databases. PHP is not the only programming language that can be used with HTML and MySQL is not the only database query language, but this combination is one of the most popular and widely available. PHP can also be used very effectively without MySQL to give a similar effect to having a database available using merely a plain text file on the server as will be illustrated in Chap. 7. PHP is easy to use and has many powerful features. The language was invented by Rasmus Lerdorf in 1994 as an aid to maintaining his personal webpage. It has since expanded into a very powerful general-purpose programming language. The name PHP originally stood for Personal Home Page, but we are now told that PHP stands for 'PHP: Hypertext Preprocessor'.

A note on terminology: Programs written in PHP or similar languages are generally called *scripts* rather than programs and the languages are generally called *scripting languages* rather than *programming languages*. Those familiar with other languages will soon realise that PHP is not just a programming language in the standard usage of the term but a very well-designed and powerful one, which has several unusual features. In this book we will use the terms 'program' and 'script' interchangeably. For the benefit of those readers who know the difference, PHP is an interpreted language not a compiled one.

This book is about PHP and its use with the MySQL[2] language for manipulating relational databases. The latter can be used in a flexible way via a PHP script. It is not a book about creating static web pages in HTML. Readers are expected already to be reasonably familiar with the latter. Section 19.6 gives basic information about the most important HTML tags.

1.1 How a Web Browser Processes an HTML File

An HTML file corresponding to the webpage shown as Fig. 1.1 is given in Fig. 1.2 below.

When a user points his or her web browser to an HTML file stored on a web server, a sequence of events occurs that is approximately as follows. The web server passes the contents of the file as a stream of characters to the web browser. As long as a sequence of consecutive characters received does not form an HTML tag such as <b>, </b> or <p>, the browser replaces any consecutive combination of newline characters, tabs and spaces by a single space and outputs the resulting text to the user's screen. If a number of consecutive characters received forms a tag, the action taken by the browser depends on which tag it is. If a <p> tag is received the browser outputs two newline characters to take the screen output to a new paragraph. If a <br> tag is received a single newline character is output. If a <b> (i.e. a 'start bold') tag is received the browser outputs all further characters in bold type until the next </b> ('end bold') tag is reached, etc.

In the case of the HTML file given in Fig. 1.2, the browser outputs the webpage shown in Fig. 1.1 to the user's screen.

```
<html>
<head>
<title>The Erewhon Society</title>
</head>
<body>
The Erewhon Society<p>
Welcome to our home page<p>
<p>Today is Tuesday</p>
<p>Our next meeting is on December 12th at the usual venue</p>
</body>
</html>
```

Fig. 1.2 HTML file corresponding to webpage shown as Fig. 1.1

[2] MySQL is pronounced my-ess-cue-ell.

1.2 Notation

It is important to be able to distinguish between an HTML file, which generally will have one or more HTML markup tags such as <html> or <b>, and a webpage, which has no tags but will often have effects such as bold and italic text, tables and hyperlinks. *The convention that will be used throughout this book is that lines of HTML or PHP will be enclosed in a regular text box with a standard single-thickness border. The words, images, etc. that would appear in the web browser are displayed in a box with a triple-thickness border.*

1.3 Creating an HTML File

It is assumed that as well as knowing at least the basics of HTML you are able to create an HTML file as a plain text file. There are two main ways of doing this. The first and most obvious is just to type the HTML code line-by-line into a text editor such as WordPad and then save it as a text file. The second is to use a visual authoring tool such as Dreamweaver, which enables you to indicate passages of bold, italic, etc. using a mouse in the same way as with a word processor and then save your work in the form of an HTML text file with the correct HTML mark up tags, <b> for 'start bold', </b> for 'end bold', etc., inserted for you.

For HTML files that are more than trivial, for example anything involving tables (writing the code for which is tedious and error-prone in HTML), the latter approach is strongly recommended. If you are familiar with that approach and would prefer not to have to learn much about the minutiae of HTML, the good news is that a little knowledge will go a long way. You can create a very complex HTML file using a visual authoring tool, perhaps one involving multiple fonts, colours, tables, images, etc. and then add special – but crucial – effects such as reading client information from a database, just by making a small PHP insertion into your HTML code at the right place. You just need to know enough HTML to locate that place; there is no need to know what all the rest of the HTML means in detail. The examples in this book will make it clear how this is done.

1.4 How PHP Files Are Processed

It is conventional for an HTML file to be given a name with the file extension htm or html, e.g. mypage1.htm. However most (if not all) browsers will accept any (reasonable) extension, e.g. mypage1.xyz. If the file extension chosen is php we will call the file a *PHP file* instead of an HTML file. Having a file name with extension php enables a file to be processed by the PHP interpreter (on the server) as well as the user's web browser. A PHP file can contain any of the following:

- Nothing but HTML (i.e. it is just an HTML file with a php file extension). This is unusual but possible.
- A single PHP script with no HTML.
- One or more (generally short) PHP scripts, which can be placed anywhere in the file, including at the beginning and/or at the end, the remainder of the file being HTML. Such short scripts are often called *scripting blocks*.

  Each PHP scripting block begins with the five-character combination
  <?php
  and ends with the two-character combination
  ?>
  These are called the *opening PHP tag* and the *closing PHP tag*, respectively.

The effect of pointing a web browser at an HTML file has been explained previously. When a web browser points to a PHP file, the file contents are assumed to be HTML and the same sequence of actions is performed as before. However if the web server finds an opening PHP tag then rather than sending the character stream to the web browser as usual it sends everything from the opening PHP tag to the next closing PHP tag to the PHP interpreter (which is located on the server). The PHP interpreter treats everything between the tags as a sequence of PHP statements (also called instructions) and processes them one by one. (This is called 'executing the script' or 'executing the statements'.)

The point of doing this is to achieve either or both of the following.

(1) Usually (but not invariably) a PHP script will include one or more instructions to send a string of characters to the web browser. If there are two such statements in a scripting block and executing them causes the two strings of characters

    Hello world!<p>
    and
    My name is John Smith

    to be output, the effect is exactly the same as far as the web browser is concerned as if the PHP scripting block were replaced by the HTML characters

Hello world!<p>My name is John Smith

(2) For most (but not all) scripts, executing the PHP statements will cause a number of other actions to take place, for example values may be calculated and compared, with the output produced depending on the values calculated or the results of the comparisons. As well as or instead of this, executing a script may cause (amongst other possibilities) information to be read from or written to a database, text files to be created, read or deleted on the server, emails to be sent or file protections on the server to be changed from 'read only' to 'read/write' or vice versa. Such actions are often referred to by the slightly dismissive term 'side effects', but in some cases may be much more important than the output (if

any) that is sent to the web browser. They are clearly all impossible with a static webpage.

When the PHP interpreter has completed its task of executing the PHP statements in the script, the web server resumes processing what is once again assumed to be HTML, sending characters to the web browser in the usual way until any further opening PHP tag is encountered.

The effect of all this is to insert pieces of HTML (frequently whole lines, but sometimes just a few characters) into a webpage displayed on the user's screen that were not present in the HTML part of the PHP file stored on the server. This is not apparent to the user of the web browser who has no way of knowing that the output was not all produced by a static webpage written solely in HTML, except that such a file would be very unlikely to include today's date or details of say the user's holiday preferences or favourite author. The user will also be entirely unaware that PHP has been used and needs no special software on his or her computer to make it happen. Everything that is needed is installed on the web server.

1.5 Exercise: The Erewhon Society's Home Page

This exercise will enable you to check that your web server is able to run PHP scripts and will illustrate how a valuable improvement to a web page can be made using only a single line of PHP.

As an experiment we would like you to type the contents of Fig. 1.2 above into your favourite text editor, save it with the name erewhon.htm and upload it to your web server. When doing this be careful to use a text editor, such as WordPad, not a Word Processor, such as Microsoft Word.

Now point your web browser to the erewhon.htm file on your server. You should see a display identical to Fig. 1.1 above.

Assuming that pointing your browser to the file erewhon.htm that you uploaded has produced the expected result, now rename your file erewhon.php on the server and point your web browser at the file named erewhon.php. The output to the web browser should be exactly the same as before.

We use the term *PHP file* for any file with extension 'php', even when (as here) it contains only HTML. So far we have not used any PHP of course, but we have established that a web page can be displayed from a file with extension 'php' as well as from files with the usual 'htm' and 'html' extensions. Most web browsers will accept almost anything as a file extension for an HTML file, but choosing to use the extension 'php' has the considerable advantage that we can now use the PHP language to enhance the flexibility of our web pages.

The usefulness of the Erewhon Society home page is rather lessened by the presence of the line

```
Today is Tuesday
```

Although undeniably true one day out of seven, this statement is very misleading on the other six. It would be far more useful for it to say whichever day of the week it really is.

Before showing how to do this we will change the code of erewhon.php to give exactly the same effect as before but now using a little PHP. Having done that the stage is set for us to change the page to insert something more useful.

We start by changing the PHP file erewhon.php to have slightly different (but functionally equivalent) contents.

We replace the HTML line

```
<p>Today is Tuesday</p>
```

by the one-statement PHP scripting block

```
<?php
print "<p>Today is Tuesday</p>\n";
?>
```

The Print statement will be explained in Chap. 3. At this point all you need to know is that it will send the characters enclosed in double quote symbols to the web browser.

If you now point your web browser to the file erewhon.php you should now see exactly the same output as before. However it is possible that you will instead see something like this.

```
The Erewhon Society

Welcome to our home page

\n"; ?>

Our next meeting is on December 12th at the usual venue
```

This would indicate that your web server does not have PHP installed.

Assuming that you do indeed have PHP installed, select the View Source (or equivalent) option from your browser's menu to see the HTML code. It should be identical to Fig. 1.2.

We are now finally ready to use PHP to do something a little more useful. We can improve the value of the information output to the user's screen by replacing the scripting block by

```
print "<p>Today is ".date("l F jS")."</p>\n";
```

Here the Print statement has been split into three parts joined by dots (called *concatenation operators*). Change your file erewhon.php accordingly and upload it to your web server.

Assuming that you are doing this on the penultimate day of the tenth month of the year and that this day is a Friday, pointing your browser at erewhon.php should now display the text

> The Erewhon Society
>
> Welcome to our home page
>
> Today is Friday October 30th
>
> Our next meeting is on December 12th at the usual venue.

The mysterious-looking item date("l F jS") is a call to a very useful system function named 'date' which uses the system clock to extract information about the date and/or time and returns it in a variety of possible formats. How to use it to produce output such as 'Friday October 30th' will be explained in Chap. 5.

1.6 About This Book

In this book a description of the main features of PHP and MySQL will be augmented by a series of examples chosen to clarify any difficult areas.

The first half of the book will cover the principal features of PHP. The second half will concentrate on the facilities available in MySQL and will illustrate how manipulating a relational database can be accomplished using a PHP script. A number of appendices will pull the technical information together for reference.

The longer examples in this book are all based on PHP scripts created by the author and used on live websites, but of course all the details have been changed. The main constraint is that of a published book with book-size pages and black and white printing. This has meant that most of the examples given are text based for reasons of space and readability, but there is no reason at all why PHP cannot be used with the most elaborate web pages imaginable to extend their functionality.

As well as knowing the basics of HTML and being able to create an HTML file in either of the ways given above, it will be assumed that you know how to upload pages to your web server, generally by using FTP or one of the variants that are available, in many cases free of charge.

If your organisation or the commercial web hosting company you use does not allow you to use PHP scripts on your web server together with at least one MySQL database our advice is to find a service provider that does. There are many companies that will provide you with both at very little (if any) extra cost.

Inevitably, there are different versions of PHP available, with new features being added with each new release. You are very likely to be using PHP 5 or possibly the older PHP 4. The examples in this book are designed to work in both versions and should still work in later versions of the language when they come out. They have all been checked using PHP version 5.6.12 with MySQL version 5.5.42.

Chapter Summary
This chapter introduces the PHP scripting language as a way of enhancing the functionality of webpages, especially by providing facilities to create, maintain and interrogate databases. It describes the way that a web browser processes an HTML file and how PHP files are processed. Finally an example is given to illustrate how an improvement to a webpage can sometimes be made using only a single line of PHP.

Chapter 2
PHP Fundamentals

Chapter Aims
After reading this chapter you should be able to:

- describe the basic structure of a PHP script or scripting block
- understand how a PHP file containing a mixture of HTML and PHP is processed
- discriminate between valid and invalid names for variables and functions
- explain the similarities and differences between a scalar variable and an array
- explain the differences between strings enclosed in single and double quotes and the use of escape sequences in strings
- explain the importance of system functions to programming in PHP

2.1 Structure of a PHP Script

As stated in the introduction, a PHP *scripting block* comprises a sequence of PHP statements (sometimes also called 'instructions') starting with an *opening PHP tag* <?php and ending with a *closing PHP tag* ?>. The letters php in the opening tag can be written in any combination of upper and lower case. This is a simple example of a PHP script comprising only a single statement.

```
<?php
print "Hello world!";
?>
```


M. Bramer, *Web Programming with PHP and MySQL*,
DOI 10.1007/978-3-319-22659-0_2

We will call any file stored on a web server that has a name with the extension 'php' a *PHP file*. However – and probably surprisingly – this name does not imply that the file comprises only a single PHP scripting block. It may do so, but it is also perfectly possible that only part of the file may be lines of PHP or there may be no PHP at all. This is considerably different from the normal situation with programming languages. If we refer to a program written in the language Java, say, we expect that the whole program will be written in that language. PHP is different.

It is certainly possible to develop a whole website as one or more large PHP files, generating web pages that link to one another. It is also possible that an entire website is written in HTML (or using some package that automatically generates HTML) with the exception of just one single line of PHP.

At one extreme, a PHP file can comprise just a single *PHP scripting block* (to be defined below) or at the opposite extreme solely lines of HTML.[1] More generally a PHP file can comprise a number of PHP statement blocks alternating with groups of lines of HTML. (The file can begin and end with either lines of HTML or a PHP statement block.) The only restriction on where a PHP scripting block can be placed in a PHP file is that it must not be inside another scripting block.

The term *PHP script* is often used as well as PHP scripting block. There is no difference as far as their working is concerned. The term 'script' seems more appropriate when a PHP file consists solely of lines of PHP and the term 'scripting block' seems more suitable when it contains only a few lines of PHP. We will use the two terms fairly interchangeably in this book.

2.1.1 Blank Lines and Layout

Blank lines in a PHP script are ignored altogether. PHP is also very liberal about the use of tabs and spaces within statements to improve the readability of a script. They can be placed anywhere that most people would be likely to consider reasonable, but not inside the names of variables, arrays or functions (all to be defined later) or inside system keywords such as 'Print'. It is probably easiest to experiment to find out what is permitted rather than memorise a precise specification. The examples in this book will help to illustrate what is considered reasonable usage.

2.1.2 Comments

Two types of comment are permitted in PHP scripts:

Single-line comments: Two consecutive slash characters (//) on a line indicate that those characters and everything that follows on the same line is to be treated as a

[1] In this extreme case there is no benefit in using the file extension php rather than htm or html.

comment and ignored. A single-line comment can alternatively begin with a hash (#) character.

Multi-line comments: Comments that go over more than one line are permitted. The character combinations /* and */ are used to signify the start and end, respectively, of a multi-line comment.

Thus the following is a valid scripting block.

```
<?php
$x=1;   // this is a comment


$y=2;

/* This is
a comment that
    goes over more than one line
*/

?>
```

In this book we will normally place the opening and closing PHP tags on separate lines and we recommend this as standard practice in the interests of clarity. However PHP is very flexible and we can choose whether to write even a small scripting block as a single line such as

```
<?php print "Hello world!"; ?>
```

or as two lines

```
<?php print "Hello world!";
?>
```

or in many other possible ways. As blank lines are ignored, another alternative would be

```
<?php
print "Hello world!";

?>
```

There must always be at least one space or new line after the opening PHP tag.

When showing just a few lines of PHP rather than an entire scripting block in this book we will often omit the opening and closing tags altogether to save space on the printed page.

Everything between the opening and closing PHP tags (apart from comments) is taken to be a sequence of PHP statements. Statements are often written one per line to aid legibility, but this is not essential.

Statements are generally terminated by semicolons. However some of the more complex statements may optionally also end in a 'statement group' enclosed in brace characters { }, as will be explained in Chap. 3.

2.2 How a 'Mixed' PHP File Is Processed

The effect of pointing the web browser to a PHP file with a mixture of HTML and PHP is to make the following sequence of events occur:

(a) If the file begins with HTML text, everything up to but not including the next <?php tag is passed to the browser unchanged and displayed on the user's screen in the usual way.
(b) Once a <?php tag is encountered everything between it and the next ?> tag is treated as a sequence of PHP statements. These are performed or *executed* one by one. This can have many possible effects, such as giving values to variables (this will be explained soon) and updating a database, but the only ones that directly affect the web browser are when a print statement[2] is executed. The resulting string of characters is passed to the web browser as if it had been entered as HTML.
(c) After the closing PHP tag is encountered any following lines are treated as HTML once again and are passed to the browser unaltered until any further opening PHP tag is found and so on.

Once this process is completed the web browser displays the HTML it has been given (including HTML generated by PHP) in the form of a webpage in the usual way.

2.3 PHP: Basic Components

In this chapter we will set out some of the fundamental language features of PHP. Most of it will come as no surprise at all to those who are experienced in other languages. As with all programming/scripting languages the basic building blocks are *constants* of a number of kinds and *variables* of different kinds which are used to store those constant values. An invaluable part of the language is pre-written

---

[2] Print statements in PHP have no connection with printing on paper. In early programming languages the word 'print' did have that meaning, but in more modern languages it has come to mean outputting to the user's screen. For PHP it simply means send a string of characters to the user's web browser, which will display it on the screen or otherwise depending on the contents.

system functions which make it easy to perform complex operations, such as calculating the square root of a number or updating a database.

This and the next few chapters will cover the main building blocks of PHP but in the interests of avoiding 'information overload' some important parts of the language will be deferred until later in the book when we can more easily illustrate why they are needed. Material from different parts of the book will be pulled together in Chap. 19 (Appendices).

This may be a good place to point out that this book is not envisaged as an encyclopaedic collection of every minute detail of this very elaborate language and some of the more obscure features are deliberately left out, especially one or two that anyone but an expert would be ill-advised to use, but we do aim to include enough information for you to construct a wide range of PHP scripts of your own and in later chapters to give you practical examples of how to do it.

2.4 Variables

A basic feature of all but the simplest scripts is the manipulation of one or more *variables*. A variable is a part of the computer's memory that can be used to store a value. A set of variables can be thought of as a set of boxes or pigeonholes, each labelled with the name of one of the variables.

In PHP the name of a variable must start with a dollar sign, which is followed by a sequence of one or more upper case letters, lower case letters, digits and/or underscores. The character immediately after the $ sign must not be a digit.

It is a matter of personal taste whether to use long and meaningful variable names such as $the_occupation_of_my_father (which are prone to typing errors), short but meaningless names such as $x, or something in between. In this book we will frequently use short names in the interest of saving space.

$yourname	$year	$forename	$age	$surname	$alpha
"John"	2099	"Mary"	27	"Smith"	true

This example represents six variables held in the computer's memory. The variable named $yourname has the value "John" and so on. Two of the variables have values that are numbers, three have values that are strings, such as "John", and one has a logical value *true*. These three types of constant value will be discussed in Sect. 2.5.

When a variable is given a value (or 'assigned a value') for the first time, a pigeonhole with its name is created and the value is entered. Subsequently the value in the pigeonhole may be replaced by a different value by another assignment (the previous value being destroyed). This can happen an unlimited number of times.

A variable such as $x can be given a value by an *assignment statement*[3] such as

[3] Assignment statements and the other statements described briefly in this section will be discussed in more detail in later sections.

```
$x="this is a string example";
```

or

```
$x=27.4;
```

or

```
$x=$x+100;
```

The = sign in an assignment statement should be read as 'is set to', so variable $x is set to the value 27.4, etc. Note that a variable can appear on both sides of an assignment, so the final example should be read as 'variable $x is set to the existing value of $x plus 100'.

Other ways of using a variable include the following:

The value of the variable can be sent to the web browser using a *print statement*, such as

```
print $x;
```

An *If statement* (often called a 'conditional') can be used to test the value of the variable with the action taken next depending on what value it has. For example[4]:

```
if ($x==1) print "You win!"; else print "You lose!";
```

2.4.1 Uninitialized Variables

If a script refers to a variable which has never been given a value, called an *uninitialized variable*, this does not cause an error to occur. If the context expects a numerical value it will be assumed that an uninitialized variable has the value zero. If a string value is needed it will be assumed to be "", i.e. a pair of double quotes with nothing inside them, which is called a *null string* or an *empty string*.

2.4.2 Variable Names: A Warning

Variable names are 'case-sensitive', so that $Surname is a different variable from $surname. It is very unwise to have two variables with names that are identical except for a change of case, which almost invites confusion. However you may

[4] The operator == (two 'equals' signs) is used here to test whether the value of variable $x is the constant 1. It is not to be confused with the = operator used in an assignment.

accidentally create two such variables by mistyping a lower case letter in upper case or vice versa. Unlike some other languages a PHP script does not include a list of all the variables that will be used in it, and there is no error created by trying to use the value of an uninitialized variable, so if a variable name is mistyped PHP will not recognise this as a mistake, with problems likely to result at a later stage. Errors caused by mistyping of this kind can be very difficult to spot.

2.4.3 Types of Variable

A variable that has a number as its value is called a *numeric variable*. A variable that has a string value is called a *string variable*, etc. Unlike many other languages the writer of a PHP script does not have to specify the type of each variable used. PHP recognises which type of variable it is using automatically. It is also permitted for a variable that has (say) a numeric value at one point to be assigned a value of another type, say string, subsequently.

This may all seem very reasonable or even obvious but many other languages place strong restrictions on the types of the variables used with the aim of making it harder to make errors. In practice the laudable aim of saving software writers from themselves often seems to be achievable only at the expense of making a language very cumbersome to use. There is an unavoidable trade-off between flexibility and the risk of making mistakes, which the present author would generally prefer to make on the side of flexibility.

2.4.4 Arrays

The variables described above are basic ones that hold a single value, sometimes called *scalar variables*. This is entirely satisfactory for most applications but PHP also has a 'structured' kind of variable called an *array*, which can store many values, using a single variable name.

Previously we suggested that variables are similar to pigeonholes, each of which can hold a value such as a number or a string. They might also be thought of as similar to the houses in a street, for example:

$yourname	$year	$forename	$age	$surname	$alpha
"John"	2099	"Mary"	27	"Smith"	true

It is fine to give variables individual names such as $yourname, $year, etc. if there are only a few, but what if there are dozens, hundreds or even thousands of them, especially ones we wish to relate together? We can draw inspiration from the way that houses in the same street are generally named. Although for a short street it may be preferable to give each house its own name, the most convenient approach beyond a certain size is generally to give the street as a whole a name (e.g. 'High

Street') and then number the houses within it 1 High Street, 2 High Street, 3 High Street, etc.

PHP and many other languages allow related variables to be grouped together in a similar way to the houses in a street, but in PHP it is usual for the numbering to begin at zero (don't ask why!). For example here is an array $info which can hold six separate values.

$info[0]	$info[1]	$info[2]	$info[3]	$info[4]	$info[5]
−8.3	"dog"	27	"cat"	true	647.142

The individual components of an array are known as *array elements*. Array elements are written in a special notation using square brackets, e.g. $info[2]. The first (left-most) element is called $info[0], the next is $info[1], etc. and so on.

Here there are six array elements named from $info[0] to $info[5], stored in a single array named $info. The names of arrays follow the same rules as the names of variables (as arrays are a type of variable). Like the names of other variables, the names of arrays are case-sensitive.

We can use an array element in an assignment statement (and most other PHP statements) in just the same way as a variable. If we want to give an array element a value, we write, e.g.

```
$info[4]="this is an example";
```

or

```
$info[4]=27.3;
```

depending on whether the value is a string or a number.

If we want to use the value of an array element, we write, say

```
$x=$info[4];
```

or

```
$new[7]=$info[4]+2;
```

A PHP script can use a mixture of any number of arrays and any number of (scalar) variables. However they must have different names. A sequence of statements such as

```
$x=99;
$x[3]=88;
```

will produce an error message.

Although arrays are a kind of variable, from now on we will normally use the term 'variable' to refer to a scalar variable, which can be used to store only a single value at any time. This is because arrays are different in many respects from (scalar) variables. The individual elements of an array are far more similar to (scalar) variables. As a general principle an array element, but not an entire array, can be used anywhere in a script that a scalar variable can.

2.4.5 *Variable Variables*

A very unusual feature of PHP is the 'variable variable', which takes the value of a variable and treats it as the name of a variable. To explain what this means, suppose that variable $myvar has the value "val" and $val has the value 27.3. What is the value of $$myvar?

In most languages this question would be meaningless. Writing $$myvar would simply generate an error message. However in PHP the double $ sign has a special meaning. $myvar has value "val" so $$myvar has the value of variable $val, i.e. 27.3.

This facility is probably not used very often but it can be useful occasionally.

In reading a PHP script it is easy to overlook the double dollar sign. To make a script easier to read $$myvar can also be written using a pair of braces as ${$myvar}.

The $$ notation can also be used when there is an array element involved. However there is a possible ambiguity. Should $$abc[6] mean the value of the variable the name of which is held in $abc[6] or should it mean element 6 of the array $$abc?

We can distinguish between the two cases by using braces.

- If $abc[6] is "xyz" and $xyz is "alpha" the value of ${$abc[6]} is alpha. (The notation $$abc[6] would also be interpreted as meaning alpha.)
- If $pqr is "myarray" and $myarray[6] is 123.97 the value of ${$pqr}[6] is 123.97.

2.5 Constants

The principal types of constant available in PHP are numbers, string constants (often simply called *strings*) and logical values.

2.5.1 *Numbers*

Examples of numbers in PHP are: 27, −8 and 57.36 and 7.6E−4

The last of these uses *exponent notation*. It stands for $7.6*10^{-4}$. The letter E can be written in lower case if preferred, so −8e5 is also a valid number standing for $-8*10^5$.

It is also possible to use numbers written in binary, octal or hexadecimal notation, but these will not be discussed in this book.

2.5.2 Strings

An example of a string constant is "this is a piece of text".

In PHP, strings can be enclosed in either single quotes, e.g. 'Hello World' or double quotes, e.g. "Hello World". (Note that the " character in the latter – called a *double quote* – is a single character on the keyboard.) For most strings it makes no difference which of the two types of enclosing quote is used, as long as the opening and closing quotes are the same. However in other cases there can be a considerable difference.

(i) *Single Quotes*

When a string is enclosed in single quotes its contents are exactly what they appear to be, with just two exceptions. If the string includes a single quote it must be 'escaped' by being preceded by a backslash character \. So the combination \' represents a single quote character. If the string includes a backslash character that is not followed by a single quote character it should be 'escaped' by being entered twice, i.e. \\. Both three and four consecutive backslashes inside a string enclosed in single quotes represent the two characters \\.

So the string written as 'abc\'def\\ghi' represents the 11 characters abc'def\ghi. Note that any other use of the \ character is treated as meaning the backslash character itself. So \t means the two characters \ and t.

(ii) *Double quotes*

When a string is enclosed in double quotes it is 'evaluated' before it is used. There are two aspects to this. First, certain combinations of characters beginning with a backslash, called *escape sequences*, are treated as having special meanings.

The following table shows how various escape combinations are interpreted.

\"	" (double quote)
\\	\ (i.e. a single backslash)
\n	new line
\r	'carriage return', often used in combination with \n
\t	tab
\$	$ (dollar sign)

Any use of the \ character followed by a character that does not have special significance is treated as meaning the backslash character itself. So \xyz just means the four characters \xyz.

Note that a single quote character ' enclosed in double quotes should not be 'escaped'. The combination \' simply means the two characters \'.

The instruction

```
print "abc\n\t\tdef\xyz";
```

will send to the web browser the three characters abc, followed by a newline character, followed by two tab characters,[5] followed by def\xyz. By contrast the instruction

```
print 'abc\n\t\tdef\xyz';
```

will output the sixteen characters

```
abc\n\t\tdef\xyz
```

The instruction

```
print "abc\"def\\ghi\jkl\$\xyz";
```

will output

```
abc"def\ghi\jkl$\xyz
```

The second difference when double quotes are used is that any variable name appearing in the quotes (without a preceding backslash character) is replaced by its value. So if $xyz has the value 123.4 the string "abc$xyz" stands for "abc123.4".

When using this facility it is important (and usually easy) to avoid the variable name being followed by a letter, digit or underscore, as these characters could be part of a longer variable name. For example, if we write "abc$xyzdef" we may intend the part after abc to be variable $xyz followed by the characters def, but the PHP system will interpret it as the (probably non-existent) variable $xyzdef. If we really want the value of $xyz to be followed by the characters def we can achieve this in several ways, e.g. by placing a space character between them. If the variable name is followed by the end of the string or a space or punctuation symbol, as is usually the case, there is no problem.

To illustrate this further, if $xyz has the value 123.4 the sequence

[5] The web browser will convert the newline character, followed by two tab characters to a single space on the user's screen.

```
print "abc$xyz<br>";
print "abc$xyzdef<br>";
print "abc$xyz def";
```

will output the three lines

```
abc123.4
abc
abc123.4 def
```

The unwelcome second line is caused by the system printing the value of non-existent (and therefore uninitialized) variable $xyzdef which is taken to be an empty string. The embedded space before def in the third print statement solves the problem.

Finally, If we want $xyz to be treated as the four characters $xyz, rather than being replaced by the value of variable $xyz, we can escape the $ sign by prefixing it by \. This causes it to be interpreted as the character $ itself rather than the first character of a variable name. For example

```
print "abc\$xyz def";
```

will output the characters

```
abc$xyz def
```

Despite these possible small complications, for most of the examples in this book we will enclose the strings in double quotes not single quotes, as this generally gives us more flexibility.

2.5.3 *Logical Constants*

There are two logical constants: TRUE and FALSE, which can be written in any combination of upper and lower case letters.

2.6 Functions

Functions are an important part of virtually any language. They enable an operation to be carried out by a single statement that would otherwise require several separate statements, or in some cases a very large number of separate PHP statements. In the case of some functions (e.g. to find the current day of the week) the operation would not be possible at all if the function were not available.

A function name follows the same rules as a variable name but does not have the initial $ sign. However, unlike variable names, function names are not case-sensitive. When used, the function name is followed by zero, one or more variables, constants or expressions in parentheses. These are known as the *arguments* of the function. If there is more than one argument they are separated by commas.

As an example, the *sqrt* function is used to calculate square roots. The statement

```
$x=sqrt($y+2.4);
```

assigns to variable $x the value of the square root of its argument, which is the value of the expression $y+2.4.

A function can be thought of as a 'black box' with its arguments as 'inputs'. The function takes in these values, processes them and 'returns' a value, generally either a number or a string, which effectively replaces the function and its arguments in the statement in which they appear. For example, the statement

```
$x=sqrt(36);
```

is effectively replaced by

```
$x=6;
```

The function *min* takes two numerical values as arguments and returns the value of the smaller. The statements

```
$x=12;
$y=min($x+3,29.7);
```

are effectively the same as

```
$x=12;
$y=15;
```

A function followed by its arguments is often called a *function call*. It may appear anywhere in a statement that a constant of the same type could appear, for example

```
$x=min(12.4,sqrt($y));
```

It was stated above that a value returned by a function call effectively replaces it in the statement in which it appears. However a function call may also cause one or more actions to take place, such as writing to a text file or reading from a database.

The functions used so far are technically called *system functions*. (The terms *internal function* and *built-in function* are also used.) Many of them are used in this book. They are collected together for reference and summarised in Chap. 19. There are many other system functions that are used more rarely, which can be found in the extensive PHP documentation available on the Internet.

As well as using system functions the PHP programmer can define his or her own functions. This can save a great deal of time when writing complex programs. This will be discussed further in Chap. 8.

2.7 A Note on Brackets

So far we have seen two types of bracket used: conventional round ones, which are used with functions such as sqrt (and in many other places) and square ones, which are used with arrays. There are in fact three types of bracket used in PHP. To avoid confusion we will call them by different names.

We will call () *parentheses*
We will call [] *square brackets*
We will call {} *braces*

2.8 Some Combinations of Quote Characters

In PHP strings can be enclosed either in single quote characters ' or by double quote characters ", the latter being a single character on the keyboard. Some combinations of single and double quotes, with or without other characters can be difficult to read on the printed page as well as on a screen. For example, is "'" five characters, three characters or something else? There is very little visual difference between a double quote character and two single quote characters but the difference in meaning can be considerable.

In this book some potentially confusing combinations are used. They should be interpreted like this.

Combination	Usual interpretation
""	An opening and closing pair of double quotes with nothing between them, i.e. a null string
"'"	An opening and closing pair of double quotes enclosing a single quote
"\""	An opening and closing pair of double quotes enclosing a backslash + double quote combination - a way of getting a double quote into a string enclosed in double quotes
''	An opening and closing pair of single quotes with nothing between them, i.e. a null string
'\''	An opening and closing pair of single quotes enclosing a backslash + single quote combination - a way of getting a single quote into a string enclosed in single quotes

Chapter Summary
This chapter describes the basic structure of a PHP script, the use of blank lines, spaces, etc. to improve readability and the forms that comments can take in a script. It explains how a PHP file containing a mixture of HTML and PHP statements is processed and goes on to describe two of the fundamental components of any language: variables (including arrays) and constants. The important distinction is made between strings enclosed in double quotes and those enclosed in single quotes and the use of 'escape sequences' in strings is explained. The chapter ends by introducing system functions.

Practical Exercise 2

Specimen Solutions to all the Practical Exercises are given in Sect. 19.7.

(1) Which of these are not valid variable names? Explain why.

$DoG
$_abCDE_1234_
$happy-BIRTHDAY
$27_Today
john
$this_is_a_long_name_
$abc!_*xyz

(2) What sequence of characters will be displayed on the user's screen as a result of printing each of these strings? Assume that variable $xyz has the value 296.4.

(a) 'I live at 26 Queen\'s Road'
(b) 'My name is John O'Brien'
(c) 'This is a backslash\\'
(d) "I live at 26 Queen\'s Road"
(e) "My name is John O'Brien"
(f) "This is a backslash\\"
(g) "He said \"Hello\" to me"
(h) "the value of the variable is $xyz"
(i) "the value of the variable is $xyzpounds"
(j) "a strange string\n\n\t\t\n\t\tabc\$xyz $xyz here is a backslash\\"

(3) Give at least four other ways in which the number –487.316 can be written.

(4) Which of these are not valid function names? Explain why.

$DoG
$_abCDE_1234_
$happy-BIRTHDAY
$27_Today
john

$this_is_a_long_name_
$abc!_*xyz
Sqrt
SQRT
sqrt2
happy-BIRTHDAY
_abCDE_123456_

Chapter 3
The PHP Language: Types of Statement

Chapter Aims
After reading this chapter you should be able to:

- understand seven of the most important statements in the PHP language
- use those statements to construct simple PHP scripts
- evaluate a complex arithmetic, string or logical expression
- understand how PHP Print statements differ from those in conventional programming languages
- understand how PHP handles and prints logical values
- understand different types of conditional statement
- understand the three types of looping statement available in PHP and the difference between them
- understand the use of the 'include' statement to 'include and evaluate' the contents of a PHP file while a PHP script is executing.

3.1 Overview of Statements

PHP has eight principal types of statement (some with slight variants):

- Assignment statements: to give a value to a variable
- Print statements: to send a string of characters to the user's web browser
- If statements: to test the value of a condition and take action that depends on its value
- Switch statements: an alternative to using an If statement when the value of a variable is repeatedly tested
- For statements: to perform one or more instructions until a variable reaches a given value

M. Bramer, *Web Programming with PHP and MySQL*,
DOI 10.1007/978-3-319-22659-0_3

- While and Do…While statements: to perform one or more instructions while or until a condition is satisfied
- Include, Require, Include_once and Require_once statements: to 'include and evaluate' the contents of a PHP file while a PHP script is executing
- Foreach statements: to perform one or more instructions for each of the elements in an array in turn

The first seven will be described in this chapter; the final one will be described in Chap. 4 which is about arrays.

PHP also includes a number of functions to perform operations that in other languages would probably be carried out by language statements. We will describe the main ones of these in Chap. 5.

3.1.1 PHP Keywords

The PHP 'syntax words' such as PRINT, IF, ELSE, SWITCH, FOR and WHILE used in the statements introduced in this chapter and elsewhere in this book are called 'PHP keywords'. They are not case-sensitive. So for example PRINT can be written as print or even as PrInT.

3.2 Assignment Statements

An assignment statement comprises a variable name or array element followed by an equals sign (=) followed by an arithmetic expression, a string expression or a logical expression. The value of the expression is calculated and then assigned to the variable or array element on the left-hand side of the = sign. We will go through each type of expression in turn.[1]

3.2.1 Arithmetic Expressions

An arithmetic expression can take several forms, each of which can optionally be enclosed in parentheses.

(a) A number which may be unsigned or prefixed by a + or – sign, for example 6, –85.4, 0, +12.97

---

[1]Assignment statements with a function call on the right-hand side of the = sign can be used to create variables that are not of the types described in Chap. 2. These include arrays, file pointers (used to access text files) and 'resources' (which hold references to system software used for purposes such as accessing an external database). These will be described in later chapters.

(b) A variable or an array element that has a number as its value, and which may be prefixed by a + or – sign, for example $x, +$var or –$arr[7].

(c) A function call that has a number as its value, and which may be prefixed by a + or – sign, for example sqrt($x), +sqrt(5.36) or –sqrt(3).

The + or – sign as used above is called a *unary operator*. It is applied to the value of the number, variable or array element immediately to its right. The + operator has no effect; the – operator negates the value.

(d) Any two arithmetic expressions joined by an *arithmetic operator*. A table of these is given below.

Operator	Example	Meaning
+	expr1 + expr2	expr1 plus expr2
–	expr1 – expr2	expr1 minus expr2
*	expr1 * expr2	expr1 times expr2
/	expr1/expr2	expr1 divided by expr2
%	expr1 % expr2	The remainder when expr1 is divided by expr2. (% is called the 'modulus operator'.)

The modulus operator % is likely to be the least familiar of these. If the values on both sides of the % operator are positive integers the value is the remainder when the first is divided by the second, for example 17 % 3 returns 2.

If either value is not an integer it is first converted into one by dropping the decimal part, e.g. 17.9 % 3.1 is treated as 17 % 3, i.e. 2. If either value is negative the result takes the same sign as the value to the left of the operator. So –17.9 % –3.1 is –2, –17.9 % 3.1 is –2 and 17.9 % –3.1 is 2.

An example of an expression using an arithmetic operator is –85.4 * $z. Spaces are allowed to either side of an arithmetic operator to aid readability.

The arithmetic operators are known as *binary operators*. This term implies that they are placed between the two arithmetic expressions.

The above definition is *recursive* at step (d), i.e. an arithmetic expression can be a combination of arithmetic expressions using an arithmetic operator. This can lead to some very complex expressions. The following are all valid arithmetic expressions:

```
-23*$a
$b/$arr[6]
(-23*$a)+($b/$arr[6])
(-23*$a)+($b/$arr[6])
((-23*$a)+($b/$arr[6]))
(-23*$a)+($b/$arr[6])+$z
$q/$var[99]
($q/$var[99])*sqrt(297)
((-$x*$a)+$b/$arr[6]-$z)-($q/$var[99]*sqrt(88.36))
```

3.2.2 Evaluating an Arithmetic Expression

To evaluate a complex arithmetic expression, the PHP system works systematically through a number of steps, replacing variables, array elements and function calls by their values as it comes to them. To illustrate these we will go back to this expression:

```
((-$x*$a)+$b/$arr[6]-$z)-($q/$var[99]*sqrt(88.36))
```

We will assume that the variables and array elements have the following values $x: 23 $a: 5.5 $b: 6 $arr[6]: 7.5 $z: 10 $q:170 $var[99]: 8.5

PHP eliminates all the expressions in parentheses in turn, replacing each one by its value. If there is a parenthesised expression inside another parenthesised expression, the innermost one is evaluated first, working outwards. At each stage of this process the system will be evaluating a parenthesis-free expression and the end result will inevitably be a parenthesis-free expression.

In our expression (repeated below)

((**-$x*$a**)+$b/$arr[6]-$z) - ($q/$var[99]*sqrt(88.36))

the innermost parenthesised expression (without the parentheses) is shown in bold. This has two operators: unary minus – and multiplication *. (We know that the minus sign is unary as there is nothing to its left-hand side.)

When evaluating a parenthesis-free expression we deal with operators in the following order:

- Apply any unary + or – operator to the value on its right-hand side.
- Apply any * / or % operator to the values immediately to either side of it. If there is more than one, work from left to right.
- Apply any binary + or – operator to the values immediately to either side of it. If there is more than one, work from left to right.

The value of –$x*$a is therefore –23 multiplied by 5.5, i.e. –126.5.
Our expression has now become:

(**-126.5+$b/$arr[6]-$z**) - ($q/$var[99]*sqrt(88.36))

The expression in the left-most set of parentheses is now –126.5+$b / $arr[6] – $z.

Using the rules given above, we start by dividing $b by $arr[6], giving 0.8. This reduces the expression to −126.5+0.8 − 10. We next apply the + and − operators from left to right. We take −126.5, add 0.8 and then subtract 10, giving −135.7.

Our expression has now been transformed to

```
-135.7 - ($q/$var[99]*sqrt(88.36))
```

We next need to evaluate the part shown in bold. We apply the / and * operators from left to right. Dividing $q by $var[99] gives 20. Multiplying this by sqrt(88.36), i.e. 9.4, gives 188.

The expression has now become

```
-135.7 – 188
```

This is parenthesis-free. We subtract 188 from −135.7, giving −323.7.

It is not necessary for arithmetic expressions to be fully parenthesised, e.g. $a + $b/$c is a valid expression. If you are uncertain whether this means ($a + $b)/$c or $a + ($b/$c), you are strongly advised to include parentheses to make your intended meaning clear. If there are no parentheses, the standard rule applies: division is performed before addition.

3.2.3 *Arithmetic Functions*

The sqrt function is an example of a function that returns a numerical value. PHP has many other functions for manipulating numbers including some such as trigonometric functions that are likely to be of interest mainly to mathematicians. The most important ones are listed in Chap. 5.

3.2.4 *Simplified Notation for Assignment*

An optional simplified notation is available for some of the most common types of assignment statement involving arithmetic operators, where the same variable would otherwise appear on both sides of the equals sign.

	Is an abbreviation for this assignment statement
$x++;	$x=$x+1;
$x– –;	$x=$x–1;
$x += $y;	$x=$x+$y;
$x –= $y;	$x=$x–$y;
$x *= $y;	$x=$x*$y;
$x /= $y;	$x=$x/$y;
$x %= $y;	$x=$x%$y;

Here $y can be replaced by any arithmetic expression.

3.2.5 String Expressions

A string expression can take several forms:

(a) A string constant (often called simply a *string*), for example "dog".
(b) A variable or an array element that has a string constant as its value.
(c) A function call that returns a string constant as its value, for example date("ymd").
(d) Two or more of the above joined by the *string concatenation operator* (a dot), for example
"Hello ".$yourname." – my name is ".$myname

If $yourname and $myname have the values "John" and "Louise" respectively, the above expression is equivalent to "Hello John – my name is Louise".

An unusual but sometimes very helpful feature of PHP is that in a chain of items separated by dots as in (d) above, any or all of the values can instead be a number,[2] variable or array element with a numerical value. These are automatically converted to strings before the concatenation takes place, e.g. −128.3 is converted to "−128.3".

If $x is 87.4 and $y[7] is −128.3, the string "hello ".56.$x. " world ".$y[7] is equivalent to "hello 5687.4 world −128.3" and $x.$y[7] is equivalent to "87.4-128.3".

It is even possible to include an arbitrarily complex arithmetic expression in a string expression of type (d) provided it is enclosed in parentheses, e.g.
"hello ".(13.5+4−sqrt(9))." world" is equivalent to "hello 14.5 world"

3.2.6 String Functions

So far the only function we have seen which returns a string as its value is *date*, e.g. date("ymd") returns "191225" (if today is Christmas Day, 2019). PHP has many other functions that return a string value. The most important ones are listed in Chap. 5.

3.2.7 Simplified Notation for Joining Strings

There is an optional simplified notation for joining strings, using the .= operator. For example,

---

[2]A number that begins with a minus sign or that includes a decimal point needs to be enclosed in parentheses.

```
$x.=" and more";
```

is equivalent to

```
$x=$x." and more";
```

3.2.8 *Logical Expressions*

A logical expression can take several forms, each of which can optionally be enclosed in parentheses:

(a) One of the logical constants TRUE and FALSE. These can be written in any combination of upper and lower case letters and are not enclosed in quotes.
(b) A variable or an array element that has a logical constant as its value.
(c) A function call that returns a logical constant as its value.
If any variable or array element used in (b) or (c) has a value that is not a logical constant, it is treated as having the value TRUE, with the important exception that the null string "" is treated as having the value FALSE. (Rather surprisingly, the value "0", i.e. a string containing only a single zero digit, is also treated as FALSE and so is the number zero.)
(d) A logical expression prefixed by the unary operator ! (read as NOT), which negates its value (TRUE becomes FALSE and vice versa).
(e) Two logical expressions joined by one of the *logical operators* &&, || and XOR.

value1 && value2 is TRUE if value1 and value2 are both TRUE. Otherwise it is FALSE. (&& is the 'logical and' operator.)
value1 || value2 is TRUE if either value1 or value2 is TRUE (or both). Otherwise it is FALSE. (|| is the 'logical or' operator.)
value1 XOR value2 is TRUE if either value1 or value2 is TRUE, but not both. Otherwise it is FALSE.
(XOR is the 'exclusive OR' operator. It can be written in any combination of upper and lower case letters.)

The above definition is *recursive* at steps (d) and (e), i.e. a logical expression can be a combination of logical expressions using a logical operator. This can lead to some very complex expressions. The following are all valid logical expressions:

TRUE && $x
(TRUE && $x) || $arr[16]

((TRUE && $x) || $arr[16]) && ! ($p XOR $q)

The operators && (two ampersands) and || (two vertical bars) can also be written as AND and OR, respectively, but we do not recommend this. AND and OR can be written in any combination of upper and lower case characters. For reasons which we will not go into here any logical expression that includes an AND, OR or XOR operator should be enclosed in an outer set of parentheses, for example:

```
$xyz= (((TRUE AND $x) OR $arr[16]) AND !($p XOR $q));
```

or sometimes unexpected results may occur.

The conditional expressions described in Sect. 3.4 below can also be placed in parentheses and treated as logical expressions. For example if $x and $y are 6.3 and 8.2 respectively, the statement

```
$z= ($x+$y<5);
```

will assign the value FALSE to $z.

3.2.9 Evaluating Logical Expressions

Evaluating logical expressions is carried out using the same principles as evaluating arithmetic expressions, described in Sect. 3.2.2.

We apply any && operators before any || operators and any || operators before any XOR operators. If there is more than one of the same kind of operator we work from left to right.

Thus FALSE && TRUE XOR TRUE is interpreted as (FALSE && TRUE) XOR TRUE, i.e. FALSE XOR TRUE, which is TRUE.

3.2.10 Logical Function

One very useful function that returns a logical value is isset. This takes the name of a variable as its argument and returns FALSE if the variable is uninitialized. Otherwise it returns TRUE. So if $x has the value 8.3, isset($x) is TRUE.

The isset function can also be used in conjunction with the ! operator. If $y is uninitialized, !isset($y) will be TRUE.

3.3 PRINT Statements

The general form of a PRINT statement is
print *expression*;
where *expression* can be any of the types of expression described under 'The Assignment Statement' in Sect. 3.2.

The expression can also be enclosed in parentheses, e.g.

```
print ("Hello World");
```

but we will not do so in this book.

As in all languages the print statement is of fundamental importance as the only means of communicating the result of possibly extensive calculation to the user. However PHP differs from conventional languages in that the characters output are not sent directly to the user's screen. Rather they are handed to the web browser which interprets them as HTML. So if variable $name has the value "Martin Williams" and the variable $day has the value "Tuesday" the print statement

```
print "Welcome <b>".$name."</b>.Today is ".$day."<p>";
```

will send the fragment of HTML
Welcome **Martin Williams**.Today is Tuesday <p>
to the web browser. This will cause

Welcome **Martin Williams**.Today is Tuesday

to be displayed by the browser, followed by a paragraph break.

There are other print statements that will not cause anything to be displayed by the browser immediately, for example

```
print "<table border=1><tr><td>";
```

which is just the first part of a construct that will cause a table to be displayed. Nothing will be displayed until the remainder of the information necessary to construct a table, ending in a </table> tag, is received by the browser.

It is important to appreciate that the HTML sent to the web browser when a PHP file such as file1.php is invoked may be a combination of 'plain' HTML and HTML generated by a PHP script. For example a table such as this one

Forename	Surname	Membership Type	Date of Birth
Marianne	Jones	Full Member	January 6th 1992

may be produced by plain HTML in file file1.php such as

```
<table border=1>
<tr>
<td>Forename</td><td>Surname</td><td>Membership Type</td>
<td>Date of Birth</td>
</tr>
<tr>
<td>Marianne</td>
<td>Jones</td>
<td>Full Member</td>
<td>January 6th 1992</td>
</tr>
</table>
```

or by a mixture of HTML and PHP such as

```
<?php
$forename="Marianne";
$surname="Jones";
$memtype="Full Member";
$dob="January 6th 1992";
?>
<table border=1>
<tr>
<td>Forename</td><td>Surname</td><td>Membership Type</td>
<td>Date of Birth</td>
</tr>
<tr>
<?php
print "<td>".$forename."</td>";
print "<td>".$surname."</td>";
print "<td>".$memtype."</td>";
print "<td>".$dob."</td>";
?>
</tr>
</table>
```

It is even possible to use PHP only to print the values of the four variables.

```
<?php
$forename="Marianne";
$surname="Jones";
$memtype="Full Member";
$dob="January 6th 1992";
?>
<table border=1>
<tr>
<td>Forename</td><td>Surname</td><td>Membership Type</td>
<td>Date of Birth</td>
</tr>
<tr>
<td><?php print $forename?></td>
<td><?php print $surname?></td>
<td><?php print $memtype?></td>
<td><?php print $dob?></td>
</tr>
</table>
```

At the other extreme we can output the entire table using PHP print statements like this.

```
<?php
$forename="Marianne";
$surname="Jones";
$memtype="Full Member";
$dob="January 6th 1992";

print "<table border=1>";
print "<tr>";
print "<td>Forename</td><td>Surname</td><td>Membership Type</td>";
print "<td>Date of Birth</td>";
print "</tr>";
print "<tr>";
print "<td>".$forename."</td>";
print "<td>".$surname."</td>";
print "<td>".$memtype."</td>";
print "<td>".$dob."</td>";
print "</tr>";
print "</table>";
?>
```

The final version seems fine, but there is a hidden problem. Web browsers normally have a facility for viewing the 'source code' of a web page, i.e. the HTML, complete with tags, that was used to generate it. Most users never look at this and you may have no interest in it too, but it can often be useful for debugging incorrect scripts.

In this case the source code looks like this:

```
<table border=1><tr><td>Forename</td><td>Surname</td><td>Membership Type</td><td>Date of
Birth</td></tr><tr><td>Marianne</td><td>Jones</td><td>Full Member</td><td>January 6th
1992</td></tr></table>
```

It is all run together into a single line, wrapped around (and printed in this book) on to more than one line. It would be far easier to read if there were new lines after some of the tags, especially the </td> tags.

To get round this problem (if we consider it a problem) we can add \n at the end of some or all of the print statements to send a newline character to the web browser, like this:

```
print "<table border=1>\n";
print "<tr>\n";
print "<td>Forename</td><td>Surname</td><td>Membership Type</td>\n";
print "<td>Date of Birth</td>\n";
print "</tr>\n";
print "<tr>\n";
print "<td>".$forename."</td>\n";
print "<td>".$surname."</td>\n";
print "<td>".$memtype."</td>\n";
print "<td>".$dob."</td>\n";
print "</tr>\n";
print "</table>\n";
```

When the browser interprets the HTML it ignores newlines[3] so this has no effect at all on what is displayed on the user's screen. However the newline characters have a significant effect on the source code which now looks like this.

```
<table border=1>
<tr>
<td>Forename</td><td>Surname</td><td>Membership Type</td>
<td>Date of Birth</td>
</tr>
<tr>
<td>Marianne</td>
<td>Jones</td>
<td>Full Member</td>
<td>January 6th 1992</td>
</tr>
</table>
```

[3] To be accurate, the browser treats any number of newlines and space characters as equivalent to a single space. Placing a space between one tag and another in a table has no effect.

How far it is worthwhile adding newline characters like this is a matter of taste. In this book we will occasionally use it. The main point to bear in mind is that outputting newline characters like this only affects the source code and not what is displayed on the user's screen. If we want the text displayed on the screen to go to a new line or a new paragraph we need to print the HTML tags <br> or <p>.

3.3.1 *Printing Logical Values*

One unusual feature of PHP is the way that it prints logical values. If variable $x has the value TRUE you might expect that printing $x would output the word TRUE. However this is not the case, as this example shows.

```
$x=TRUE;
$y=FALSE;
print "x=".$x."<br>";
print "y=".$y."<br>";
```

Produces the output

```
x=1
y=
```

A logical value of TRUE is printed as the number 1 and a logical value of FALSE is printed as an empty string.

3.4 IF Statements

The basic form of an 'if' statement comprises the word 'if' followed by a conditional expression in parentheses, followed by a statement that should be executed if the conditional expression is true, for example:

```
if ($x+$y-4>$z*8.3+2*min($p,$q)) print "success!\n";
```

The simplest form of conditional expression is a comparison between two expressions of the same type (string, numerical etc), which may be either true or false. It comprises two expressions separated by a *relational operator*. The main six of these are:

Operator	Example	Meaning
==	exp1==exp2	The two expressions are equal
!=	exp1!=exp2	The two expressions are not equal

Operator	Example	Meaning
>	exp1>exp2	exp1 is greater than exp2
>=	exp1>=exp2	exp1 is greater than or equal to exp2
<	exp1<exp2	exp1 is less than exp2
<=	exp1<=exp2	exp1 is less than or equal to exp2

The == (two 'equals' signs) in 'if ($name=="Henry")' etc. should not be confused with the = sign used in assignment statements. The double = indicates a test of whether two values are equal.

In the case of string expressions, the operators >, >=, < and <= refer to the alphabetical ordering of the characters in the strings. For example "abd" is greater than "abc".

A conditional expression can also comprise:

- a conditional expression prefixed by a logical 'not' operator (written as !), optionally enclosed in parentheses
- two conditional expressions joined by a 'logical and' or a 'logical or' operator (written as && or || respectively), optionally enclosed in parentheses.

This can give some quite complex conditions such as:

```
if (($x==1.5 && $name=="Jane") || ($y>27.3 && $surname!="Wilson" &&
    !($j<44 || $abc==0)))
```

3.4.1 Statement Groups

The statement after the conditional expression may instead be a *statement group*, i.e. a sequence of statements enclosed in a pair of brace characters, i.e. {}. For example:

```
if ($x+$y-4>$z*8.3+2*min($p,$q)) {
  $q=1;
  $z=0;
  print "success!\n";
}
```

Any type of statement can be included in a statement group, including another 'if' statement.

3.4.2 Augmenting an 'if' Statement with 'elseif' and 'else' Clauses

The basic form of 'if statement' can optionally be augmented by one or more 'elseif clauses' followed optionally by an 'else clause'. These indicate what should happen if the condition specified by the 'if clause' is false. The structure is essentially:

if (*condition is satisfied*) *do something*;
elseif (*another condition is satisfied*) *do something different*;
else *do something else*;

Each of the conditions tested is enclosed in parentheses.

This example shows a compound if statement comprising an if clause followed by two elseif clauses and a final else clause.

```
if ($x+$y-4>$z*8.3+2*min($p,$q)) print "success!";
elseif ($s=="yesterday") $n=$k+1;
elseif ($x<$y) $m=min($a,$b);
else print "end of example";
```

If the condition specified by the if statement is false, the condition specified in the first elseif clause is tested. If $s=="yesterday" is true, the specified assignment is performed. If it is false, the condition specified in the second elseif clause is tested. If $x<$y is true the specified assignment to $m is performed. If all three of the specified tests prove false the 'else' clause is invoked as a 'catchall' and the string 'end of example' is output. Note that a 'compound if statement' of this kind can have elseif clauses but no else clause, or vice versa. The keyword 'elseif' can alternatively be written as the two words 'else if'.

There must be a statement, terminated by a semicolon, after each part of an 'if … elseif … else' construct. However this may be just an 'empty statement', i.e. a semicolon on its own. More importantly each one can also be a statement group, i.e. a sequence of statements enclosed in 'brace' characters { }. For example:

```
if ($x==1) {
  $y=2;
  print "if was satisfied";
}
else if ($z!="dog") {
  $y=4;
  print "else if was satisfied";
}
else {
  $w="cat";
  print "else was satisfied";
}
```

Each statement within the brace characters must be terminated by a semicolon, unless it is itself one that ends in a statement group enclosed in brace characters. The indentation of the lines between the braces is solely for readability.

Braces can also be placed around a single statement if you choose. As usual PHP is very tolerant about the use of newlines and spaces, so this is one of many alternative layouts of the first four lines that are also valid.

```
if ($x==1) {$y=2; print "if was satisfied";}
```

3.4.3 Dealing with Variable Values in Conditional Expressions

Variables are most commonly used in conditional expressions on one or both sides of a relational operator such as >. However they can also be used in a 'standalone' fashion, e.g.

```
if ($x && $y==1) xxxxxx
```

or simply

```
if ($x) xxxxxx
```

If $x has previously been assigned a logical value it is clear that this value will be used in evaluating the conditional expression, but what if it has a numerical value or a string value instead? We can answer this question using this test script

```
$x=TRUE;
print "x=".$x." "; if ($x) print "true<p>"; else print "false<p>";
$x=FALSE;
print "x=".$x." "; if ($x) print "true<p>"; else print "false<p>";
$x=1;
print "x=".$x." "; if ($x) print "true<p>"; else print "false<p>";
$x= -27;
print "x=".$x." "; if ($x) print "true<p>"; else print "false<p>";
$x=0;
print "x=".$x." "; if ($x) print "true<p>"; else print "false<p>";
$x="abcde";
print "x=".$x." "; if ($x) print "true<p>"; else print "false<p>";
$x="0";
print "x=".$x." "; if ($x) print "true<p>"; else print "false<p>";
$x="";
print "x=".$x." "; if ($x) print "true<p>"; else print "false<p>";
```

which outputs the following:

```
x=1 true
x= false
x=1 true
x=-27 true
x=0 false
x=abcde true
x=0 false
x= false
```

From this we can see that

- The logical constants TRUE and FALSE behave as expected
- The number zero is treated as false
- Any number except zero is treated as true
- The strings "0" and "" are treated as false
- Any string except "0" and "" is treated as true

3.5 The Switch Statement

The SWITCH statement is an alternative to an IF … ELSEIF … ELSE statement when repeated tests on the value of the same variable are required. The following example illustrates its structure.

```
switch ($day) {
    case "Saturday":
        statement1;
        statement2;
        statement3;
        break;
    case "Sunday":
        statement4;
        statement5;
        break;
    default:
        statement6;
        statement7;
        break;
}
```

The PHP system finds the case that matches the value of the specified variable. If it cannot find one it goes to the default case. It then goes through the statements one by one until it reaches the next break statement or the closing brace. (Note that it does not stop when it reaches the next case, hence the break statements are required.) There can be any number of statements for each case. They are not enclosed in braces.

The above statement is equivalent to the if … elseif … else statement

```
if ($day=="Saturday") {
    statement1;
    statement2;
    statement3;
}
elseif ($day=="Sunday"){
    statement4;
    statement5;
}
else{
    statement6;
    statement7;
}
```

3.6 Loops in PHP 1: For Loops

Sometimes we need to repeat the same sequence of statements repeatedly, for example to print out a number of elements of an array. There are several facilities for implementing 'loops' such as this in PHP. The most fundamental one of these is the FOR loop, which involves repeating one or more instructions, with a variable used for counting being increased or decreased at each stage until a final 'terminating value' is reached.

The following is a typical example of the use of a 'for' loop with an array.

```
for ($i=0;$i<=9;$i++) print $arr[$i]."<br>";
```

The value of variable $i increases from a starting value of zero, increasing in steps of 1, continuing as long as the value of $i is less than or equal to 9.

The effect is to give $i the values 0, 1, 2 … up to 9 in turn. For each one, the value of $arr[$i] is printed, followed by a
 tag, signifying 'go to a new line'.

This gives the same effect as the ten lines

```
print $arr[0]."<br>";
print $arr[1]."<br>";
print $arr[2]."<br>";
print $arr[3]."<br>";
print $arr[4]."<br>";
print $arr[5]."<br>";
print $arr[6]."<br>";
print $arr[7]."<br>";
print $arr[8]."<br>";
print $arr[9]."<br>";
```

After the keyword *for* there are three components enclosed in parentheses and separated by semicolons.

- The first is a variable, which we will call the *looping variable*, which is assigned its initial value, e.g. $i=0. This will frequently be zero or 1 but can be any value. There can be any arithmetic expression after the equals sign.
- The second component is a test which examines the value of the looping variable. This may be a simple test such as $i<=9 but can be any conditional expression, as described in Sect. 3.4, provided it includes the looping variable. Before each pass through the loop the condition is evaluated. If it is true the instruction or instructions after the parentheses is/are executed. If not, the loop terminates.
- The third component is an assignment statement to vary the value of the looping variable. If the variable is $i this will often be $i++ but it may be, say, $i=$i+2 or $i−−.

After the 'for (xxxxxx)' component there can be either a single statement or a statement group, i.e. a set of statements enclosed in braces. These statements can include additional for statements.

If we want to print out the squares of all the odd integers less than 10 we could use the instruction

```
for ($i=1;$i<10;$i=$i+2) print $i*$i."<br>";
```

which produces the output

```
1
9
25
49
81
```

A common use of for loops is to work through the elements of an array one at a time. This is such a common requirement that there is a special alternative statement (the foreach statement) available for it. This will be discussed further in Chap. 4.

3.7 Loops in PHP 2: WHILE Loops

A WHILE loop is similar to a FOR loop, but this time a sequence of instructions is repeated indefinitely provided a condition remains satisfied.

We can use a WHILE loop as an alternative (but more cumbersome) way of doing anything that could be done with a FOR loop. For example to print out the first ten elements of an array we can say

```
$i=0;
while ($i<10) {
  print $arr[$i]."<br>";
  $i++;
}
```

If we want to print out the squares of all the odd integers less than 10 we could use the instruction

```
$i=1;
while ($i<10) {
  print $i*$i."<br>";
  $i=$i+2;
}
```

These examples illustrate the structure of a WHILE statement. There are usually one or more assignment statements that set the initial conditions. Then there is the keyword WHILE followed by a condition in parentheses. After that there is a statement or more often a statement group, i.e. a set of statements enclosed in braces. The statement or statements following while (xxxxxx) is executed indefinitely as long as the condition remains satisfied. It follows from this that those statements need to include some way in which the while condition can become satisfied. In the above example $i increases from 1 in steps of 2 until it becomes 10 after which the condition $i < 10 is no longer satisfied.

There are many other situations when a while loop can be used where a for loop would not be possible. For example to output all the perfect squares less than 90 we can write:

```
$i=1;
while ($i*$i<90) {
  print $i*$i."<br>";
  $i=$i+1;
}
```

A more valuable use of a while loop is to find a value in an array. For example a club may have a list of members stored in array $members and a related list of membership numbers in the same order stored in array $memnums. We are given a name held in variable $mem and wish to find out whether or not he or she is a member and if so what the corresponding membership number is.

Realistically, the data in the arrays may come from a membership list held in a text file. As this topic has not yet been covered we will simulate it in a small way by defining two arrays listing the names of members and their corresponding membership numbers. (The *array* function will be explained in detail in Chap. 4.)

```
$members=array("Max Bramer","Jane Roberts","Martin Williamson","Henry Peters",
  "Jane Bryant", "Sarah Dobson","Olivia Martens","Erin Tompkins",
  "Francesca Roberts","James Stephenson","Helen Chapman");

$memnums=array(623,184,456,390,817,464,311,290,565,333,221);
```

We can now look for a member $mem using a while loop as follows

```
$found="no";
$i=0;
while ($i<count($members) && $found=="no"){
  if ($members[$i]==$mem) $found="yes";
  else $i++;
}
if ($i==count($members)) print $mem." is not a member";
else print $mem." found at position ".$i."<br>The membership number is ".$memnums[$i];
```

If $mem has the value "Henry Peters" executing this script will give the output:

```
Henry Peters found at position 3
The membership number is 390
```

If instead $mem has the value "Simone Gilligan" the output will be:

```
Simone Gilligan is not a member
```

3.8 Loops in PHP 3: Do…While Loops

Do … While loops are similar to While loops with one significant difference: the truth of the condition is tested at the end rather than the beginning of the loop, with the result that the statements in the loop are always executed at least once.

In many cases this makes no difference. For example to output the first ten elements of an array, we can say:

```
$i=0;
do {
  print $arr[$i]."<br>";
  $i++;
} while ($i<10);
```

The final example in the previous section would also take a very similar form if written using a do … while loop:

```
$found="no";
$i=0;
do {
  if ($members[$i]==$mem) $found="yes";
  else $i++;
} while ($i<count($members) && $found=="no");
if ($i==count($members)) print $mem." is not a member";
else print $mem." found at position ".$i."<br>The membership number is ".$memnums[$i];
```

In some other languages a do…while loop is called an 'until' loop. In most cases it makes little difference whether a while or a do … while loop is used, but it may sometimes be significant whether or not the loop should be executed at least once.

3.9 The Include and Require Statements

These two statements are very similar and can often be used to very valuable effect. The PHP statement

```
include "file1.php";
```

tells the PHP system to 'include and evaluate' the contents of an external file "file1.php".

To illustrate what this means we will start with an example where file1.php contains only PHP statements. Suppose that file1.php contains

```
<?php
$forename="John";
$surname="Smith";
?>
```

The following script

```
<?php
print "Hello world<p>\n";
include "file1.php";
print "My name is ".$forename." ".$surname;
?>
```

is equivalent to a script containing

```
<?php
print "Hello world<p>\n";
$forename="John";
$surname="Smith";
print "My name is ".$forename." ".$surname;
?>
```

The statements in an included 'PHP only' file will often be definitions of one or more 'user-defined functions', which will be discussed in a later Chapter. Another possibility is that the file may contain frequently used statements, e.g. to produce standard headings and/or a standard menu at the top of all of a company's web pages. Another example relating to accessing a MySQL database is given in Chap. 15.

The situation is more complicated when an included file contains HTML (outside PHP tags of course) as well as (possibly) one or more PHP scripting blocks. In this case any HTML will be passed directly to the web browser to interpret. To illustrate this, suppose that file2.php contains

```
<?php
$forename="John";
print "abcde<br>";
?>
First line of HTML<p>
Second line of HTML<p>
<?php
$surname="Smith";
print "fghij<br>";
?>
```

The following script

```
<?php
print "Hello world<p>\n";
include "file2.php";
print "My name is ".$forename." ".$surname;
?>
```

will produce the output

```
Hello world

abcde
First line of HTML

Second line of HTML

fghij
My name is John Smith
```

The sequence of events when file file2.php is 'included' is as follows:

- The two statements in the first PHP scripting block are executed. Variable $forename is given the value "John" and the string abcde
is sent to the web browser and displayed as abcde followed by a newline character.
- Next the two lines of HTML after the closing PHP tag are 'evaluated', i.e. they are passed to the web browser and displayed as the two lines

```
First line of HTML
Second line of HTML
```

with each line of text followed by a paragraph break.

- Next the two statements in the second PHP scripting block are executed. Variable $surname is set to "Smith" and the string fghij
is sent to the web browser and displayed as fghij followed by a newline character.
- As file file2.php has now been fully 'included and evaluated' the original PHP script continues execution. The words 'My name is John Smith' are sent to the web browser and displayed.

Although an included PHP file generally contains only PHP or a mixture of PHP and HTML, it is also possible for it to contain no PHP at all, just HTML. This can be used to valuable effect.

The HTML source text of every webpage begins in a standardised way, similar to:

```
<!DOCTYPE HTML PUBLIC "-//W3C//DTD HTML 4.0 Transitional//EN">
<html>
<head>
<META http-equiv=Content-Type content="text/html; charset=iso-8859-1">
<META content="MSHTML 6.00.2900.2769" name=GENERATOR>
<LINK href="mystyle.css" type=text/css rel=stylesheet>
</head>
<body>
```

and ends in a standardised way, i.e.

```
</body>
</html>
```

To save the bother of typing this every time we can put the former into a file start.php and the latter into a file end.php (both without PHP tags).

Then if we wish to use a PHP script to create a complete webpage we can include the two files in our PHP like this.

```
<?php
include "start.php";

// put other PHP statements here

include "end.php";
?>
```

The sixth line of start.php refers to a style sheet file mystyle.css. If the approach shown above is used to generate a large number of webpages and later it is decided to use a different style sheet, all that has to be altered is one line in file start.php, not one line in each of many files.

The *require* statement is identical to the *include* statement with one difference. If the specified file cannot be loaded or does not exist an include statement will generate a warning message but the script will continue. The require statement will terminate execution. Although the latter seems generally preferable, in practice we are most unlikely to try to include a non-existent file and for all practical purposes we can use include and require interchangeably.

There are two other variants: the *include_once* and *require_once* statements. If these statements are used and for any reason the contents of the file specified have already been 'included and evaluated' it will not be loaded again. These forms of the statement are unlikely to be of more than very marginal benefit in practical applications.

Chapter Summary

This chapter describes seven of the eight principal types of statement in PHP and their variants: assignment, Print, If, Switch, For, While/Do…While and Include/Require/Include_once/Require_once. (The eighth statement, Foreach, will be described in Chap. 4.) Rules for evaluating complex arithmetic, string and logical expressions are described in detail and a simplified notation for some of the most common types of assignment is described. The significant role of the Print statement and alternative ways in which it may be used in generating the output displayed in the user's web browser are explained. The chapter goes on to explain the If statement and the closely related Switch statement. Three types of looping statement: For, While and Do…While are then described. The chapter concludes with a description of the Include statement and its variants.

Practical Exercise 3

(1) What is the value of this arithmetic expression?
(−$x*$y+$val[23]*$x−2.5)/($x+$y−$x*$y+38.5)
Assume that $x, $y and $val[23] are 4.5, −2 and 3.0 respectively.

(2) Why is this assignment statement invalid?
$res="the value is ".$x+$y." pounds";

(3) What is the value of this logical expression?
$x && $y XOR ($x||$y)
Assume that $x is TRUE and $y is FALSE

(4) Write a For loop to output the squares of the first 20 even numbers.

(5) Given an array of numbers $numbers and a variable $val write PHP statements to output the position of $val in array $numbers or a statement that it is not in the array. Do this (a) using a While loop and (b) using a Do…While loop.

(6) Write an If statement that takes a variable $month containing the name of a month, e.g. "October", and outputs the number of days it contains.

Chapter 4
More About Arrays

Chapter Aims
After reading this chapter you should be able to:

- use arrays when writing PHP scripts, especially in conjunction with the Foreach statement
- use the various sort functions available in PHP and understand the differences between them
- distinguish between indexed arrays and associative arrays
- use the explode and implode functions to convert strings with internal separator characters, such as commas, into arrays and vice versa.

Arrays were introduced in Chap. 2 as a form of variable in which many values, known as array elements, can be referred to using the same name, distinguished by a numerical index contained in square brackets. There is much more to arrays than this, as we will illustrate in this chapter.

4.1 The *Array* Function

In Chap. 2 we saw the example of array $info with the following contents

$info[0]	$info[1]	$info[2]	$info[3]	$info[4]	$info[5]
–8.3	"dog"	27	"cat"	true	647.142

M. Bramer, *Web Programming with PHP and MySQL*,
DOI 10.1007/978-3-319-22659-0_4

These values could have been assigned by a series of six assignment statements:

```
$info[0]= -8.3;
$info[1]="dog";
$info[2]=27;
$info[3]="cat";
$info[4]=true;
$info[5]=647.142;
```

However, if the number of elements in an array is fairly small there is a much neater way of creating it. This uses the function *array*, which takes a number of values as its arguments and returns an array with those values as the values of the array elements. For example the above array of six elements could have been constructed by the single statement:

```
$info=array(-8.3,"dog",27,"cat",true,647.142);
```

Warning – if you have previously given values to any elements of an array with the same name (using assignment statements or otherwise) using the *array* function will automatically delete them. Incidentally, it is possible to use a non-integer index value, if only by mistake. $info[3.1] and $info[4.9] will be treated as $info[3] and $info[4] respectively.

4.2 The *Count* Function

The function *count* is used to count the number of elements in an array, so for array $info the value of count($info) is 6.

Assuming that all the values in our array are numbered consecutively starting from zero, as is often the case, we can work through them one at a time using the FOR statement defined in Chap. 3 in conjunction with the count function. For example

```
for ($i=0;$i<count($info);$i++) print $i."...".$info[$i]."<br>";
```

gives the output

```
0...-8.3
1...dog
2...27
3...cat
4...1
5...647.142
```

However the situation is not always so straightforward. It is possible for array elements to be non-consecutive or to have a negative index value. For example we may have this sequence of assignments:

```
$alpha[0]=1100;
$alpha[1]=200;
$alpha[2]=300;
$alpha[-1]=1400;
$alpha[3]=500;
$alpha[4]=600;
$alpha[8]=1900;
$alpha[-11]=1400;
$alpha[13]=500;
```

The value of count($alpha) is now nine, and the instruction

```
for ($i=0;$i<count($alpha);$i++) print $i."...".$alpha[$i]."<br>";
```

will produce

```
0...1100
1...200
2...300
3...500
4...600
5...
6...
7...
8...1900
```

which is most unlikely to be what is wanted.

4.3 The PHP *Foreach* Statement

The PHP *foreach* statement is invaluable for situations such as that illustrated above. It enables us to work through all the elements of an array without knowing in advance what their index values are.

There are two forms of the statement. The first is
foreach (*arrayname* as *variable1=>variable2*) *statement*;
The second is just
foreach (*arrayname* as *variable2*) *statement*;

The space between the keyword foreach and the opening parenthesis is optional.

For each array element, the two variables *variable1* and *variable2* are called the *key* and the *value* respectively. For an array element such as $alpha[1] the key is 1 and the value is 200.

As for the FOR statement, the *statement* after foreach (xxxxx) can be either a single statement or a statement block enclosed in braces.

If we enter the instruction

```
foreach ($alpha as $k=>$v) print $k."...".$v."<br>";
```

the output is

```
0...1100
1...200
2...300
-1...1400
3...500
4...600
8...1900
-11...1400
13...500
```

This gives all the array values in the order in which they were assigned.

If instead we enter the instruction

```
foreach ($alpha as $v) print $v."<br>";
```

the output is simply

```
1100
200
300
1400
500
600
1900
1400
500
```

which is considerably less informative.

4.4 Sort Functions

Another useful facility that applies to arrays is the function *sort*, which will sort an array into ascending order of its values. If we sort array $alpha and then again print out its constituent values by

```
sort($alpha);
foreach ($alpha as $k=>$v) print $k."...".$v."<br>";
```

we obtain

```
0...200
1...300
2...500
3...500
4...600
5...1100
6...1400
7...1400
8...1900
```

Note that not only have the values been placed in ascending numerical order but the original keys have all been replaced by the consecutive range of integers from 0 to 8.

If instead we had sorted using the *asort* function the sorting would still have been in ascending order of the values but the key values would have been retained. If we had used the *ksort* function the sorting would have been in the order of the key values.

So this sequence of instructions

```
$alpha[0]=1100;
$alpha[1]=200;
$alpha[2]=300;
$alpha[-1]=1400;
$alpha[3]=500;
$alpha[4]=600;
$alpha[8]=1900;
$alpha[-11]=1400;
$alpha[13]=500;

print "Example of asort<p>";
asort($alpha);
foreach ($alpha as $k=>$v) print $k."...".$v."<br>";

print "<br>Example of ksort<p>";
ksort($alpha);
foreach ($alpha as $k=>$v) print $k."...".$v."<br>";
```

would produce the output

```
Example of asort
1...200
2...300
13...500
3...500
4...600
0...1100
-11...1400
-1...1400
8...1900

Example of ksort
-11...1400
-1...1400
0...1100
1...200
2...300
3...500
4...600
8...1900
13...500
```

There are three other functions: *rsort, arsort* and *krsort* which work in the same way as *sort, asort* and *ksort*, respectively, except that the sorting is carried out in descending order rather than ascending order.

All six variants of the sort function are examples of what in this book we will call *standalone functions*, i.e. functions that do not need to appear on the right-hand side of an assignment statement.

Instead of

```
sort($alpha);
```

we can write

```
$res=sort($alpha);
```

if we wish, but the variable $res will just hold the value TRUE or FALSE, depending on whether the sort was successful or not. Unless we are sorting a particularly large array we can safely assume that the process will succeed, so setting and testing $res is of little if any value.

4.5 Associative Arrays

The arrays discussed so far are technically known as *indexed arrays*. Their keys are numeric and generally start with zero. A more general type of array is known as an *associative array*. Here the keys can have non-numerical values. For example we might have an array where the keys were French words and the values were the corresponding words in English. We can create a simple version of this by

```
$convert=array("chien"=>"dog","homme"=>"man","cuisine"=>"kitchen",
   "femme"=>"woman","livre"=>"book");
```

Note that the keys are separated from the values by => symbols (two characters which together resemble an arrow).

Entering the further instruction

```
print "The English word for the French word cuisine is ".$convert["cuisine"];
```

will produce the output

```
The English word for the French word cuisine is kitchen
```

If we want to see the complete set of French words in our array, in alphabetical order, each with its English translation we can use the ksort function and enter

```
ksort($convert);
foreach ($convert as $k=>$v) print $k."...".$v."<br>";
```

This will produce the output

```
chien...dog
cuisine...kitchen
femme...woman
homme...man
livre...book
```

Here is a slightly more complicated example.

Suppose that we have a set of names, say the forenames of all the pupils in a school, and that we want a list of all the different names and how many times they each occur.

We might obtain the names from a text file or a database but as these topics will not be covered until later in the book, we will instead assume that they are held in an array $names defined as follows:

```
$names=array("frances","john","gavin","max","mary","frances","bryony",
    "gavin","max","dawn","max","frances","dawn","john","frances",
    "mary","max","frances","bryony","frances");
```

The first step is to go through the names in $names one by one and count how many times each one occurs. We can do this with just a single foreach statement using an associative array $namecount.

```
foreach ($names as $newname) $namecount[$newname]++;
```

The default value of $namecount for any element, e.g. $namecount["frances"] is zero. Each time a name appears in $names the corresponding value in $namecount is increased by one.

We can now use a foreach statement to list the contents of $namecount. We will do this first without any change. The key values come out in the order in which they appeared in the argument list of the array function, but only once each. Next we will show the effect of sorting the names by frequency of occurrence using asort. Finally we will list the names in ascending alphabetical order using ksort. Entering the instructions

```
print "Values in array namecount<p>";
foreach ($namecount as $k=>$v) print $k."...".$v."<br>";
print "<br>Values after sorting with asort<p>";
asort($namecount);
foreach ($namecount as $k=>$v) print $k."...".$v."<br>";
print "<br>Values after sorting with ksort<p>";
ksort($namecount);
foreach ($namecount as $k=>$v) print $k."...".$v."<br>";
```

produces the output

```
Values in array namecount

frances...6
john...2
gavin...2
max...4
mary...2
bryony...2
dawn...2

Values after sorting with asort

mary...2
dawn...2
gavin...2
john...2
bryony...2
max...4
frances...6
Values after sorting with ksort

bryony...2
dawn...2
frances...6
gavin...2
john...2
mary...2
max...4
```

4.5.1 *Using Associative Arrays with Dates*

There are several examples in this book which represent dates in numerical form, with January represented by the string "01", February by "02", etc. This works well until we come to printing out the name of the month which we would generally prefer to print in its full textual form rather than as a number. We can do this easily using an associative array $monthnames defined like this.

```
$monthnames = array (
'01' => 'January',
'02' => 'February',
'03' => 'March',
'04' => 'April',
'05' => 'May',
'06' => 'June',
'07' => 'July',
'08' => 'August',
'09' => 'September',
'10' => 'October',
'11' => 'November',
'12' => 'December');
```

Now if we have a month stored as a string in variable $month we can print out its equivalent month name by just

```
print $monthnames[$month];
```

4.6 Two Dimensional Arrays

So far all the arrays described have been one-dimensional, similar to a row of boxes or pigeonholes. Sometimes it is helpful to be able to store a two-dimensional table of values such as the one below, which we can think of as the results obtained by five students on three examinations.

10	15	20
100	115	120
200	215	220
300	315	320
400	415	420

For this we can use a two-dimensional array.

If the number of elements is small we can use the array function to define the contents of a two-dimensional array in terms of a number of one-dimensional arrays.

For the table above we can define the five one-dimensional arrays

```
$arr1=array(10,15,20);
$arr2=array(100,115,120);
$arr3=array(200,215,220);
$arr4=array(300,315,320);
$arr5=array(400,415,420);
```

and then define a two-dimensional array $marks by

```
$marks=array($arr1,$arr2,$arr3,$arr4,$arr5);
```

Essentially $marks is an array comprising five one-dimensional arrays, each corresponding to a row of the table. Each row (such as $arr1) comprises three elements. This gives us a 5 X 3 table. The rows are numbered from zero downwards and the columns are numbered from left to right starting at zero. The array element in row 4 column 1 is referred to as $marks[4][1]. It has the value 415.

The count function can be applied either to the array as a whole or to an individual row. The value of count($marks) is 5, the number of rows, and the value of count($marks[1]) is 3, i.e. the number of columns in row 1.

We can use a foreach statement with a two-dimensional array but only with a single row at any time. For example the statement

```
foreach ($marks[2] as $kkk => $val) print $kkk."...".$val."<br>";
```

will produce the output

```
0...200
1...215
2...220
```

If we wish to find the average mark scored on the examination listed in the middle column (i.e. column 1) we can do it using a FOR loop by

```
$sum=0;
for ($i=0;$i<count($marks);$i++) $sum+=$marks[$i][1];
print "Average mark is: ".($sum/count($marks));
```

which gives

```
Average mark is: 215
```

4.7 The Explode and Implode Functions

PHP has two useful functions which enable a string to be converted to an array (explode) or an array to be converted to a string (implode).

The first can be used for any string which has a structured form, with items separated by, say, commas, spaces or tab characters (\t). Lines read from text files (which will be covered in Chap. 7) are often of this form.

Suppose the value of variable $s is a string with values separated by commas, e.g.

"malcolm,johnson,male,1997,associate,2012,married,2,melbourne"

The statement

```
$newarray=explode(",",$s);
```

will create an array with nine values, with $newarray[0], $newarray[1] etc. being "malcolm", "johnson" etc.

If we want to display the nine values as a table of an array we can do so with this script

```
<?php
$s="malcolm,johnson,male,1997,associate,2012,married,2,melbourne";
$newarray=explode(",",$s);
?>
<table border=1>
<tr>
<?php
for ($i=0;$i<count($newarray);$i++){
   print "<td>".$newarray[$i]."</td>\n";
}
?>
</tr>
</table>
```

which produces the output

malcolm	johnson	male	1997	associate	2012	married	2	melbourne

Note the use of HTML interspersed with PHP. As previously pointed out there is no need for a PHP script to comprise only PHP statements.

To take the elements of an array and convert them into a string we can use the *implode* function. For example

```
$strNew=implode("*",$newarray);
print $strNew;
```

will output

```
malcolm*johnson*male*1997*associate*2012*married*2*melbourne
```

The first argument of explode and implode does not have to be a single character. It can be any string. Escape sequences can be included, e.g. \r, \n or \t.

A very important use of associative arrays automatically provided by the PHP system will be described in Chap. 10.

Chapter Summary

This chapter extends the description of arrays started in Chap. 2. It introduces the *array* function, which can be used to create an array with a (usually small) number of elements and the *count* function which returns the number of elements in an array, and goes on to describe the *Foreach* statement for working through the elements of an array. It goes on to describe functions available for sorting elements of an array into either ascending or descending order. Next two types of array are distinguished: *indexed arrays* and *associative arrays*, followed by arrays with two dimensions. The chapter concludes with a description of the *explode* and *implode* functions which enable a string with internal separator characters, such as commas, to be converted to an array or vice versa.

Practical Exercise 4

(1) Using the results table in Sect. 4.6 write a script to calculate the total score of each of the five students.

(2) What would be the effect of applying (a) the sort or (b) the asort function to array $monthnames given in Sect. 4.5.1?

(3) Write a script to convert a string such as $s in Sect. 4.7 to an equivalent string with each comma replaced by two asterisks and with the first element (malcolm in our example) removed.

Chapter 5
Some Important Functions

Chapter Aims
After reading this chapter you should be able to:

- understand and use the most important functions available in PHP for manipulating both numbers and strings
- use the *date* function to generate the date and/or time in any of a wide variety of formats
- understand the system functions *header*, *die* and *echo*
- obtain detailed information about the configuration of the version of PHP you are using, including the version number.

5.1 System Functions Applied to Numbers

PHP has many functions for manipulating numbers. The most important ones are listed below.

Value returned	Function	Meaning
number	abs(num)	Absolute value of argument abs(–4.3) = abs(4.3) = 4.3
integer	ceil(num)	Ceiling function The smallest integer ≥ the argument
number	exp(num)	Exponent function e to the power of the argument
integer	floor(num)	Floor function The largest integer ≤ the argument

(continued)

M. Bramer, *Web Programming with PHP and MySQL*,
DOI 10.1007/978-3-319-22659-0_5

Value returned	Function	Meaning
number	log(num)	Logarithm to base e (natural logarithm)
number	log10(num)	Logarithm to base 10
number	pow(num,num)	The first argument raised to the power of the second argument
number	pi()	Return value of pi to 13 decimal places, i.e. 3.1415926535898 (Argument list must be empty)
number	round(num)	The argument rounded to an integer (if it is half-way between two integers it is rounded up)
number	round(num,posint)	The argument rounded to the number of decimal places specified by second argument (zero means round to integer). If the argument is half-way between two values, it is rounded up
number	sqrt(num)	Square root of the argument (must be non-negative)

num: a floating point number
posint: a positive or zero integer

5.1.1 Mathematical Constant

Although strictly outside the scope of this chapter, this is a convenient place to mention that another way of obtaining the value of pi is to use the PHP 'mathematical' constant M_PI. This has the value 3.14159265358979323846 (i.e. pi to 20 places of decimals). The name is case-sensitive.

5.2 Trigonometric Functions

PHP has a range of trigonometric functions, which will be of value to those with a mathematical background but will probably be largely meaningless to everyone else. They are listed in table form below.

An important point to note is that functions such as sin, cos and tan assume that their argument is in radians. If you have an argument in degrees you should first convert it to radians using the deg2rad function. Similarly the inverse sin, cos, tan, etc. functions (called asin, acos, atan, etc.) all return angles measured in radians. To convert them to degrees you can use the rad2deg function.

Value returned	Function	Meaning
number	sin(angleRad)	Sine of the argument
number	cos(angleRad)	Cosine of the argument
number	tan(angleRad)	Tangent of the argument
angleRad	asin(num)	Inverse sine (arc sine) of the argument
angleRad	acos(num)	Inverse cosine (arc cosine) of the argument
angleRad	atan(num)	Inverse tangent (arc tangent) of the argument

(continued)

Value returned	Function	Meaning
number	sinh(angleRad)	Hyperbolic sine of the argument
number	cosh(angleRad)	Hyperbolic cosine of the argument
number	tanh(angleRad)	Hyperbolic tangent of the argument
angleRad	asinh(num)	Inverse hyperbolic sine of the argument
angleRad	acosh(num)	Inverse hyperbolic cosine of the argument
angleRad	atanh(num)	Inverse hyperbolic tangent of the argument
angleRad	deg2rad(angleDeg)	Convert a number of degrees to the equivalent in radians
angleDeg	rad2deg(angleRad)	Convert a number of radians to the equivalent in degrees

num: a floating point number
angleRad: an angle measured in radians
angleDeg: an angle measured in degrees

5.3 System Functions Applied to Strings

Many applications involve the manipulation of strings of characters: to compare one string with another, to make systematic changes to a string or to extract some of the characters from a string, amongst other purposes. For example a customer may enter their name into a form on a webpage and we may then wish to compare it with a succession of strings corresponding to the names of previous customers obtained from a database or a text file used for data collection. (We will show how to use databases, text files and web forms in later chapters.) PHP provides a large number of system functions for manipulating strings and new ones are likely to be added in later releases of the language. Many of the functions are for esoteric purposes that will never concern most users. Rather than trying to be encyclopaedic we will describe the functions that you are most likely to need to use.

5.3.1 Trimming a String

A common requirement, especially with data entered by a user into a web form is to trim a string to remove leading or trailing spaces. For example we may have a file of usernames and wish to check whether a user name entered on a web form is included in that file. This is quite easy if the (new) username is entered as say "johnson617" but what if it is entered as " johnson617   " with spaces at the beginning and/or the end? It is usually best to 'trim' user input to remove leading and trailing spaces before it is entered into a database or stored in a text file. We can do this using a statement such as

```
$newname=trim($newname);
```

The *trim* function removes not only spaces, but also tabs and 'newline' and 'carriage return' characters. If for some reason we want to remove characters only at the start of a string or only at the end of a string we can do so using the *ltrim* and *rtrim* ('left trim' and 'right trim') functions. So the scripting block

```
$str="   abcde   ";
$x=ltrim($str);
$y=rtrim($str);
```

gives $x and $y as "abcde   " and "   abcde", respectively.

5.3.2 Changing Case

Another issue when comparing strings is that we may have a stored value $str1 such as the username "johnson617" and wish to compare it with an input value $str2 which (possibly after trimming) is "Johnson617" or perhaps "JOhnson617". Are these the same? In most cases we will want to treat different capitalisations of the same characters as equivalent. To do this we can convert both strings to lowercase letters before comparing them. We recommend storing names, passwords, etc. in lower case form in databases and text files, so we will assume that the stored value $str1 is already in lowercase form and will change the input value $str2 before comparing it with $str1. To do this we can use the *strtolower* function, e.g.

```
$str3=strtolower($str2);
if ($str1==$str3) print "Same"; else print "Different";
```

or just

```
if ($str1== strtolower($str2)) print "Same"; else print "Different";
```

If for any reason we want to convert a string to upper case we can use the *strtoupper* function, for example

```
$s="it was the best of times; it was the worst of times";
$news=strtoupper($s);
```

will return $news as

```
IT WAS THE BEST OF TIMES; IT WAS THE WORST OF TIMES
```

5.3.3 *Converting Initial Letters to Uppercase*

An obvious drawback to storing a surname in lowercase such as "robinson" is that we may wish to output a message beginning Dear Mr. Robinson with an initial capital letter for the surname. We can do this using the *ucfirst* function. If variable $name has the value "robinson" then

```
print "Dear Mr. ".ucfirst($name);
```

will output

```
Dear Mr. Robinson
```

In some applications we may wish to convert the first letter of every word in a string to uppercase. We can do this using the *ucwords* function. This takes a string as its argument and returns the same string with the first character of each word capitalized, if that character is alphabetic. The definition of a word (after the first) is any string of characters that comes immediately after a space, tab, newline or carriage return. For example:

```
$s="my name is john smith. i am 27 years old.";
print ucwords($s)."<p>";
```

produces the following output

```
My Name Is John Smith. I Am 27 Years Old.
```

5.3.4 *Replacing One Substring by Another*

It is sometimes useful to be able to replace every occurrence of a substring of one or more characters in a string by another substring (which may be just an empty string). The *str_replace* function takes three arguments (all of them strings). Every occurrence of the value of the first argument is replaced by the value of the second argument in the string given as the third argument. For example

```
$sss="Tuesday,June,3rd,john,smith";
$newstr=str_replace(",","**",$sss);
```

will return $newstr with the value "Tuesday**June**3rd**john**smith", where each comma in the original string has been replaced by two asterisks.

5.3.5 *Reversing a String*

The *strrev* function returns a string with the characters in the original string in reverse order. For example

```
$s=strrev("abcde");
```

will return $s as "edcba";

The ideal use for this function is to check whether a string of characters is a palindrome, i.e. it reads the same both forwards and backwards. If $s is the string "redivider", the test

```
if ($s==strrev($s)) print "Palindrome"; else print "Not a palindrome";
```

will produce the output

```
Palindrome
```

5.3.6 *Manipulating a Substring*

We often have a string of characters with a known internal structure. For example we may have a date stored as "181225" where the first two characters correspond to the year (18, representing 2018), the next two to the month (12) and the last two to the day (25th).

We can regard the characters in a string as numbered from left to right, starting at zero. (The enclosing double quotes are not part of the string itself.) For example

Position	0	1	2	3	4	5
Character	1	8	1	2	2	5

If we want to extract a substring comprising the final two characters, here representing the day, we can do this using the *substr* function:

```
$date="181225";
$day=substr($date,4,2);
```

returns $day with the value "25". The second argument of substr is the position (numbering from zero) of the first character of the substring required. The third argument is the number of characters in the substring.

As an alternative we may have a string with a number of fields of variable length, such as "Tuesday**March**23rd". If we wish to extract the day of the week (Tuesday) we can do so by finding the position of the (first character of the) first double asterisk combination, which is position 7 counting from zero, and then extracting the substring that starts at position zero and is seven characters long. To do this we use the *strpos* function. The function call strpos(str1,str2) returns a numerical value, the position of the (first character of the) first occurrence of substring $str2 in string $str1.

```
$date="Tuesday**March**23rd";
$pos=strpos($date,"**");
$weekday=substr($date,0,$pos);
```

returns $weekday with value "Tuesday".

If we want to extract the day (23rd) we can do this using the *strrpos* and *strlen* functions.

The *strrpos* function works in the same way as the *strpos* function but instead of returning the position of the (first character of the) first occurrence of the second argument substring in the first argument string it returns the position of the last occurrence. For our example strrpos($date,"**") will be the number 14. We would like to extract the day as substr($date,16,4). The second argument is just strrpos($date,"**")+2, but how can we tell that the third argument (i.e. the number of characters in the substring) should be 4?

This is where the *strlen* function is helpful. The function takes a string as its argument and returns the number of characters it contains. The value of strlen($date) is 20 which means that the third argument of substr should be 20 – 16=4. We can now write

```
$pos=strrpos($date,"**");
$day=substr($date,$pos+2,strlen($date)-$pos-2);
```

To obtain variable $day with value "23rd".

5.3.7 Converting a String to an Array and Vice Versa

Although using strpos and strrpos can be very helpful in extracting substrings they are not always sufficient. Suppose we have a string such as "john**smith**male**plumber**london**46" how can we extract the fourth element, representing the person's occupation?

The *explode* function takes two arguments, both strings. It treats the first string as a separator and returns an array containing the component parts of the second string that are separated by the first string. As usual the array elements are numbered beginning with zero. For example:

```
$str="john**smith**male**plumber**london**46";
$parts=explode("**",$str);
```

returns an array $parts with six strings as elements

$parts[0]	$parts[1]	$parts[2]	$parts[3]	$parts[4]	$parts[5]
"john"	"smith"	"male"	"plumber"	"london"	"46"

Now the fourth component of the original string is just the value of $parts[3].

It is also possible to go in the opposite direction. So if we have an array $parts with six elements as shown above we can convert it to a string with the six components separated by (say) a comma using the *implode* function.

```
$str2=implode(",",$parts);
```

would return string $str2 with value "john,smith,male,plumber,london,46".

5.3.8 *Wrapping Text*

Sometimes it is helpful to be able to display a line of text in the user's web browser so that it fits neatly into a column of width no more than a specified number of characters.

The *wordwrap* function takes three arguments: a string, a number and another string. If variable $str has the value "The time has come, the Walrus said, to talk of many things" the function call wordwrap($str,15,"<br>") will return a string broken up every 15 characters at most by the replacement of a space character by the separator "<br>". For this example the string returned will be "The time has <br> come, the
 Walrus said, to <br> talk of many <br> things". The reason why "<br>" was chosen as the separator was that when output in a web browser this string is displayed in 'word wrapped' form as

The time has
come, the
Walrus said, to
talk of many
things

Note that the lines are not all 15 characters long – that is the maximum length. The wrapping takes place before a word is displayed that would take the width past the specified maximum.

This function is particularly useful when a long string is output in a cell of a table.

```
$str="The time has come, the Walrus said, to talk of many things";
$s1=wordwrap($str,15,"<br>");
$s2=wordwrap($str,20,"<br>");
$s3=wordwrap($str,25,"<br>");
$s4=wordwrap($str,30,"<br>");
print "<table border=1><tr>\n";
print "<td>".$s1."</td>";
print "<td>".$s2."</td>";
print "<td>".$s3."</td>";
print "<td>".$s4."</td>";
print "</tr></table>\n";
```

gives a tabular display of the same string wrapped to four different column widths.

The time has come, the Walrus said, to talk of many things	The time has come, the Walrus said, to talk of many things	The time has come, the Walrus said, to talk of many things	The time has come, the Walrus said, to talk of many things

5.4 The *rand* Function

It is sometimes useful to be able to generate a random number. PHP provides the *rand* function for doing this. It takes two positive or zero integers as its arguments, the second being larger than the first. If the arguments are say 1 and 7, then the value of rand(1,7) is an integer in the range from 1 to 7 inclusive, with each value having an approximately equal probability of being generated.

Example 1
We can use the rand function to generate a random password, for example comprising four random letters followed by four random digits.

If we have a string $alpha with the value "abcdefghijklmnopqrstuvwxyz" then the characters are automatically numbered from 0 to 25, working from left to right. We can find a random letter using the function call substr($alpha,rand(0,25),1), denoting a string of one character at a random position from 0 to 25 in string $alpha. The PHP instructions needed to generate a random password are then

```
$alpha="abcdefghijklmnopqrstuvwxyz";
$pwd=substr($alpha,rand(0,25),1).substr($alpha,rand(0,25),1)
  . substr($alpha,rand(0,25),1).substr($alpha,rand(0,25),1)
  .rand(1001,9999);
```

We use rand(1001,9999) rather than rand(0,9999) for the final part of the string to ensure that there are always four digits.

Example 2
We can use the rand function to generate a randomly selected picture, for example to display on the home page of an organisation's website. The HTML to display a picture is similar to

```
<img src="myfiles/pix/picture.jpg" width=150 height=150>
```

If we have six pictures of flowers and wish to display one of them chosen at random each time our webpage is visited we can do this by

```
$arr=array("iris.jpg","rose.gif","daffodil.gif","tulip.jpg","poppy.jpg","orchid.gif");
$num=rand(0,5);
print "<img src=\"myfiles/pix/".$arr[$num]."\" width=150 height=150>";
```

Note the use of \" to include a double quote character inside a string enclosed in double quotes.

5.5 The *max* and *min* Functions

It is often useful to be able to find the largest or the smallest of a set of numbers. PHP has functions max and min, which return the largest and smallest values of its arguments, respectively. Unlike most functions these can both take any number of arguments, provided there are at least two. For example

```
print max(34.2,-8.2,27.3,0,55.91)."<br>";
print min(34.2,-8.2,27.3,0,55.91);
```

outputs

```
55.91
-8.2
```

As an alternative the two functions may instead take a single argument, the name of an array. In this case they return the largest and smallest array elements, respectively.

```
$myarray=array(34.2,-8.2,27.3,0,55.91);
print max($myarray)."<br>";
print min($myarray);
```

outputs

```
55.91
-8.2
```

5.6 The *date* Function

PHP has a very powerful function named *date* which enables information about the current date and time to be obtained and displayed in a very flexible way. The *date* function takes one argument, which can be a string of any length. It reads the system clock to find out the date and time and then returns a string constant with part or all of that information presented in a suitable form, which depends on the string that was given to it as its argument.

We will start by illustrating the effect of calling the function with a one-character string as its argument. If we assume that today is Christmas Day 2018, the function call date("d") will return the string "25", date("F") will return "December" and date("Y") will return "2018".

If the argument is more than one character the string returned is the combination of all the strings returned by the individual characters joined together. So date("dFY") returns the string "25December2018".

A list of the main characters that can be used in the argument of a date function and the outputs they produce is given at the end of this section. Any other characters can also be used. Those that do not have a special meaning return themselves. These include characters such as space, colon, dot and minus (or hyphen), which can be used as separators. Thus executing the instruction

```
print date("d F Y");
```

will output

```
25 December 2018
```

The argument "l F jS" looks (and is) obscure, but consulting the table below will reveal its meaning, character-by-character:

l (lower case 'L') means display the day of the week in the form Sunday, Monday, etc.

F means display the month in the form January, February, March, etc.
j means display the day of the month in the form 1, 2, 3, etc.
S means display the suffix st, nd, rd or th depending on the value given by j
The two spaces each just mean display a space.

So executing the instruction

```
print date("l F jS");
```

will output

```
Friday December 25th
```

The effect is just the same as if instead of print date("l F jS"); we had written print "Friday December 25th"; in the original script, except that the current date is used of course.

The PHP statement

```
print date("g:i a … D M j Y");
```

would give an output such as

```
6:18 pm … Fri Dec 25 2018
```

A common way of storing dates is in six digit form such as 181225 for December 25th 2018. This can easily be achieved using the instruction

```
$thisdate=date("ymd");
```

The value of date("L") is the number 1 if the current year is a leap year and zero otherwise. We can test which it is by using the script

```
$leap=date("L");
if ($leap==1) print "This is a leap year<p>\n";
else print "This is not a leap year<p>\n";
```

To test the day of the week we can use a script such as this

```
$today=date("D");
if ($today=="Sat") print "This is Saturday.\n";
else if ($today=="Sun") print "This is Sunday.\n";
else print "This is a weekday.\n";
```

5.6.1 *List of Special One-character Arguments for the* date *Function*

The following table is based on the online PHP manual available on the web at http://uk.php.net/.

Character	Description	Values returned
d	Day of the month, two digits with leading zeros	01 to 31
D	A textual representation of a day, three letters	Mon through Sun
j	Day of the month without leading zeros	1 to 31
l (lowercase 'L')	A full textual representation of the day of the week	Monday through Sunday

(continued)

Character	Description	Values returned
N	Numeric representation of the day of the week	1 (for Monday) through 7 (for Sunday)
S	English ordinal suffix for the day of the month, two characters (normally used immediately after j)	st, nd, rd or th
w	Numeric representation of the day of the week	0 (Sunday) through 6 (Saturday)
z	The day of the year (starting from 0)	0 through 365
W	Week number of year (weeks starting on Mondays)	e.g. 42 (the 42nd week of the year)
F	A full textual representation of a month, such as January or March	January through December
m	Numeric representation of a month, with leading zeros	01 through 12
M	A short textual representation of a month, three letters	Jan through Dec
n	Numeric representation of a month without leading zeros	1 through 12
t	Number of days in the given month	28 through 31
L	Whether it is a leap year	1 if it is a leap year, 0 otherwise.
Y	A full numeric representation of a year, four digits	Examples: 1999 or 2003
y	A two digit representation of a year	Examples: 99 or 03
a	Lowercase am or pm	am or pm
A	Uppercase AM or PM	AM or PM
g	12-hour format of an hour without leading zeros	1 through 12
G	24-hour format of an hour without leading zeros	0 through 23
h	12-hour format of an hour with leading zeros	01 through 12
H	24-hour format of an hour with leading zeros	00 through 23
i	Minutes with leading zeros	00 through 59
s	Seconds with leading zeros	00 through 59

5.7 The *header* Function

The header function is used to send a HTTP header to the web browser, for example an error message such as

```
<?php
```

```
header("HTTP/1.0 404 Not Found");
?>
```

It is quite possible that you have no intention of ever doing this. However there is one very valuable use of a header that is certainly worth using and that is to redirect the web browser to a new page. For example

```
<?php
// many lines of PHP here
header('Location: http://www.newsite.com/');
?>
```

will execute many lines of PHP, possibly to update a database or write a text file, and then will effectively 'jump' to a new page http://www.newsite.com, without the user having to click on a link to make it happen.

An important condition is that the header must be the first output sent to the web browser. It must be sent before any blank lines, HTML tags, text generated by PHP and anything else, or an error message will result.

5.8 The *die* Function

Using the *die* function, for example

```
die("Unable to connect to database");
```

will output a message and immediately terminate execution of the script (and any further HTML or PHP scripts in the same file).

We will see how this is used in conjunction with a function to connect to a database in Chap. 15. Doing so enables us to terminate a script immediately if for any reason the database connection cannot be made, the alternative in many cases being to carry on attempting to process non-existent data.

5.9 The *echo* Function

As an alternative to the print statement, PHP has an *echo* function, e.g.

```
echo ("The answer is ".$x."\n");
```

The difference between using the echo function and the print statement is slight, in fact so slight that we will consider them as effectively equivalent and will not use echo in this book.

5.10 The *phpinfo* Function

Executing this small script

```
<?php phpinfo() ?>
```

will produce a large amount of detailed information about the configuration of PHP that you are using. At or near the top will be a statement indicating the version of PHP that you are using.

The *phpinfo* function takes no arguments and returns a logical value: either true if it succeeds or false if it fails. However it is normally used in standalone mode.

Chapter Summary

This chapter describes some of the most important functions available in PHP for manipulating numbers and strings. It goes on to describe the very powerful function *date* which enables information about the current date and/or time to be displayed in a very flexible way. The chapter ends by describing four other functions: *header*, which can be used to redirect a web browser to a new page, *die*, which terminates the execution of a script, the *echo* function, which can be used as an alternative to the Print statement and the *phpinfo* function which outputs detailed information about the configuration of PHP, including the version number.

Practical Exercise 5

(1) Write a PHP statement that will replace every occurrence of the letter 'a' in a string by two asterisks.

(2) Write a PHP statement that will take a string representing a name, remove any leading spaces and convert it to lower case letters, except for the first character which should be in upper case.

(3) Given a string of the kind shown in Sect. 5.3.6, say $date with value "Tuesday**March**23rd", write PHP statements that will create a new string with the name of the month replaced by December.

(4) Write a PHP statement that will display the date in the form dd/mm/yyyy.

Chapter 6
Formatted Print Functions

Chapter Aims
After reading this chapter you should be able to:

- use the printf function to output numbers in a structured form
- understand the meaning of a format string and the various kinds of specifier
- use the sprintf function to assign a formatted string to a variable

6.1 Standalone Functions

In the next section the *printf* function

```
printf("The first value is %.2f and the second is %d. There are no more answers.",$b,$c);
```

will be introduced as a more flexible alternative to the Print statement. Printf is another example of what was described in Chap. 4 as a 'standalone' function. The function value is generally not assigned to a variable (although it can be) and it would be easy to assume that the statement shown above was a language statement not a function call. The distinguishing feature is that functions are always followed by a list of arguments in parentheses, or occasionally by (), signifying an empty list of arguments.

This is quite an unusual feature of the PHP language. Normally we would expect to see the value of a function assigned to a variable, for example

```
$z=max($x,$y);
```


M. Bramer, *Web Programming with PHP and MySQL*,
DOI 10.1007/978-3-319-22659-0_6

Leaving out the assignment to variable $z would produce just

```
max($x,$y);
```

which would be a meaningless statement.

However for certain functions either there is no value returned or we have little (if any) interest in that value and simply omit the '*variablename* =' part. Whereas this would not make sense for most functions, it is appropriate in some contexts, such as when outputting a string using function printf, or when performing certain operations on either a text file or a database. In such cases the importance of the function is that it performs an action such as outputting a string or closing a text file. These actions are often referred to by the rather dismissive name 'side effects', but they are the main reason for using several functions, rather than the values they return.

In this book we will coin the name *standalone functions* for those such as printf that can sensibly be used (and often are) without any assignment of a value to a variable.

6.2 The printf Function

The *printf* function is used when we want a number to be printed in a way that is different from the way the PHP system would normally output it by default when executing a *print* statement. The function returns an integer value (of little interest): the number of characters output. It is generally used as a 'standalone' function, as defined above.

As an example, suppose we want to calculate the average mark (out of 10) scored by 13 students on a test. We first calculate that the total mark is 97 and this value is stored in variable $a. We can now calculate the average mark by

```
$b=$a/13;
print "The average mark is $b<p>\n";
```

but are probably not going to be satisfied with the output

```
The average mark is 7.46153846154
```

This has no fewer than 11 decimal places and is most unlikely to be the number we wanted printed. Rounding to two decimal places, i.e. 7.46 is almost certainly entirely sufficient.

Using the printf function rather than a print statement allows us to specify the way that numbers are printed. The printf function takes at least two arguments: a *format string* followed by one or more variables, all separated by commas and enclosed in parentheses. We can write this as:

printf (*format string*, *variable 1*, *variable2*, ...)

The format string is an adjusted form of the string we would use if we were not concerned about the format of the numbers. For example we might start with a standard print statement such as

```
print "The first value is $x and the second is $y. There are no more answers.";
```

and adjust it to:

```
printf("The first value is %.2f and the second is %d. There are no more answers.",$b,$c);
```

Here each variable has been replaced by a *format specifier*, such as %.2f, in the format string. Each format specifier begins with % and continues up to and including the next letter. There are two format specifiers in this example: %.2f and %d. These tell PHP how to output the values of the first two variables listed as the arguments of printf, i.e. $b and $c respectively. The two specifiers mean 'print the number rounded to two decimal places' and 'print the number as an integer' respectively. So if $b is 7.46153846154 and $c is 123.456 the output from the printf function is

```
The first value is 7.46 and the second is 123. There are no more answers.
```

There are four types of format specifier, relating to type, sign, precision and padding. We will go through them all in turn. (Note that the following is not an exhaustive list.)

6.2.1 *Type Specifiers*

In this book we are concerned with three ways of representing numbers[1]:

- integers such as −3, 0, 27 and +429
- floating point numbers, i.e. non-integers written with decimal places such as 123.456
- numbers in 'scientific notation', also known as 'e-notation', such as 1.23456e+3, which means $1.23456*10^3$ (i.e. 1234.56), or 1.23456e−3 which means $1.23456*10^{-3}$ (i.e. 0.00123456).

Any numbers of the above three kinds can be either positive or negative. If they are positive they can be written with or without an initial + sign. We can use the *type specifiers* d, e and f to display numbers in any of these three forms. They represent

[1] We will ignore other possibilities available in PHP such as outputting numbers in binary, octal and hexadecimal notation.

integer, floating point and scientific notation, respectively. The following table shows the effect of each one on the three different types of number.

If $x has this value	This format specifier	Will output this string	Comments
123	%d	123	Non-integer numbers are truncated
123.456	%d	123	
1.23456e+2	%d	123	
123	%e	1.230000e+2	Numbers are displayed to six decimal places (rounded if necessary)
123.456	%e	1.234560e+2	
1.23456e+2	%e	1.234560e+2	
123	%f	123.000000	Numbers are displayed to six decimal places (rounded if necessary)
123.456	%f	123.456000	
1.23456e+2	%f	123.456000	

6.2.2 *The Sign Specifier*

Any negative numbers displayed in the above way will be prefixed by a minus sign. However positive numbers will not be prefixed by a plus sign. If it is important that they are we can place a plus sign, called the *sign specifier*, between the % symbol and the following letter, e.g. %+e.

If $x has this value	This format specifier	Will output this string	Comments
123.456	%+e	+1.234560e+2	The same applies to type specifiers %d and %f.
–123.456	%+e	–1.234560e+2	

6.2.3 *Precision Specifiers*

When outputting numbers in %f format, i.e. floating-point form, PHP displays six decimal places as a default. If we want this to be some other number of places we can insert a dot followed by the number of places required between the % and the f characters. The combination .0 means no decimal places, i.e. output as an integer.

The same precision specifiers also apply with the %e type specifier, but the results may not always be as expected. The table below summarises the possible cases.

If $x has this value	This format specifier	Will output this string	Comments
123.456	%.2f	123.46	Numbers are rounded as necessary
123.456	%.12f	123.456000000000	
123.456	%.0f	123	
123.456	%.2e	1.23e+2	The number is truncated to an integer and then converted to e notation
123.456	%.12e	1.234560000000e+2	The number is converted to e notation with 12 decimal places
123.456	%.0e	1e+2	This may be surprising. There are no decimal places before the letter e, i.e. the number has effectively been converted from 123 to 100

6.2.4 *Padding Specifiers*

Sometimes we may wish to pad out a number, either before or after the value, so it always occupies the same number of characters. For example we may want the number 234 to be output as "00000234" or as "234   " or as "*****234". We can do this by inserting a padding specifier between the % character and the type specifier. A padding specifier comprises two parts: first a value indicating which character is used. This can be

- a space character
- nothing (equivalent to a space)
- a zero
- a quote symbol followed by the character to use (e.g. '*).

After this we put the number of characters to which the number is to be padded. This can be a positive integer signifying that the padding should be added to the left or a negative integer signifying that the padding should be added to the right.

Here are some examples

If $x has this value	This format specifier	Will output this string (without the enclosing quotes)	Comments
123	% 6d	" 123"	
123	% –6d	"123 "	
123	%6d	" 123"	
123	%–6d	"123 "	
123	%06d	"000123"	

If $x has this value	This format specifier	Will output this string (without the enclosing quotes)	Comments
123	%0–6d	"123 "	Spaces have been used for padding rather than zeroes, which would otherwise make the number 123000
123	%'*6d	"***123"	
123	%'*–6d	"123***"	
1234	%03d	"1234"	Padding a number cannot reduce it to a smaller number of characters than is needed to display the integer part correctly
1234	%0–3d	"1234"	
123.4	% 14f	" 123.400000"	
123.4	% –14f	"123.400000 "	
123.4	%14f	" 123.400000"	
123.4	%–14f	"123.400000 "	
123.4	%014f	"0000123.400000"	
123.4	%0–14f	"123.4000000000"	
123.4	%'*14f	"****123.400000"	
123.4	%'*–14f	"123.400000****"	
123.4	% 16e	" 1.234000e+2"	Note that the 16 characters includes the e+2 (for all examples using e)
123.4	% –16e	"1.234000e+2 "	
123.4	%16e	" 1.234000e+2"	
123.4	%–16e	"1.234000e+2 "	
123.4	%016e	"000001.234000e+2"	
123.4	%0–16e	"1.234000e+200000"	NB – this is not likely to be the effect required!
123.4	%'*16e	"*****1.234000e+2"	
123.4	%'*–16e	"1.234000e+200000*****"	

If a number is negative or if the sign signifier is used to ensure that a sign (either + or –) is always output, the sign occupies one of the characters of the specified field width. It is placed to the right of any padding to the left of the number unless the padding character is a zero, in which case it is placed to the left of the leftmost zero.

6.2.5 *Padding Strings*

The same method for padding numbers can be used for padding strings. In this case the insertions are made into specifier %s. The following table gives examples of the output obtained.

If $x has this value	This format specifier	Will output this string (without the enclosing quotes)	Comments
Tuesday	% 10s	" Tuesday"	
Tuesday	%10s	" Tuesday"	
Tuesday	%'*10s	"***Tuesday"	
Tuesday	% −10s	"Tuesday "	
Tuesday	%−10s	"Tuesday "	
Tuesday	%'*−10s	"Tuesday***"	

6.2.6 *Outputting a Percent Sign*

If it is required to include a 'real' % sign in a format string it should be written as two characters, i.e. %%.

Example

```
$a= 1.28e-3;
$b= -467.8;
$c= 99;
$d= 0;
$e= 844;
printf("The values are %+.4f then %e, then %04d%%, then %+d and finally %.2f",$a,$b,$c,$d,$e);
```

gives the output

```
The values are +0.0013 then -4.678000e+2, then 0099%, then +0 and finally 844.00
```

6.2.7 *Specifying Variables Explicitly*

We can choose to associate a format specifier explicitly with a variable in the argument list by referring to its position in the list (not counting the format string).

To refer to the first variable, i.e. $a, we insert the characters 1$ immediately after the % sign. To refer to $b we use 2$, etc. So the statements

```
printf("The values are %+.4f, then %04d<p>",$a,$b);
```

and

```
printf("The values are %1$+.4f, then %2$04d<p>",$a,$b);
```

are equivalent.

Alternatively we could output the second variable before the first, e.g.

```
printf("The values are %2$04d preceded by %1$+.4f<p>",$a,$b);
```

We can also refer to the same variable twice. For example

```
printf("The values are %1$+.4f, which in e notation is %1$+.4e and then %2$04d<p>",$a,$b);
```

refers to the first variable twice and then the second variable. It produces the output

```
The values are +0.0013, which in e notation is +1.2800e-3 and then -467
```

6.2.8 *Combining Options*

The options described above can be used in combination provided they are placed in the format specifier string in the right order, as listed below.

%	compulsory
variable number plus $ sign	optional
sign specifier	optional
padding specifier	optional
precision specifier	optional
type specifier (d, e, f, s, etc.)	compulsory

6.2.9 *List of Type Specifiers*

There are several other type specifiers available. Here is a complete list.

b	An integer presented as a binary number
c	An integer presented as the character with that ASCII value
d	An integer presented as a (signed) decimal number
u	An integer presented as an unsigned decimal number
o	An integer presented as an octal number
x	An integer presented as a hexadecimal number (with lowercase letters)
X	An integer presented as a hexadecimal number (with uppercase letters)
e	A number presented in scientific notation (e.g. 6.34e+4)
E	Like e but uses a capital letter (e.g. 6.34E+4)
f	A number presented in floating point form
g	The shorter of %e and %f
G	The shorter of %E and %f
s	The argument is treated and presented as a string

The only ones used in this chapter are d, e, f and s.

6.3 The sprintf Function

The *sprintf* function is very similar to the *printf* function but instead of a formatted string being output it is assigned to a variable. For example

```
$a= 1.28e-3;
$b= -467.8;
$xyz=sprintf("The values are %+.4f and then %e",$a,$b);
```

is equivalent to

```
$xyz="The values are +0.0013 and then -4.678000e+2"
```

If we have a string $num containing the number of a month from "1", "2" up to "12" and would prefer to have the variables in two character form, from "01", "02" up to "12", we can achieve this by the statement:

```
$newnum=sprintf("%02d",$num);
```

Chapter Summary

This chapter describes the *printf* function, which can be used to display numbers in a more structured fashion than is possible with the Print statement. *Format specifiers* used to specify a required layout in a *format string* are introduced and described in detail. The chapter ends with a description of the *sprintf* function, which is similar to printf but instead of outputting a formatted string assigns it to a variable.

Practical Exercise 6

Given a variable $x with the value 62.917, write a statement that uses the printf function to output the value of $x in at least three different formats.

Chapter 7
Using Files

Chapter Aims

After reading this chapter you should be able to:

- understand the organisation of the files making up a website in a hierarchy of directories and sub-directories
- understand the concepts associated with the creation and use of text files
- understand the principles of file protection
- use the many functions provided in PHP to manipulate files and directories.

7.1 Directories and Sub-directories

When we refer to a website we actually mean a (usually large) collection of files in a filestore on an external server. These can include files containing lines of HTML, PHP files, plain text files or documents in formats such as Word or Acrobat. These are most unlikely all to be together in a single directory.[1] All servers use the same approach, which is to place files and subdirectories in a hierarchical structure. The user of a website is likely to have little or no knowledge of or interest in the file and directory structure, but for system developers it is most important.

Here is a typical example of part of a website for our imaginary organisation The Erewhon Society, which we will call *erewhonsoc.org*.

The uppermost directory is traditionally known as the 'root'.

[1] Directories are often referred to by the alternative name 'folders'.

M. Bramer, *Web Programming with PHP and MySQL*,
DOI 10.1007/978-3-319-22659-0_7

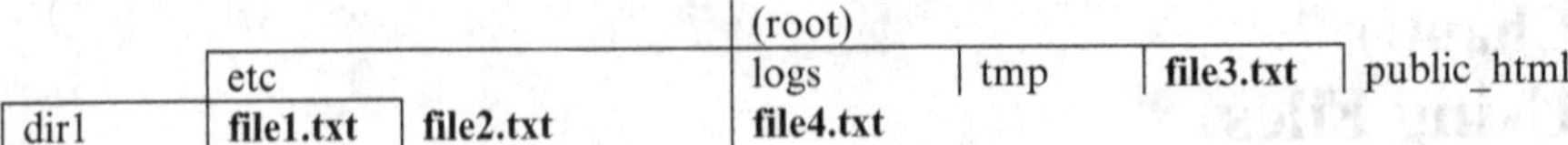

This figure shows the root directory containing four sub-directories and a file named file3.txt. (In this and the next figure the names of files are given in bold.) Sub-directory *logs* contains the file file4.txt. Sub-directory *etc* contains three members: directory dir1 and files file1.txt and file2.txt. The contents of sub-directories dir1, tmp and public_html are not shown. (A full expansion of the figure to show the entire hierarchy and all the individual files located in sub-directories of sub-directories of sub-directories etc. might be very large indeed.) Sub-directories are a form of directory in their own right and will often be referred to in that way.

From the point of view of the system programmer (as opposed to a member of the public using a web browser) the address of the root directory is / (a forward slash character). The addresses of directories etc and dir1 are /etc and /etc/dir1, respectively. The address of the file named file1.txt is /etc/file1.txt. These are called *absolute addresses*.

It is also possible to use *relative addresses* to refer to one file relative to another.

- The address of file2.txt relative to file file1.txt in the same directory is just file2.txt.
- Its address relative to file file3.txt in the root directory is etc/file2.txt.
- Its address relative to any file in the dir1 directory would be ../file2.txt
- Its address relative to file file4.txt in the logs directory would be ../etc/file2.txt

The notation .. (two dot characters) refers to the parent directory. So to refer to file2.txt in the etc directory starting at file file4.txt in the logs directory, we first go up to the parent directory, i.e. root, then down to directory etc, then to file file2.txt.

The server on which a website is stored will have a special directory which it treats as the *home directory* for the website. This is often called public_html, but sometimes has other names such as www or web. We will assume that it is called public_html.

To represent the structure of the website in a diagram we redraw the hierarchical structure to place directory public_html at the top and work downwards, ignoring all the other files and directories shown in the previous diagram.

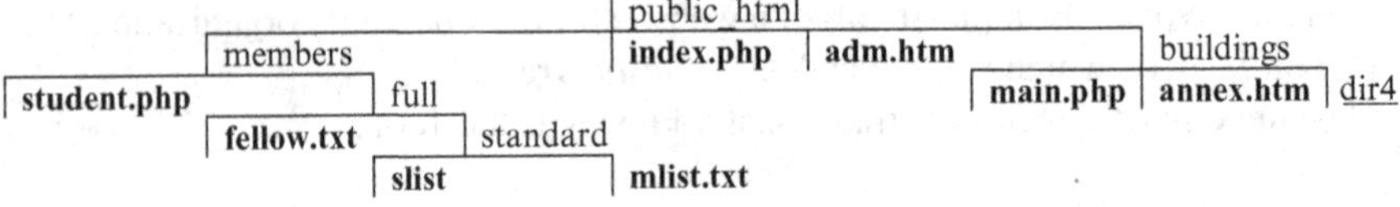

All files are shown in bold. In this small example we have files with three different extensions (htm, php and txt) and also with no extension at all. We have four levels of directory and also a directory (dir4) with no contents. The latter is indicated by underlining the directory name.

Directory public_html contains four items: files index.php and adm.htm and sub-directories *members* and *buildings*. Directory 'members' contains two items: file student.php and sub-directory *full*. The latter contains file fellow.txt and subdirectory *standard*. Directory 'standard' contains two files: slist and mlist.txt. Directory 'buildings' contains files main.php and annex.htm, plus an empty directory dir4.

When the user's web browser is pointed to http://www.erewhonsoc.org it examines the website's home directory and searches for a file called index.php, index.htm or index.html (there are a few other possibilities). If it finds index.htm or index.html it displays the contents in the usual way. If it finds index.php it executes it as a PHP script. So for our example website the address http://erewhonsoc.org (with or without a final slash character) is equivalent to http://erewhonsoc.org/index.php.

An address such as http://erewhonsoc.org/members/student.php is treated as a reference to the PHP file located at the position members/student.php relative to the home directory.

Note that any attempt to enter the address of a file at the same level as or a higher level than public_html (the home directory) in a web browser, e.g. http://erewhonsoc.org/../logs/file4.txt, will generate an error.

7.2 Relative Addressing Using Paths

Let us assume that our web browser is currently pointing to the webpage named index.php on the Erewhon Society website. We will call the directory in which the corresponding file is located, i.e. public_html, the *current directory*. (In this case this is also the home directory for the site.)

We will also assume that the page displayed has a link to another page on the same site, such as main.php in directory buildings. In the HTML for the displayed page the link from index.php to the file main.php will either take the form of an *absolute link* such as

<a href="http://www.erewhonsoc.org/buildings/main.php"> Click here</a>

or a *relative link* which simplifies the address to just

<a href="buildings/main.php"> Click here</a>

Having clicked on the link to main.php the *current directory* will now be buildings. If we want to place a link from there to annex.htm we can refer to it by the *relative address* "annex.htm". Any file name written like this is assumed to be in the current directory.

If instead we wished to link to file index.php back in directory public_html, we would refer to it as "../index.php". To link to the file student.php instead we would write the relative address as "../members/student.php".

Relative addresses are not only used for links to HTML and PHP files. They can also be used when referring to files or directories on the same server from a PHP script, as we shall see later in this chapter.

If the current directory were 'standard' the relative address of the file student.php would be ../../student.php and the relative address of directory dir4 would be "../../../

buildings/dir4". The three sets of double dots in the latter case signify go up three levels to reach public_html and then down one into directory buildings, where dir4 is located.

We use the term *path* of a file or directory to mean its address (in the case of a directory) or the address of the directory in which it is located (in the case of a file), in both cases relative to the current directory.

So if the current directory were 'standard':

- The path of the file student.php would be ../../
- And the path of directory dir4 would be ../../../buildings/dir4/.

(Paths can be written either with or without the final slash character.)

For a file such as mlist.txt in the current directory (which we will again assume is 'standard'), the relative name can be written either as just mlist.txt or as ./mlist.txt. Here the dot denotes 'the current directory'. The path of the file is taken to be a dot character with or without a following slash (. or ./).

7.2.1 *Relative and Absolute Addresses*

In the remainder of this chapter we will describe a number of functions that take relative addresses of files and/or directories as arguments. For completeness we should mention that absolute addresses are also permitted. For example we can refer to the file main.php in directory 'buildings' as /public_html/buildings/main.php, giving the full address starting at the root directory. However we do not recommend doing this. Using relative addresses such as ../buildings/main.php makes your scripts (and your entire website) far more portable. Should you ever move your website to a new server which uses slightly different standards or should your system administrator decide to restructure the directory structure of the site the absolute address of your home directory might change to say /web or /system/public_html. This ought to be a minor change but if you have used absolute addresses you will need to search through every one of your PHP scripts and change every absolute address. By contrast if you have relative addresses you should not need to make any changes at all.

7.3 Storing Data in Text Files

Although the topic of storing information in and retrieving it from a database will be covered in detail in later chapters of this book, the use of plain text files on the server to store data of a fairly basic kind is well worth knowing about and for newcomers to PHP has the advantage of avoiding the need to learn another language (mySQL or something similar) at the same time as learning PHP.

Organising data in plain text files is a very basic but often very useful way of storing it. In some cases we will use a PHP script to read a file that already exists. At other times we will use a script to write a new file or to add to a file that already exists. We will assume that a text file is broken up into a number of lines separated by newline characters.

Note that although it is not possible to use a web browser to access files such as file1.txt and directories such as tmp (both shown in the first figure in Sect. 7.1) that are not part of the hierarchy starting at directory public_html, it **is** entirely possible for a PHP script to do so. If the current directory is 'members' we can legitimately refer to file "../../etc/file1.txt" or directory "../../tmp".

7.3.1 Opening a File

Before we can write to or create a file, we first have to *open* it, i.e. establish a link to the file from a PHP script. We do this using the system function *fopen*, which takes two arguments. The first is the (relative) name of the file, the second is a string constant called the *mode*, which indicates how we intend to use the file. By the name of the file we mean its address relative to the current directory, including the path.

For example fopen("mydir/myfile.txt","a") indicates that we wish to open (i.e. use) a file with name myfile.txt in directory mydir relative to the current directory and if the file already exists we intend to *append* to it, i.e. write additional records (lines of text) to it, which are to be placed after those already there. If no file of the given name exists, an empty file with the specified name but no contents will first be created.

Another possible value for the second parameter is "w" (write), meaning if the file exists start by deleting all its contents before anything is written. If not, create an empty file.

A third possibility for the second argument is "r", meaning that the file should be opened for reading only. The use of the system function 'file' described later in this chapter is easier than opening the file using the "r" option and we will adopt that approach in this book.

We can also combine the "r" and "w" options to give "w+" or combine "r" and "a" to give "a+". There are other possible modes but these are the most important ones.

The fopen function returns a value of a special kind known as a *resource*, which must be assigned to a variable, which is then known as the *file pointer* for the specified file. The name of a file pointer variable can be any valid PHP variable name, but in this book we will generally call it $fp. Thus we can write the statement

```
$fp=fopen("mydir/myfile.txt","a");
```

to open file mydir/myfile.txt for 'appending' with file pointer $fp (assuming that directory *mydir* already exists).

7.3.2 Closing a File

Having opened a file for appending or writing, we can then write lines of text to it using the *fwrite* system function, as will be described below. Once we have finished doing this we should 'close' the file again, i.e. make it unavailable for use (until and unless it is opened again). We can do this using the *fclose* function, which takes the file pointer as its only argument.

```
fclose($fp);
```

Function fclose returns TRUE for success or FALSE for failure, but is normally used as a 'standalone' function, i.e. its value is not assigned to a variable.

Warning - files should always be closed promptly as soon as reading and/or writing operations are concluded. If the PHP script should contain an error leading the PHP interpreter to 'crash' while a file is open it is possible that its contents can be corrupted.

7.3.3 Writing to an Open File

Assuming that a file with file pointer $fp has been opened for appending (or writing) we can write a line of text to it by using the *fwrite* system function. This takes two arguments: the first is the file pointer; the second is the string of characters we wish to write to the file, e.g.

```
fwrite($fp,"This is an example line");
```

We usually want the output string to end with an end of line character or characters. Unfortunately there are two 'standards' for this. For a Windows server we place the two characters[2] denoted by \r\n at the end of the line, e.g.

```
fwrite($fp,"This is an example line\r\n");
```

For all other kinds of server we output the single character denoted by \n.

---

[2] It is important to appreciate that the combination \r\n represents two characters that will be stored in the text file and not four. We cannot type these characters directly into a PHP script (or a page of this book) so instead type the characters \r\n which requires four keystrokes.

```
fwrite($fp,"This is an example line\n");
```

The combinations \r and \n are both 'escape sequences'. They cause special characters (not the actual letters r and n) to be written to the file, corresponding roughly to 'carriage return' and 'newline'. In practice it does little if any harm to standardise on using just one of the newline sequences irrespective of the server. The only (fairly minor) problem that arises is if a file written on a server using one operating system is downloaded to a computer that uses the other. If the file is displayed on the 'wrong' system it is likely not to look entirely as expected.

As a way round the problem of different end of line sequences, from PHP version 5.0.2 onwards it has been possible to use the PHP constant PHP_EOL which corresponds to the correct end of line sequence for the server on which the script is run. So we can write

```
fwrite($fp,"This is an example line".PHP_EOL);
```

Note that PHP_EOL is a name and so is not enclosed in quotes and that PHP_EOL is case-sensitive.

Function fwrite returns the number of bytes written, or FALSE if an error occurs, but is normally used as a standalone function.

7.3.4 *Formatted Writing to an Open File*

The printf function was introduced in Chap. 6 as a formatted print function. A typical example is the function call

```
printf("The first value is %.2f and the second is %d. There are no more answers.",$b,$c);
```

The parts of the first argument (string) beginning with % and ending in a letter are format specifiers. The specifier %.2f stands for 'the value of $b rounded to two decimal places'. Specifier %d stands for 'the value of $c printed as an integer'.

Function printf displays output in the user's web browser. The function *fprintf* is the equivalent when writing to a text file. It has an additional first argument which is the name of a file pointer for an open file. For example

```
fprintf($fp, "The first value is %.2f and the second is %d. There are no more answers.",$b,$c);
```

7.3.5 Reading an Open File

The *fread* function reads a specified number of characters from an open file. It takes a file pointer and an integer as its arguments and returns a string. For example

```
$s=fread($fp,30);
```

reads 30 characters (starting at the beginning of the file) or up to the end of the file whichever is reached sooner. The 30 characters include the end of line character(s) at the end of each line. A subsequent fread will begin where the last one ended.

The *filesize* function takes a relative filename as its argument and returns the size of the corresponding file in bytes (i.e. characters) of storage. Thus to read all the characters in a text file (including end of line characters) we can use an instruction such as

```
$longstring=fread($fp,filesize('../mydir/myfile.txt'));
```

For reading text files it is frequently much more convenient to use the *file* function described below rather than using fopen, fread and fclose.

7.3.6 The File Function

PHP has a very powerful function named *file* which takes the (relative) name of a text file as its argument and returns an indexed array with one element for each line of the file. Let us assume that file1.txt is a text file in the same directory as the current PHP script and has the following contents

```
The time has come, the Walrus said,
To talk of many things:
Of shoes and ships and sealing-wax
Of cabbages and kings
And why the sea is boiling hot
And whether pigs have wings.
```

(Each line is assumed to end with the appropriate end of line character(s).)

Executing the PHP statement

```
$arr=file("file1.txt");
```

will copy the contents of the file into the first six elements of array $arr1.

- $arr[0] is now "The time has come, the Walrus said,"
- $arr[1] is now "To talk of many things:"

and so on.

Note that there is no need to use fopen and fclose with the file function. The file is automatically opened and closed.

It is important to remember that there is an 'invisible' end of line character or characters at the end of each line. Because of this, if we have a comparison such as

```
if ($arr[0] == "The time has come, the Walrus said,") print "matched!";
```

the test will fail. To avoid this problem it is good practice to trim each line before using it to remove the end of line character(s) at the end of the string. Strictly only rtrim ('right trim') is necessary.

It is also important to realise that the web browser does not display characters such as 'carriage return' and 'newline' on the user's screen. It treats any number of them, together with any number of spaces as equivalent to a single space. So

```
print $arr[0];
print $arr[1];
```

will print the first and second lines of text as one long line, with a space separating the two parts. To separate them by a line break we must output the HTML tag <br>.

7.3.7 Examples

Given file file1.txt as before we wish to output its contents line by line. We can do this by this two-line script.

```
$arr=file("file1.txt");
for ($i=0;$i<count($arr);$i++) print trim($arr[$i])."<br>";
```

If for some reason we wish to output all the contents of file1.txt except the first line to a new file file2.txt (e.g. to remove a header line) we can do so using the following script. In this case we retain the end of line character(s) at the end of each line.

```
$arr=file("file1.txt");
$fp=fopen("file2.txt","w");
for ($i=1;$i<count($arr);$i++) fwrite($fp,$arr[$i]);
fclose($fp);
```

7.3.8 *Using the Explode and Implode Functions*

Text files often have a fixed structure for each line, for example 12 values separated by commas or tab characters. If we want to change them all in a systematic way we can often do so easily using the explode and implode functions.

Suppose we have a club membership file named memfile.txt, with the first three records as follows:

```
john,smith,1982,fellow
olivia,Williams,1985,associate
erin,bryce,1990,student
```

We wish to put the members' full names as the first component of each record, i.e.

```
john smith,john,smith,1982,fellow
olivia williams,olivia,williams,1985,associate
erin bryce,erin,bryce,1990,student
```

We start by converting the text file into an array using the *file* statement and then create a loop to process each of the records one by one, create a new record named $newRecord and write it to a new text file memfile2.txt.

```
$arr=file("memfile.txt");
$fp=fopen("memfile2.txt","w");
for ($i=0;$i<count($arr);$i++){
    $next=$arr[$i];
    // create $newRecord from $next
    fwrite($fp,$newRecord);
}
fclose($fp);
```

To create $newRecord from $next we first use the *explode* function to convert string $next into the elements of an array $nextArray. We set the first element of a new array, $secondArray[0], to the full name and then copy elements $nextArray[0], $nextArray[0] etc. into $secondArray[1], $secondArray[2] etc.

```
$nextArray=explode(",",$next);
$secondArray[0]=$nextArray[0]." ".$nextArray[1];
for ($j=0;$j<count($nextArray);$j++)$secondArray[$j+1]=$nextArray[$j];
```

All that remains is to 'implode' $secondArray into a string with values separated by commas:

```
$newRecord=implode(",",$secondArray);
```

If we wanted to use a tab character rather than a comma as a separator we would replace "," by "\t".

Putting the fragments together gives the following complete script:

```
$arr=file("memfile.txt");
$fp=fopen("memfile2.txt","w");
for ($i=0;$i<count($arr);$i++){
    $next=$arr[$i];
    $nextArray=explode(",",$next);
    $secondArray[0]=$nextArray[0]." ".$nextArray[1];
    for ($j=0;$j<count($nextArray);$j++)$secondArray[$j+1]=$nextArray[$j];
    $newRecord=implode(",",$secondArray);
    fwrite($fp,$newRecord);
}
fclose($fp);
```

7.4 File and Directory Protections

Each file or directory has three 'permissions', which determine how it can be used. These correspond to the powers given to the owner who uploaded it to the server, the members of a group set by the server administrator and the rest of the world (or in short, the owner, the group and the world). In the case of a PHP script reading or writing a file the important part of this is the permission given to 'world'.

The owner, the group and the world all have permission to do some or all (or none) of the following to a file or directory: read it, write to it and execute it as a program (if it is a file). The execute option relates to programs and is not applicable to PHP scripts.

The three permissions are usually written as three integers from 0 to 7 inclusive, corresponding to the permissions given to the owner, the group and the world in that order. The permissions use a numerical coding based on 4 meaning read, 2 meaning write and 1 meaning execute.

By adding the numbers together we can get all possible combinations from zero to seven:

0: nothing at all
1: execute
2: write
3: 2+1, i.e. write and execute
4: read
5: 4+1, i.e. read and execute
6: 4+2, i.e. read and write
7: 4+2+1, i.e. read, write and execute (everything)

If we write the three protection numbers in the order owner, group and world and place a zero in front of them (required for rather obscure historical reasons) we have the *protection mode* of the file or directory, expressed as a number such as 0777 or 0776.

The owner and the group typically have permissions to do anything or almost anything. When using a PHP script the most important digit is the final one. If the mode of a file or directory is say 0774 a PHP script will be able to read it. If it is 0776 the script will be able to both read and write it. If the mode is 0772 the script will be able to write to it but not read it and so on. For some of the functions described in this chapter it is necessary for a file or a directory to be readable and/or writeable.

7.5 Checking Existence and Protection Status of Files and Directories

PHP has a number of functions for checking whether a file or directory exists and if so its status. The main ones are:

- file_exists. This takes a relative file or directory name as its argument and returns true if either a file or a directory with that name and path exists. Otherwise it returns false.
- is_file. This takes a relative file name as its argument and returns true if a file with that name and path exists. Otherwise it returns false.
- is_dir. This takes a relative directory name as its argument and returns true if a directory with that name and path exists. Otherwise it returns false.
- is_readable. This takes a relative file or directory name as its argument and returns true if a file or directory with that name and path exists and is readable. Otherwise it returns false.
- is_writable. This takes a relative file or directory name as its argument and returns true if a file or directory with that name and path exists and is writeable. Otherwise it returns false.
- is_writeable. This is an alias for function is_writable.

Whether or not a file or directory is readable or writeable depends on its protections, as described in Sect. 7.4. The name of a directory can be written with or without a final / character.

7.6 Other Functions Applied to Files or Directories

All the functions listed in this section return TRUE for success or FALSE for failure, but they are normally used as 'standalone' functions, i.e. the value is not assigned to a variable.

7.6.1 Changing File or Directory Protections

Function chmod takes a relative file or directory name as its first argument. Its directory permissions are changed to the values specified by the second argument which is the protection mode. An example is

```
chmod('../buildings',0666);
```

7.6.2 Creating and Deleting Directories

To create a new directory we can use the mkdir function. This takes two arguments. The first is the relative name of the new directory, which has to be a subdirectory of one that already exists and has writeable status. The second argument is the 'protection mode' of the new directory. If in the example structure given in Sect. 7.1 the current directory is 'members' then the instruction

```
mkdir("../buildings/dir2",0666);
```

will create an empty directory dir2 in directory 'buildings' with protection 0666.

The second argument is optional. If omitted a default value of 0777 is assumed.

To delete a directory that is empty and has writeable status we use the rmdir function. For example, to delete the directory just created we can say

```
rmdir("../buildings/dir2");
```

The value of the function can also be assigned to a variable and returns true if the deletion succeeds and false otherwise.

7.6.3 Renaming Files and Directories

We can rename a file or directory using the *rename* instruction. This takes two arguments: the relative names of the old and new files or directories, in that order. The paths do not have to be the same, which means that either a file or a directory (together with its contents) can be moved from one directory to another, provided that both parent directories are writable. So with the directory structure given in Sect. 7.1, if the current directory is 'members' and the following instructions are executed:

```
rename("student.php","student2.php");
rename("student2.php","full/standard/student3.txt");
rename("full/standard","../buildings");
```

the following sequence of actions occurs. First file student.php is renamed student2.php (in the current directory), then the file is moved to the 'standard' directory and renamed student3.txt. Finally the 'standard' directory and its contents are moved into the 'buildings' directory.

7.6.4 Getting and Changing the Current Directory

To find the name of the current directory from a PHP script we can use the *getcwd* function.

```
$thisdir=getcwd();
```

sets $thisdir to the address of the current directory ('cwd' stands for 'current working directory', which is another name for the current directory). The function takes no arguments, but the opening and closing parentheses must still be present. The string returned is the absolute address of the directory. Thus for working directory 'full' the value returned is "/public_html/members/full".

If we wish to change to a new current directory this can be done using the chdir function which takes the relative name of the new current directory as its argument. For example

```
chdir("../buildings");
```

The new directory name can also end with a slash character, e.g. "../buildings/".

7.7 Decomposing a Relative File or Directory Name into its Components

Occasionally it is useful to be able to decompose the name of a file or directory into its component parts.

Function *dirname* takes a relative file or directory name as its argument and returns the path as a string. For example if the current directory is 'members' then

```
$s=dirname("../buildings/main.php");
```

returns the string "../buildings". The value of dirname("../buildings") is also "../buildings". The value of dirname("student.php") is the string ".", which contains only a dot. Note that directory names are returned without a final / character.

The function *pathinfo* takes a relative file or directory name as an argument and returns an associative array giving its component parts. For example (taking 'members' as the current directory):

```
$arr=pathinfo("student.php");
foreach ($arr as $key => $val) print $key." => ".$val."<br>";
```

outputs

```
dirname=>.
basename=>student.php
extension=>php
filename=>student
```

Here the value of dirname (the path) is the dot character, signifying the current directory.

The next example shows a file in a different directory, referred to by its relative name.

```
$arr=pathinfo("full/standard/mlist.txt");
foreach ($arr as $key => $val) print $key." => ".$val."<br>";
```

outputs

```
dirname=>full/standard
basename=>mlist.txt
extension=>txt
filename=>mlist
```

If we apply pathinfo to a file without an extension, such as

```
$arr=pathinfo("full/standard/slist");
foreach ($arr as $key => $val) print $key." => ".$val."<br>";
```

the output is

```
dirname=>full/standard
basename=>slist
filename=>slist
```

Finally we apply pathinfo to a directory

```
$arr=pathinfo("../buildings/dir4");
foreach ($arr as $key => $val) print $key." => ".$val."<br>";
```

outputs

```
dirname=>../buildings
basename=>dir4
filename=>dir4
```

Note that PHP refers to 'dir4' as 'filename' even though it is actually the name of a directory. In the final two examples no value is associated with the key 'extension'.

7.7.1 Example

Suppose we have a variable $fname holding a relative file name such as "../../docs/abc.pdf" and we wish to create a new relative filename with the file 'stem' (i.e. the part before the extension) replaced by the value of variable $newStem. So if $newStem were "mem2647" the new relative file name should be "../../docs/mem2647.pdf". If $fname does not have an extension, e.g. "../../docs/xyz" the value of the new name should just be "../../docs/mem2647".

We can achieve this using the PHP statements

```
$arr=pathinfo($fname);
$newName=$arr['dirname']."/".$newStem;
if ($arr['extension']!="") $newName.= ".".$arr['extension'];
```

Note the need to write a / character after the directory name and a dot character before the extension, if there is one.

7.8 Finding the Contents of a Directory

If we want to know all the contents of a directory we can find them using the *scandir* function, which takes a relative directory name as its only argument and returns an indexed array containing all its contents in ascending order. For example (with current directory 'members'):

```
$arr=scandir("..");
foreach ($arr as $k=>$v) print $k."=>".$v."<br>";
```

outputs

```
0=>.
1=>..
2=>adm.htm
3=>buildings
4=>index.php
5=>members
```

The first two elements of the array will always be . and .. signifying this directory and the parent directory, respectively. The remaining elements are the names of the files and directories in the specified directory in ascending alphabetical order. Note that files and directories are not distinguished. Also note that only the 'top-level' of directories are shown. The sub-directories of 'members' and 'buildings' are not listed.

7.9 Summary of Functions

This is a reference list of the functions described in this chapter. There are other less important functions which can be found in PHP reference material if they are needed.

Type returned	Function name and arguments	Description
logical*	chdir(dir)	Change to new current directory (returns TRUE for success or FALSE for failure)
logical*	chmod(file/dir,mode)	Change protection mode of specified file or directory (returns TRUE for success or FALSE for failure)
string	dirname(file/dir)	Return path of file or directory
array	explode(string1,string2)	Divides up string2 into parts separated by substring string1 and converts them into the elements of an array
logical	is_dir(file/dir)	Exists and is a directory
logical	is_file(file/dir)	Exists and is a file
logical	is_readable(file/dir)	File or directory exists and is readable
logical	is_writable(file/dir)	File or directory exists and is writeable
logical	is_writeable(file/dir)	File or directory exists and is writeable
logical*	fclose(filepointer)	Closes file (returns TRUE for success or FALSE for failure)
array	file(file)	Convert text file to array
logical	file_exists(file/dir)	File or directory exists
integer	filesize(file)	Returns size of file in bytes (i.e. characters) of storage
resource (file pointer)	fopen(file,mode)	Opens a text file in a specified mode

(continued)

Type returned	Function name and arguments	Description
integer*	fprintf(filepointer,format specifier, var1, var2, ...)	Prints a string in formatted form. (Returns the number of bytes written.)
string	fread(filepointer,integer)	Read specified number of characters from a text file or up to the end of file, whichever is less
integer*	fwrite(filepointer,string)	Write to specified text file (Returns number of bytes written or FALSE on error)
string	getcwd()	Returns the absolute address of the working directory
string	implode(string,array)	Combines the elements of the array into a string separated by substring string1
logical*	mkdir(dir,mode)	Create directory with specified name and path with specified protection mode (returns TRUE for success or FALSE for failure)
array	pathinfo(file/dir)	Return associative array of components
logical*	rename(file/dir,file/dir)	Rename file or a directory (including its contents). This can involve moving the file or directory to a different parent directory (returns TRUE for success or FALSE for failure)
logical*	rmdir(dir)	Delete directory with specified name and path (returns TRUE for success or FALSE for failure)
array	scandir(dir)	Return indexed array of directory contents (top-level only)

* Function generally used in 'standalone' mode
file: address of a file, relative to the current directory
dir: address of a directory, relative to the current directory
file/dir: address of either a file or a directory, relative to the current directory

Note: absolute addresses such as /public_html/buildings/main.php are also permitted, but using these is not recommended.

Chapter Summary

This chapter introduces the idea of a website as a collection of files organised in a hierarchical structure of directories and sub-directories. The use of relative and absolute addresses is explained and the *path* to a file or directory is defined. Functions for writing data to text files and reading data stored in that form are described. The use of the explode and implode functions to change a string such as a record in a text file to the elements of an array or vice versa is illustrated. The topic of file and directory protections is introduced and functions for testing the existence and protection status of files are described. The chapter ends with descriptions of other functions that can be applied to files and directories and functions for decomposing a relative file or directory name into its component parts and for finding all the contents of a directory.

Practical Exercise 7

Using the scandir function write a PHP script which takes a variable $path containing the path to a directory from the current directory and displays the names of all the files and (top-level) sub-directories in that directory in alphabetical order. The entries . and .. should be omitted. To distinguish between files and directories display the name of the latter in bold. For both types of entry display after the name the letter R and/or W indicating that it is readable and/or writeable.

Chapter 8
User-Defined Functions

Chapter Aims
After reading this chapter you should be able to:

- create and use your own user-defined functions[1]
- create and use a personal function library
- understand the difference between passing arguments by value and by reference
- understand how to give an argument of a function a default value.

8.1 Introduction

As will no doubt be clear from previous chapters, much of the power of PHP comes from the use of system functions to perform a wide variety of operations. It is also possible for PHP programmers to define their own functions as part of a script, and then to use them (possibly several times) in that script.

As an example the PHP statements shown in Chap. 7 to copy the contents of a text file to a new text file with the first line removed can be made into a function *removeHeader*, defined as follows.

```
function removeHeader($fileA,$fileB) {
   $arr=file($fileA);
   $fp=fopen($fileB,"w");
   for ($i=1;$i<count($arr);$i++) fwrite($fp,$arr[$i]);
   fclose($fp);
} //removeHeader
```

[1]To avoid any possible confusion, the term 'user' here refers to the PHP programmer, i.e. the person who writes the PHP script. Elsewhere in this book we use the term 'user' to refer to the 'end user' of a script, i.e. the person looking at a web page in a browser.

M. Bramer, *Web Programming with PHP and MySQL*,
DOI 10.1007/978-3-319-22659-0_8

Then to copy a file file1.txt to a new file file2.txt with its first line removed, all we need to write is:

```
removeHeader("file1.txt","file2.txt");
```

The first line of a function definition comprises four elements:

- The word function
- The name of the function
  Function names follow the same rules as variable names. They comprise the characters a to z, A to Z, 0 to 9 and underscore, but may not begin with a digit. Unlike variable names a function name may not begin with a $ sign. Also unlike variable names, function names are not case-sensitive, so the function names removeHeader and reMOVEheader are effectively the same.
- An argument list enclosed in parentheses. This will generally consist of one or more variable names separated by commas. However some functions may have no parameters in which case an empty pair of parentheses () is required.
- An opening brace character, signifying the start of the definition of the function.

The final line of a function definition is always a closing brace character. In the above example we have added a comment giving the name of the function, but that is solely in the interest of readability.

Between the opening and closing braces we can place any number of PHP statements with the exception of another function definition. User-defined functions can call other user-defined functions but their definitions may not be nested.

Function definitions can be placed almost anywhere in a PHP script. It is probably good practice to place all of them together either at the beginning or at the end of the script but they can also be placed between 'normal' PHP statements if you wish. (The system will not be confused if you do this, although you may find it harder to understand your own scripts if you do.) Although the PHP system generally works through a script from top to bottom, function definitions are not executed when they are encountered. A function is only executed when it is 'called', in the same way as a system function might be. Except in very early versions of PHP it is not necessary for a function to be defined in a script before it is used there.

The following example shows the removeHeader function being used from two parts of the same script.

```
<?php
function removeHeader($fileA,$fileB) {
   $arr=file($fileA);
   $fp=fopen($fileB,"w");
   for ($i=1;$i<count($arr);$i++) fwrite($fp,$arr[$i]);
   fclose($fp);
} //removeHeader

// PHP statements here
removeHeader("file1.txt","file2.txt");
// PHP statements
?>
Here is some HTML text<br>
Another line of text<p>

<?php
// PHP statements here
$fname="fname.txt";
removeHeader($fname,"file4.txt");
?>
```

Note that the presence of two lines of HTML between the two blocks of PHP does not prevent the second use of removeHeader. Wherever it is placed in one of the PHP parts of the file, the function definition is available for use throughout that and all the other PHP parts of the file.

Function removeHeader is an example of a type of function that is permitted in PHP but would not be allowed in many other languages. It does not return any value and is executed purely for what it does. To call it we simply use a function call such as

```
removeHeader($file88,"file9.txt");
```

Functions of this kind can include a RETURN statement which indicates that execution of the function should immediately stop. To illustrate this here is a revised version of function removeHeader.

```
<?php
function removeHeader2($fileA,$fileB) {
   if (!is_readable($fileA)) {
      print "File ".$fileA." is not readable!<p>";
      return;
   }
   $arr=file($fileA);
   $fp=fopen($fileB,"w");
   for ($i=1;$i<count($arr);$i++) fwrite($fp,$arr[$i]);
   fclose($fp);
} //removeHeader2

// PHP statements here
removeHeader2("file1.txt","file2.txt");

print "This line will always be reached";

// PHP statements
?>
```

Here we start by checking whether the file passed as the first argument of removeHeader2 is readable. If it is not we print out an error message and then execute the return statement which immediately terminates the execution of the statements in the function definition. Otherwise we copy the contents (less the first line) to $fileB as before. In both cases, when function execution ends the line saying 'This line will always be reached' will be the next to be executed.

There can be return statements at several different places in a function definition if required. On the other hand, for functions that do not return values it is often possible to avoid using a return statement altogether. Thus the previous definition of function removeHeader2 can be simplified to

```
function removeHeader2($fileA,$fileB) {
   if (!is_readable($fileA)) {
      print "File ".$fileA." is not readable!<p>";
   }
   else {
      $arr=file($fileA);
      $fp=fopen($fileB,"w");
      for ($i=1;$i<count($arr);$i++) fwrite($fp,$arr[$i]);
      fclose($fp);
   }
} //removeHeader2
```

The next example shows a function which returns a value. In practice this is likely to be the more common kind of function defined (and the only kind permitted by many other languages).

The function *printout* defined below starts by testing whether a file passed to it as its only argument is readable. If it is not readable, a value of zero is returned, but no error message is output. If it is readable, its contents are printed out line by line and the value returned is the number of lines of text in the file.

```
function printout($thisfile){
   if (!is_readable($thisfile)){
      return 0;
   }
   $arr=file($thisfile);
   for ($i=0;$i<count($arr);$i++) print trim($arr[$i])."<br>";
   return count($arr);
} //printout
```

As before, executing a return statement causes the function to cease execution immediately. The value of the function (in the form of a variable name, a constant or an expression) follows the word return, separated from it by at least one space.

To call the function we need to use a statement such as

```
$result=printout("docs/file99.txt");
```

which assigns the function value to a variable.

As for system functions, when a user-defined function is called the arguments of the calling function can be variables, constants or expressions that evaluate to constants. They are matched against the variables listed in the argument list of the function definition, so in the above example variable $thisfile in function printout is given the value "docs/file99.txt".

8.2 Global and Local Variables

So far there has been no clash between the variable names used in the function definitions and those used in the remainder of the scripts. To understand what happens if there is, it is necessary to introduce the concept of *global* and *local* variables. The next example (which does not make use of functions) illustrates the concept of global variables.

Let us assume that file udf1.php contains the following lines:

```
<?php

// PHP statements here

$a=100;
$b="abcde";

// more PHP statements

?>
Here is some HTML text<br>
Another line of text<p>
<?php

// Here $a and $b are still 100 and "abcde", respectively
?>
```

The file comprises two PHP scripts separated by two lines of HTML. Despite this fragmentation the values given to $a and $b in the first script are still in force in the second script. It is in this sense that variables $a and $b are called global variables: once values have been assigned to them they apply to any further PHP scripts in the same file. When the file ceases execution the variable values cease to exist, unless they are passed to a new PHP file via its URL (as described in Chap. 10) or using a web form (as will be described in Chap. 9).

The position with variables used in functions is entirely different. This example is an amended version of one given previously.

```
<?php
$aa=100;
$bb=50;

function printout($thisfile,$bb){
   $arr=file($thisfile);
   for ($i=0;$i<count($arr);$i++) print trim($arr[$i])."<br>";
   $aa=200;
   $bb=150;
} //printout

$myfile="docs/file99.txt";

printout($myfile1,-8.4);

// Here variable $aa has value 100 and variable $bb has value 50.
// Variables $arr and $i both have undefined values

?>
```

As the comments at the end of the script indicate, variables $arr and $i, which were used when the function printout was executed have no existence once the function has ceased execution.

Variable $aa was given a value (100) before function printout was executed and still had this value after the function ceased execution, even though variable $aa was assigned the value 200 during the execution of the function. The value −8.4 was passed to *printout* as the value of parameter $bb and this was increased to 150 within the function. Despite this variable $bb still had the value 50 after the function had finished executing.

This is because variables $aa and $bb used in function printout are entirely different variables from the variables $aa and $bb used outside the function. Variables $aa, $bb, $arr and $i used in function printout are called *local variables*. Global variable $bb used outside the function definition has the same name as a local variable used within the function, but they are entirely separate variables.

We can think of a function definition as being enclosed in a sealed box with its own local variables that are entirely separate from any variables of the same name used outside the box. Values are passed into the box via the argument list and a value may be passed out using a RETURN statement.

This separation between local and global variables is generally of great value to the programmer. It means that functions can be defined without any need to consider the variables that will be used elsewhere in the script from which they are called.

8.3 Returning More than One Value

Sometimes it may be desirable for a function to return more than one value. We can handle this by creating an array with the required values as its elements and then returning the array as the function's (one) return value.

In this example, two numbers and a string are returned as the elements of an array which is then assigned to variable $myarray.

```
<?php
$a=4; $b=3;
function threeRes($a,$b){
$x=$a*$a+$b*$b;
$y=$a*$a-$b*$b;
return array($x,$y,"dog");
} // threeRes

$myarray=threeRes($a,$b);
for ($i=0;$i<=2;$i++) print $i."...".$myarray[$i]."<br>\n";
?>
```

produces the output

```
0...25
1...7
2...dog
```

8.4 Creating a Function Library

If you write any significant number of PHP scripts you are likely to find that there are some sequences of statements that you use frequently in the same or nearly the same form. Such sequences are natural candidates for making into functions.

For example, if you often store numbers in the *yymmdd* form used in this book (e.g. 180624 for 24th June 2018) you are likely to find that the associative array definition given in Sect. 4.5.1 to illustrate how to convert a month number such as "02" into a month name such as "February" will prove useful in several different scripts. This makes it a good candidate for conversion to a function genMonthName, as shown below.

```
<?php
// PHP statements here

function genMonthName($monthnum){
    $monthnames = array (
    '01' => 'January', '02' => 'February', '03' => 'March',
    '04' => 'April', '05' => 'May', '06' => 'June',
    '07' => 'July', '08' => 'August', '09' => 'September',
    '10' => 'October', '11' => 'November', '12' => 'December');
    return $monthnames[$monthnum];
} //genMonthName

$month="02";
// PHP statements here

$mname=genMonthName($month);
// $mname now has the value "February"

?>
```

Functions that are likely to be needed frequently in different scripts can also be placed in special PHP files to form a personal *function library*. For example we may decide to place function genMonthName together with the original version of function printout into a function library. To do this is straightforward. We simply create a file with a name such as utils.php ('utils' standing for 'utilities') with the following contents.

```
<?php
function genMonthName($monthnum){
   $monthnames = array (
   '01' => 'January', '02' => 'February', '03' => 'March',
   '04' => 'April', '05' => 'May', '06' => 'June',
   '07' => 'July', '08' => 'August', '09' => 'September',
   '10' => 'October', '11' => 'November', '12' => 'December');
   return $monthnames[$monthnum];
} //genMonthName

function printout($thisfile){
   if (!is_readable($thisfile)){
       return 0;
   }
   $arr=file($thisfile);
   for ($i=0;$i<count($arr);$i++) print trim($arr[$i])."<br>";
   return count($arr);
} //printout
?>
```

We will never execute this PHP file in the usual sense of pointing our web browser to it, but if we did there would be nothing for the browser to display. Functions do nothing until they are called. Instead we will insert the functions into one or potentially many scripts using an INCLUDE or a REQUIRE statement. Thus the last example would become:

```
<?php
include "utils.php";

// PHP statements here

$month="02";
// PHP statements here

$mname=genMonthName($month);
// $mname now has the value "February"

?>
```

It might be objected that the definitions of both function genMonthName and function printout are inserted into the script although only the former is used. However this is a small price to pay for the convenience of using commonly needed functions this way.

8.5 Using a GLOBAL Statement in a Function Definition

Although the value of the separation between global and local variables was stressed earlier, on some occasions it may be desirable (or at least convenient) for the execution of a function to be able to use and/or change the values of some of the variables outside the sealed box. It is possible to use a GLOBAL statement in a function definition to specify that some variable names are to be treated as global.

To illustrate this we will amend an example given previously to add a GLOBAL statement to the function printout.

```
<?php
$aa=100;
$bb=50;
function printout($thisfile) {
   global $aa,$bb;
   $arr=file($thisfile);
   for ($i=0;$i<count($arr);$i++) print trim($arr[$i])."<br>";
   $aa=200;
   $bb=150;
} //printout
$myfile="docs/file99.txt";
printout($myfile1);
// Here variables $aa and $bb have the values 200 and 150
// Variables $arr and $i both have undefined values
?>
```

In this case the variables $aa and $bb used in function printout are specified as being the same as the global variables used outside the function. When their values are changed inside the function they change outside the function too.

Although this approach has been included here for completeness, it is probably best avoided. The separation between local variables inside a function definition and global variables outside it is a valuable one which makes it much easier to write functions that are reusable, especially if they are to be placed in function libraries for use by means of INCLUDE or REQUIRE. We will not use it again in this book.

8.6 Passing an Array as a Function Argument

As well as 'regular' variables it is possible for an entire array to be passed as an argument to a function. This example illustrates what happens.

```
<?php
function test($myarray){
   for ($i=0;$i<=4;$i++) $myarray[$i]=999;
} // test

$testarray=array(10,20,30,40,50);
test($testarray);

for ($i=0;$i<=4;$i++) print $i."...".$testarray[$i]."<br>";
?>
```

The output produced is

```
0...10
1...20
2...30
3...40
4...50
```

The values of the elements of $testarray are unchanged. This may be surprising to readers who are familiar with passing arrays as arguments in other languages but it is entirely consistent with passing other (non-array) variables.

8.7 Arguments Passed by Value and Arguments Passed by Reference

Up to now all variables passed into a function through its argument list are passed *by value*. Nothing the function does can change the values of variables (even those of the same name) that are outside the function.

This is generally all that is needed but there are some occasions when it is desirable to allow a function to change the value of a variable that is passed to it through its argument list. We say that such variables are passed or called *by reference*. Passing by reference is achieved by making a small change to the function's argument list. Preceding the name of a variable by an ampersand character indicates that it is to be passed by reference.

In this example, the function's argument list has two variables: $aa and $bb. The latter is preceded by & indicating that it is to be passed by reference.

```
<?php
$x=100;
$y=50;

function test($aa,&$bb){
    $aa=200;
    $bb=150;
} //test

test($x,$y);

print "x=".$x."<br>";
print "y=".$y."<br>";

?>
```

This script produces the output:

```
x=100
y=150
```

The first argument passed to function test, i.e. $x, has been treated as passed by value and so its value of 100 was not changed by the function call. On the other hand, the second argument passed to the function, i.e. $y, was passed by reference and so the assignment $bb=150 inside the function caused the value of $y to be changed to 150.

Passing some arrays by reference is likely to prove of more value in practice. This example shows two arrays passed to function test. Array $array1 is passed by value. The ampersand in the argument list shows that array $array2 is passed by reference.

```
<?php
$x=array(10,20,30,40,50,60);
$y=array(10,20,30,40,50,60);

function test($array1,&$array2){
   for ($i=0;$i<=5;$i++){
      $array1[$i]+=100;
      $array2[$i]+=100;
   }
} //test

test($x,$y);

for ($i=0;$i<=5;$i++){
   print $x[$i]."....." .$y[$i]."<br>";
}
?>
```

The output from this script is given below:

```
10.....110
20.....120
30.....130
40.....140
50.....150
60.....160
```

All the elements of array $x are unchanged by the function call, whereas all the elements of $y have been increased by 100.

The final example in this section is a function to set all the elements of an indexed array to zero.

```
<?php
function zeroize(&$array1){
  for ($i=0;$i<count($array1);$i++) $array1[$i]=0;
} //zeroize

$x=array(10,20,30,40,50,60);

zeroize($x);

for ($i=0;$i<=5;$i++){
  print $i."...".$x[$i]."<br>";
}
?>
```

The output from the script confirms that all the elements of $x have been set to zero.

8.8 Default Values for Arguments

Another unusual feature of functions in PHP is the facility to omit some of the arguments when calling a function, in which case specified default values are used.

The example below shows a function with four arguments, all passed by value. The third and fourth arguments both have specified default values.

```
<?php
function testdef($a,$b,$c=120,$d="dog"){
  print $a."...".$b."...".$c."...".$d."<p>\n";
} //testdef

testdef(10,20,90,"cat");
testdef(10,20);
testdef(10,20,500);
?>
```

The output from the three function calls is shown below. It can be seen that if the third and fourth arguments are omitted they are treated as having default values, namely 120 in the case of $c and the string "dog" in the case of $d.

```
10...20...90...cat

10...20...120...dog

10...20...500...dog
```

When a variable is passed by value the default value must be a constant, not a variable or a function call, etc. As the next example shows, the variable can also be an array of constants.

```
<?php
function test2($a,$b,$c=array(100,200,300,"yes"),$d="dog"){
  print $a."...".$b."<br>\n";
  foreach ($c as $k=>$el) print $k."=>".$el."<br>";
} //test2

test2(10,20);
?>
```

The output from this script is

```
10...20
0=>100
1=>200
2=>300
3=>yes
```

Note that when using default arguments in a function definition, any such arguments should be specified to the right of any non-default arguments. When the function is called any omitted values must be the right-most ones in the argument list. So in the case of test2 above, the function call test2(60,90,array(12,24,–6)) would be valid but test2(60,90,,"cat") would not be.

From PHP version 5 onwards it has been possible for variables passed by reference to have default values too, but that possibility will not be discussed here.

Chapter Summary
This chapter demonstrates how users can define their own functions as part of a PHP script. The concept of global and local variables is introduced and the value of creating a function library is discussed. The chapter goes on to consider related issues such as passing an array as an argument of a function and the difference between passing arguments by value and by reference. Finally it is shown how to give arguments default values

Practical Exercise 8

(1) Define a function *hypo* that takes the length of the two shorter sides of a right-angled triangle as arguments and returns the length of the hypotenuse.

(2) Define a function that prints out the contents of a two-dimensional array row-by-row.

(3) Convert your answer to (2) to print out the contents in the form of a table.

(4) Define a function that displays a specified image, with a specified width and height. The default values of width and height should be 150 and 200 respectively.

(5) Define a function that sets all the elements of a two-dimensional array to a given value (default zero).

Chapter 9
Passing Variables to a PHP Script I

Chapter Aims
After reading this chapter you should be able to:

- understand in detail the components of a web form
- write a webform of your own using a combination of HTML and PHP function calls

9.1 Introduction

In this chapter we look at the most common way of passing the values of variables into a PHP script: the use of a webform, normally written in HTML, to send values to a PHP script which we will call a *destination page*.

Although this book is not about HTML, the topic of webforms is a major exception. Unless you have previously used PHP (or some similar language) to write destination pages it is most unlikely that you have used HTML to write webforms and we will assume that you have not. We will see that even for quite basic webforms it can save a great deal of effort and avoid a lot of errors to use PHP to generate some or all of the lines of HTML.

In the next chapter we will discuss how to write the PHP statements for a destination page to make use of the values passed from a webform and will discuss two other ways in which values can be passed into a PHP script.

M. Bramer, *Web Programming with PHP and MySQL*,
DOI 10.1007/978-3-319-22659-0_9

9.2 Webforms

Many organisations now invite their users, customers etc. to provide information by filling in a form on the screen and pressing a 'submit' button. This is a typical (but simple) example of a *webform*.

Enter your details below

Forename * Surname *

Address *

Age Group ○ under 20 ○ 20 to 40 ○ 40 to 60 ○ 60+

Nationality British

I agree to the terms and conditions ☐

Submit Reset

Press the Submit button to send us your form

Filling in the form and pressing Submit will send the information to another webpage, which we will call the *destination page*, and the user's web browser will automatically move to that page. The destination page must be written in PHP or some similar language (not plain HTML). On receiving the values passed from the 'sending' page the destination page will take some action, create or update a database record or some combination of such actions. We will come on to destination pages in Chap. 10.

This simple example illustrates seven different types of box, button etc., known collectively as *form objects*.

- The one-line horizontal boxes for Forename and Surname are known as *text boxes* or *text fields*. These are each 20 characters wide but up to 50 characters may be typed in each. (When there are more than 20 characters entered, the left-most ones scroll off to the left and become unreadable.) We will see how to specify the 20 and 50 values when we look at the HTML used to generate the form.
- A common convention is to place an asterisk after a form object if it is compulsory for the user to complete it. Here we are insisting that Forename, Surname and Address are provided. There will need to be a test that these boxes are not empty in the destination page.

- The box next to Address is called a *textarea*. This one is two rows high and 24 columns wide. The user can type any amount of text into the textarea and it will automatically wrap around as the right-hand edge of the box is reached. If more than two lines are typed the uppermost ones will scroll up and become unreadable.
- The line beginning Age Group is an example of the use of *radio buttons*. The user can select at most one of the options. Selecting an option makes the small circle (the 'button') turn black. Clicking on another option makes the first button clear again and turns the second one black. The complete set of radio buttons is known as a *radio group*.
- The line beginning Nationality illustrates a 'Select Box'. Clicking on the arrow (or other marker) to the right of the word British will produce a drop-down menu with a (short) list of alternative nationalities.
- The small square to the right of the words 'I agree to the terms and conditions' is a checkbox. Clicking on it once puts a small tick (or similar symbol) into the box indicating that the option is selected. Clicking on the box again removes the contents making the option unselected.
- There needs to be a Submit button at the end of every web form. Pressing it sends all the values entered in the form to the destination page and moves the user's web browser automatically to that page.
- The Reset button can sometimes be useful, especially if the user makes mistakes in entering some of the values. Pressing it returns the web form to its original state.

Although writing a web form can be done entirely in HTML it is a tedious and error-prone task if the form is anything but trivial, and can be made considerably faster by using a PHP script, or perhaps a number of small fragments of PHP to generate the lines of HTML automatically and then output them using PHP print statements.

Apart from the buttons, most form elements can be given default values that are used if the user does not change them. In the above example the only field with a default value is the Select Box labelled Nationality, which has a default of British. Default values that are always the same for every user can be specified entirely in HTML, as will be explained below. However this is not possible when the default values may vary from one user to another, e.g. name and address values that have been taken from a database. In this case the default value needs to be entered into the form using a PHP script.

The HTML needed to generate the form given above is shown below with the lines numbered for ease of reference.

```
1  <p><strong>Enter your details below</strong></p>
2  <form name="form1" method="post" action="mydir/destin1.php">
3  Forename
4  <input type="text" name="forename" size=20 maxlength=50> * Surname
5  <input type="text" name="surname" size=20 maxlength=50> * </p>
6  <p>Address
7  <textarea name="address" rows=2 cols=24></textarea> *</p>
8  <p>Age Group
9  <input type="radio" name="agegroup" value="group1"> under 20
10 <input type="radio" name="agegroup" value="group2"> 20 to 40
11 <input type="radio" name="agegroup" value="group3"> 40 to 60
12 <input type="radio" name="agegroup" value="group4"> 60+
13 <p> Nationality <select name="nationality">
14 <option value="GB">British</option>
15 <option value="FR">French</option>
16 <option value="US">United States</option>
17 <option value="CN">Chinese</option>
18 </select>
19 <p>I agree to the terms and conditions
20 <input type="checkbox" name="tsandcs" value="terms">
21 </p><p>
22 <input type="submit" name="Submit" value="Submit">
23 <input type="reset" name="Reset" value="Reset">
24 </form>
25 </p><p>Press the Submit button to send us your form<p>
```

Every web form begins with a <form> tag and ends with a </form> tag (see lines 2 and 24 above). The <form> tag and form elements have a number of attribute=value combinations such as method="post". Some of these are compulsory, others are optional. The value given after the = sign should normally be enclosed in double quotes, unless it is purely numerical and definitely must be if it contains any embedded spaces. Apart from the right-hand side of an attribute=value pair and any default values, upper and lower case letters can be used interchangeably in a web form.

Some of the less-commonly used attributes are accepted by one web browser, but ignored by another. Naturally you will have no control over the browser a user chooses to use to access your pages, so non-standard attributes are best avoided. We will not attempt to include comprehensive details of every possible attribute here; just the ones that you are most likely to need to use and that are accepted by most or all common web browsers.

9.2.1 The <form> Tag

- The value of the name attribute is normally unimportant. However, if there is more than one form on the same page they should be given different names.
- The method attribute should normally be set to "post", which indicates that the values are to be sent to the destination page 'invisibly' and retrieved by that page as we shall illustrate in Chap. 10. Other possibilities will not be considered in this book.

- The value of the action attribute is the address of the destination page. This can either be an absolute address beginning with http:// or https:// or an address relative to the sending page. In the case of action="mydir/destin1.php" the destination page is file destin1.php in the folder 'mydir', which is a subfolder of the one in which the sending page is located. To indicate the current directory or its parent directory we can use the notation . and .. respectively. Thus to indicate that the destination page is the same as the sending page we can put action="."

9.3 Form Objects

The above example illustrates the most commonly used form objects. We will go on to describe how to write each of those used in the above example in HTML and also give a PHP function that will generate the necessary HTML using a small number of parameters. We will assume that all the functions will be gathered together into a single PHP file named wfutils.php (wf standing for 'web form'). This file can then be included in the page that generates a web form by a PHP 'include' statement or a short PHP script, such as

```
<?php include "wfutils.php" ?>
```

9.3.1 *Text Field*

The HTML statement

```
<input type="text" name="forename" size=20 maxlength=50>
```

Will produce a text box representing a variable with the name forename. In this case, the box is wide enough to accept up to 20 characters of text, the value of the size attribute. However as many as 50 characters, the value of the maxlength parameter, may be entered. (If, say, 30 characters are entered, the first ten will scroll off to the left.) If the value of maxlength is omitted, the same value as size will be assumed by default.

If the 'value' attribute has a value, as in this example:

```
<input type="text" name="forename" size=20 maxlength=50 value="What is your name?">
```

that value will appear in the box as a default value.

Here and elsewhere in this chapter it is possible that the default value you wish to set is not a string constant but the value of a variable, say $defval. (This may have been obtained from a database, a text file etc.)

Specifying a variable as the default requires some use of PHP. The easiest way is to print the entire <input> tag, for example:

```
print "<input type=\"text\" name=\"forename\" size=20 maxlength=50 value=\"$defval\">";
```

Note that all the " symbols except the outermost pair have been 'escaped', i.e. preceded by a backslash character.

Writing a succession of form objects is a tedious and error-prone task, even when there are no non-constant default values involved. The effort involved can often be reduced considerably by using PHP to generate form objects automatically.

This short PHP user-defined function will automatically generate a text box with a specified default value (which may be an empty string).

```
function wftext($name,$size,$maxlength,$default){
    print "<input type=\"text\" name=\"$name\" size=\"$size\" maxlength=\"$maxlength\"
    value=\"$default\">";
} // wftext
```

It can be used by passing it just four parameters, e.g.

```
wftext("forename",20,50,"What is your name?");
```

9.3.2 Textarea Field

Unlike a text box, a textarea box allows more than one line of text to be entered. The HTML statement

```
<textarea name="address" rows=2 cols=24></textarea>
```

will place a box with 2 rows and 24 columns on the screen. The user can type any amount of text into the textarea and, as mentioned previously, it will automatically wrap around as the right-hand edge of the box is reached. If more than two lines are typed the uppermost ones will scroll up and become unreadable.

If for any reason you want to limit the number of characters entered in a textarea box an additional attribute/value pair can be used to do this, e.g.

```
<textarea name="address" rows=2 cols=24 maxlength=150></textarea>
```

(The 'maxlength' attribute is only available with HTML 5 onwards.)

Any text that is placed between the <textarea> tag and the closing </textarea> tag is treated as a default value, for example:

```
<textarea name="name4" rows="2" cols="24" > This is a default value. It is quite long and goes over
more than one line.</textarea>
```

will produce a text area box containing the words 'This is a default value. It is quite long and goes over more than one line.'

To include a line break in a default value, either press the 'return' key or use the combination
 which inserts two special characters, essentially 'carriage return' and 'linefeed'. Other possibilities such as using the combination \r\n or the HTML tags <br> and <p> will not work. Those characters will simply be displayed unchanged.

This short PHP user-defined function will generate a text box automatically

```
function wftextarea($name,$rows,$cols,$default){
print "<textarea name=\"$name\" rows=\"$rows\" cols=\"$cols\">$default</textarea>";
} // wftextarea
```

It can be used by passing it just four parameters, e.g.

```
wftextarea("name4",2,24,"This is a default value. It is quite long and goes over more than one line.");
```

9.3.3 *Radio Buttons in a Radio Group*

The HTML statements

```
<input type="radio" name="agegroup" value="group1"> under 20
<input type="radio" name="agegroup" value="group2"> 20 to 40
<input type="radio" name="agegroup" value="group3"> 40 to 60
<input type="radio" name="agegroup" value="group4"> 60+
```

will produce a row of four radio buttons in a radio group. The buttons all have the same value of the name attribute and it is that which links them together. It is the HTML text outside the <input> tag that tells the user what meaning to give to each possible selection. The button/text combinations are generally separated by a space character or a line break <br> tag or a paragraph break <p> tag. (In the above example there is an 'invisible' space at the end of each line.)

The text following the button will necessarily need to be unique, but the values do not all have to be different. For example we may have a quiz with a number of marks awarded for each answer, such as

```
Enter answer to question 4:
<input type="radio" name="question4" value="2"> a
<input type="radio" name=" question4" value="0"> b
<input type="radio" name=" question4" value="1"> c
<input type="radio" name=" question4" value="0"> d
```

A default value may be specified by adding the attribute 'checked' to one of the buttons.

```
<input type="radio" name="agegroup" value="group1" checked> under 20
```

The corresponding button will contain a black circle to indicate that it is the default value.

Writing a PHP function to generate a group of radio buttons is more difficult than for the text box and textarea. One approach is to create an associative array, e.g. by

```
$pairs=array("a"=>2,"b"=>0,"c"=>1,"d"=>0);
```

and then use the wfbuttons function defined below

```
function wfbuttons($name,$pairs,$default,$separator){
foreach ($pairs as $text=>$value){
  print "<input type=\"radio\" name=\"".$name."\" value=\"".$value."\"";
  if ($text==$default) print " checked";
  print "> ".$text.$separator;
}
} // wfbuttons
```

by a function call such as

```
wfbuttons("question4",$pairs,"b"," ");
```

This will produce a row of four buttons with the one labelled 'b' checked by default and with a space used as a separator between them.

9.3.4 Select Box

The Select Box is one that can benefit more than probably any other from PHP assistance, as we shall soon see.

The HTML used to produce the Select Box next to the word Nationality in the figure at the start of the chapter is given below.

```
<select name="nationality">
<option value="GB">British</option>
<option value="FR">French</option>
<option value="US">United States</option>
<option value="CN">Chinese</option>
</select>
```

The value displayed, in this case British, is the default value. Clicking on the small box next to it (or other symbol such as an arrow, depending on the browser used) produces a short drop-down menu. There is a choice of four nationalities, each of which will cause a value to be sent to the destination page. Thus choosing 'Chinese' will result in the value CN being sent.

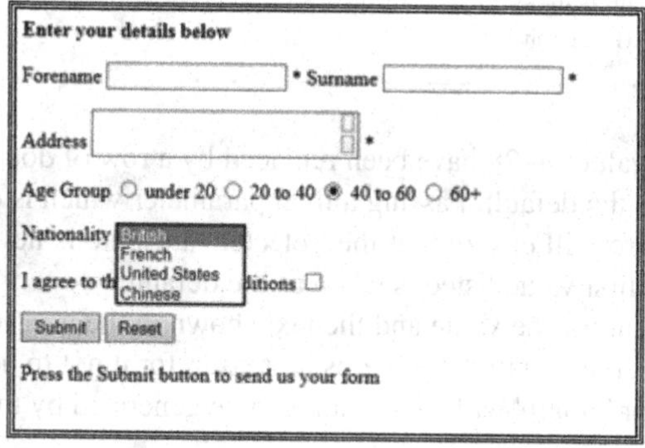

A default value can be specified by using the 'selected' attribute of the <option> tag. For example

```
<option value="FR" selected>French</option>
```

If none of the <option> tags has a 'selected' attribute, the first of them is assumed to be the default.

The main difficulty with using a Select box is that there will often be a large number of alternative options. Suppose we want a user to enter a date of birth in the order day, month and year. We need a Select box for day with values from 1 to 31, another one for month from 1 to 12 and one for year of birth from (perhaps) 100 years ago up to the current year.

The PHP function wfselectNumrange will generate a select box for a specified range of numbers.

```
function wfselectNumrange($name,$start,$end,$default){
print "<select name=\"".$name."\">\n";
for ($i=$start;$i<=$end;$i++){
  print "<option value=\"".$i."\"";
  if ($i==$default) print " selected";
  print ">".$i."</option>\n";
}
print "</select>\n";
} // wfselectNumrange
```

Calling the function by

```
wfselectNumrange("day",1,31,2);
```

will generate 33 lines of HTML

```
<select name="day">
<option value="1">1</option>
<option value="2" selected>2</option>
<option value="3">3</option>
........................................
<option value="29">29</option>
<option value="30">30</option>
<option value="31">31</option>
</select>
```

(The lines for values 4–28 have been replaced by a row of dots to save space.)

Here value 2 is the default. Passing a final parameter which is outside the specified range, e.g. zero will ensure that the 'selected' attribute is never included, with the result that the first value listed is taken as the default.

It is not essential for the value and the text shown to the user to be the same but in case of a day of the month there seems no reason for it not to be.

A select box for 'month' with no default can be generated by the function call

```
wfselectNumrange("month",1,12,0);
```

We can then use the two lines of PHP

```
$thisyear=date("Y");
wfselectNumrange("year",$thisyear-100,$thisyear,0);
```

to generate a select box for 'year' with 103 lines of HTML, with no default.

We may wish to improve on this in the case of the select box for month, by displaying the words January, February etc. to the user whilst retaining the values 1, 2 etc.

To do this we will create a separate function to generate a select box as follows.

```
function wfselectMonth($name,$default){

$month=array("January","February","March","April","May","June","July","August",
"September","October","November","December");

print "<select name=\"".$name."\">\n";
for ($i=1;$i<=12;$i++){
  print "<option value=\"".$i."\"";
  if ($month[$i-1]==$default) print " selected";
  print ">".$month[$i-1]."</option>\n";
}
print "</select>\n";
} // wfselectMonth
```

Calling the function by

```
wfselectMonth("month","February");
```

will produce 14 lines of HTML with February as the default month.

```
<select name="month">
<option value="1">January</option>
<option value="2" selected>February</option>
<option value="3">March</option>
......................................
<option value="10">October</option>
<option value="11">November</option>
<option value="12">December</option>
</select>
```

Now we have the wfselectNumrange and wfselectMonth functions we can easily write the PHP script needed to generate select boxes that can be used for inputting the date of an event we are organising, assuming it is sometime this year or in the two following years. We will make the default date displayed today's date. We can do this by:

```
$day=date("d"); $month=date("F"); $year=date("Y");
// date("F") returns the name of the month in full text form, e.g. January
print "Date of event: ";
wfselectNumrange("day",1,31,$day);
print " ";
wfselectMonth("month",$month);
print " ";
wfselectNumrange("year",$year,$year+2,$year);
print "<p>";
```

If today were July 4th 2018, the result would be a row of three select boxes like this.

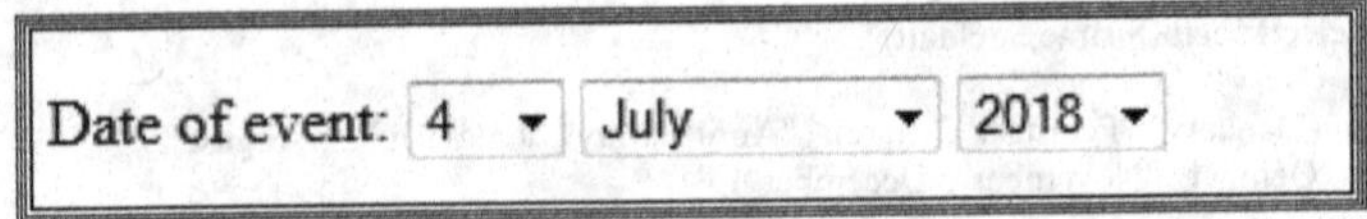

Two further attributes that can be used with the <select> tag are size and multiple.

The size attribute might be better called 'height'. The combination size=2 specifies that the select box should be two values high rather than the usual one. The HTML below

```
<select name="nationality" size=2>
<option value="GB">British</option>
<option value="FR">French</option>
<option value="US">United States</option>
<option value="CN">Chinese</option>
</select>
```

gives a form object that looks like this.

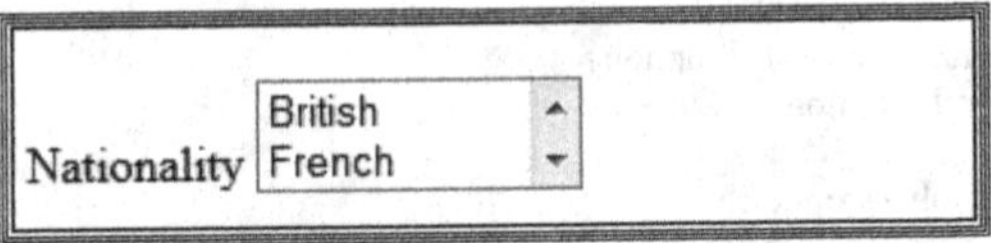

This is unlikely to be of much value and has the possible disadvantage that if no option is specified as checked, there will be nothing sent to the destination page, rather than the first item in the normal situation where size is not specified (or has the value 1).

The real value of the size attribute is when it is used in conjuction with the multiple attribute. To illustrate this we will change to a new example. The HTML below generates a select box which enables the user to specify any from zero to all seven choices in a list of possible interests.

```
<p> Please send me information about (select all that apply)
<p></p>
<select name="interests[]" size=4 multiple>
<option value="1">Sport</option>
<option value="2">Films</option>
<option value="3">Drama</option>
<option value="4">Local Events</option>
<option value="5">Services</option>
<option value="6">Education</option>
<option value="7">Transport</option>
</select>
<p>
```

There are three points to note about the <select> tag

```
<select name="interests[]" size=4 multiple>
```

The first is the use of the attribute 'multiple'. The second is the use of the 'size' attribute. This gives a larger (taller) selection box, which makes it easier to make multiple selections. The third and most important point is that instead of a name such as interests the name is given as interests[], with the opening and closing square brackets indicating that an array of options will be transferred to the destination page, rather than a single value.

The form element looks like this.

Please send me information about (select all that apply)

Sport
Films
Drama
Local Events

To make multiple selections click on the first selected item. This should cause it to become highlighted. Now hold down the 'Ctrl' key on the keyboard and click on the second and subsequent choices, which should all become highlighted too. Clicking on the same choice twice will cancel the selection. (For some keyboards, it may be that some other key needs to be used rather than 'Ctrl', possibly 'Alt'.)

We end this section by showing how to create a select box when there are a large number of options, which do not form some simple sequence such as numbers from 1 to 31. We will illustrate this by showing how to construct a select box for country of residence.

The International Standards Organisation (ISO) has a list[1] of around 240 countries, each with a corresponding unique two character code: FR for France, GB for United Kingdom etc. To enclose these country names and codes in HTML <option> tags would be an extremely tedious and error-prone task. It is much easier by means of a little cutting and pasting to create a text file, which we will call countries.txt containing 240 or so lines such as

```
United Kingdom of Great Britain and Northern Ireland*GB
Afghanistan*AF
Aland Islands*AX
Albania*AL
Algeria*DZ
```

and ending with

[1] Currently located at http://en.wikipedia.org/wiki/ISO_3166-1

```
Wallis And Futuna*WF
Western Sahara*EH
Yemen*YE
Zambia*ZM
Zimbabwe*ZW
```

Here each country name has been separated from its two-character code by an asterisk. The United Kingdom has been moved to the top of the list as the author's preferred default country. The list may also have been cut down to a more manageable one of say 100 'major' countries plus a line such as

Other*ZZ

as the final entry.

Now all we need to generate a Select box for countries is the following PHP function.

```
1   function wfselectlist($name,$listFile){
2   print "<select name=\"".$name."\">\n";
3   $arr=file($listFile);
4   for ($i=0;$i<count($arr);$i++){
5     $next=trim($arr[$i]);
6     $parts=explode("*",$next);
7     print "<option value=\"".$parts[1]."\">".$parts[0]."</option>\n";
8   } //for
9   print "</select>\n";
10  } // wfselectlist
```

which we can call by

```
wfselectlist("country","countries.txt");
```

The 'for' loop (lines 4–8) and the assignment statement in line 5 isolate each separate line of the text file. Then the use of the explode function (line 6) divides the line into the parts before and after the asterisk.

Now the wfselectlist function is available it can be used to generate other lengthy lists in a simple fashion from a text file, in the same way.

9.3.5 *Checkbox*

The checkbox next to the words 'I agree to the terms and conditions' in the figure at the start of the chapter can be generated by the HTML

```
<input type="checkbox" name="tsandcs" value="terms">
```

If the box is checked by the user the value 'terms' for variable 'tsandcs' will be passed to the destination page.

To make the default value that the box is checked we use the 'checked' attribute.

<input type="checkbox" name="tsandcs" value="terms" checked>

In this case a tick (or similar symbol) will appear in the box in the web form. The following PHP function will generate this form object.

```
function wfcheckbox($name,$value,$checked){
print "<input type=\"checkbox\" name=\"".$name."\" value=\"".$value."\"";
if ($checked=="yes") print " checked";
print ">";
} // wfcheckbox
```

To generate a checkbox where the box is checked by default we can use a PHP function call such as:

```
wfcheckbox("tsandcs","terms","yes");
```

To generate a checkbox where the box is unchecked by default we can use a PHP function call such as:

```
wfcheckbox("tsandcs","terms","no");
```

9.3.6 Submit and Reset Buttons

Submit and Reset buttons can be created by using these two lines of HTML, respectively.

```
<input type="submit" name="Submit" value="Submit">
<input type="reset" name="Reset" value="Reset">
```

In each case the value of the value attribute gives the text that is to be placed on the button. For example instead of Submit we might prefer the submit button to say 'Click here to continue', in which case we simply change the first line to

```
<input type="submit" name="Submit" value="Click here to continue">
```

To give the two buttons side-by-side, separated by a space, we can call the PHP function

```
function wfsubmitreset(){
print "<input type=\"submit\" name=\"Submit\" value=\"Submit\"> "
."<input type=\"reset\" name=\"Reset\" value=\"Reset\">";
} //wfsubmitreset
```

by the call

```
wfsubmitreset();
```

Incidentally the names given to the Submit and Reset buttons are generally of no importance, except that they must not clash with any other names used in the form. However, it is possible for a form to have more than one submit button, in which case they must all have unique names.

9.4 Other Form Objects

There are other form objects which we have not yet seen. We can illustrate the main ones by this new web form.

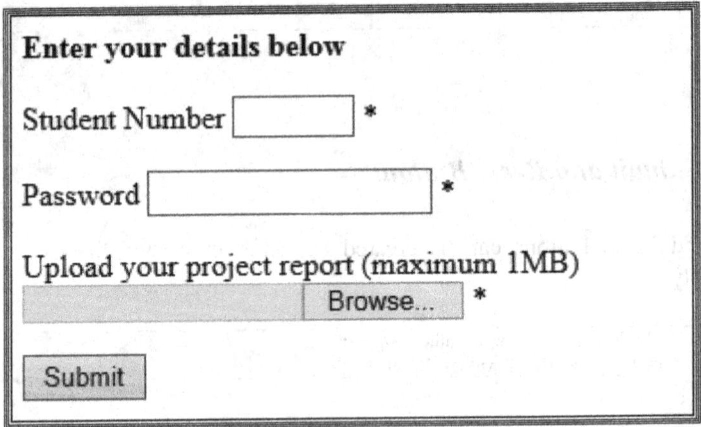

The HTML used to generate this form is given below.

```
<b>Enter your details below</b><p>
<form name="form2" method="post" action="destin1.php" enctype="multipart/form-data">
Student Number
<input type="text" name="snumber" size=6 maxlength=6> *<p>
Password
<input type="password" name="spassword" size=20 maxlength=20> * </p>
<input type="hidden" name="projectRef" value="COMP102-3">
Upload your project report (maximum 1MB)<br>
<input type="hidden" name="MAX_FILE_SIZE" value="1048576">
<input type="file" name="report"> * </p>
<p></p>
<input type="submit" name="Submit" value="Submit">
</form>
```

Note the mysterious-looking additional attribute/value pair that has appeared in the <form> tag: enctype="multipart/form-data". This is essential when there is a file to be uploaded (see Sect. 9.4.3).

9.4.1 Password Field

The box next to the words 'Student Number' is a regular text box. The box next to Password looks the same but is a variant of a text box called a *password box.*

The form of the HTML statement is the same as for a text box except that "type=text" is replaced by "type=password". For example:

```
<input type="password" name="name2" size="20" maxlength="30">
```

Characters typed into the box are not displayed on the user's screen. Instead they appear as large black dots, thus making the text typed unreadable by any onlookers. So if the name Mary Jones is entered, it will appear as 10 dots:

As for a text field, a default value may be specified:

```
<input type="password" name="name2" size="20" maxlength="30" value="mypassword">
```

The default value will appear in the box as a default value, with each of the characters replaced by a large black dot.

A default value is most likely to be used when a stored password has been read from a database and the user is given the option to change it. We will come on to databases in Chap. 12.

This PHP function can be used to generate a password box automatically.

```
function wfpassword($name,$size,$maxlength,$default){
    print "<input type=\"password\" name=\"$name\" size=\"$size\" maxlength=\"$maxlength\"
    value=\"$default\">";
} // wfpassword
```

It can be used by a function call such as

```
wfpassword("name2",20,20,"");
```

9.4.2 *Hidden Field*

The above example also illustrates the use of a hidden field.

HTML such as this

<input type="hidden" name="name3" value="my secret value">

does not place anything on the screen, but when the Submit button is pressed, the value "my secret value" will be sent to the destination page as the value of variable "name3". In the example this is used to pass the reference number for the student project to the destination page.

The main use of hidden fields is to pass values to a destination page that are important for an application but of little or no interest to the user. Note that a hidden field cannot be used to keep a value secret from the user of a web form as simply viewing the HTML source of the web page will show the value.

The following PHP function will generate a hidden field automatically.

```
function wfhidden($name,$value){
    print "<input type=\"hidden\" name=\"$name\" value=\"$value\">";
} // wfhidden
```

It can be called by e.g.

```
wfhidden("name3","my secret value");
```

9.4.3 File Field

The final box shown in the above example is called a *file box*. It is next to the text 'Upload your project report'. This provides a facility for the user to upload a file (here a file of text, but possibly an image or some other sort of file). This creates a potential security risk for the server and perhaps because of this there are restrictions on how the file box can be used. In fact, this is probably the most difficult and error-prone type of form object to use.

The HTML to generate a basic file box is very simple, for example

```
<input type="file" name="myproject file">
```

To use the facility is also straightforward. As its name suggests, pressing the Browse button (which is automatically provided as part of the form object) allows the user to browse through files on his/her hard disk and select one for uploading. Pressing the Submit button then uploads the file to the server and sends its name and other information as part of the information sent to the destination page. No default value is possible.

A major problem with this approach is that many web service providers limit the size of a file that can be uploaded this way. The limit is typically 2 MB or 5 MB. If this restriction is potentially crucial for your application, you will probably need to contact your service provider to find out the limit and (if possible) arrange for it to be increased.

It is also possible for a lower maximum limit to be specified in the HTML. This explains the second hidden field in the above example.

```
<input type="hidden" name="MAX_FILE_SIZE" value="1048576">
```

This specifies that no file larger than the specified size (measured in bytes) can be uploaded. In this case the limit is 1048576 bytes, i.e. 1 MB. It is recommended that this statement be placed before the corresponding <input type="file"> tag. Note that there is no warning message given to users about file size limits unless the designer of the web form places one on the form.

There is a serious potential confusion about what happens if the user attempts to upload a larger file. Although it is possible that not all systems work in the same way, the file will generally still be uploaded and held as a temporary file on the server while the destination page, a PHP script, is executed. When we come to look at issues related to a destination page (Chap. 10) we will see that there needs to be a PHP instruction to copy that temporary file into the website's file store as a permanent file. At that stage the PHP system will recognise that the file is too large and will fail to save it (which will later cause it to be deleted automatically). Depending on how the destination page is written the user may then be sent a message saying that the file could not be uploaded, when in fact it exceeded the maximum file size restriction.

A further issue with uploading files is whether it is possible to restrict the uploading only to files of a certain kind. This can be done in the case of a PDF file by an extension to the basic <input> statement.

```
<input type="file" name="myfile" accept="application/pdf">
```

To be precise the restriction is not to files in PDF format, simply to those with the extension pdf, which may not invariably be the same. The user can browse through directories but only files with the extension pdf (or PDF) will be made available for selection.

Restrictions to other kinds of file type can also be made, e.g. to restrict uploads to image files with the extension gif or jpeg we can use:

```
<input type="file" name="myfile" accept="image/gif, image/jpeg">
```

(Here jpeg represents files with extension either jpeg or jpg.)

How to deal with an uploaded file in the destination page will be explained in detail in Chap. 10.

9.4.4 Readonly and Disabled Fields

That completes the set of form objects we will describe in this book. However we have not yet mentioned two attributes that can be used with most of them (except for the buttons). They are readonly and disabled. These two attributes are alternatives, so at most one of them should be used with any form object.[2] The HTML

```
<input type="text" name="forename" value="John" readonly>
```

indicates that the user will not be able to change the contents of the forename field. Note that there will be nothing on the form to tell the user this unless the web form designer supplies some text such as '(this value may not be changed)'.

When the Submit button is pressed the value of forename is sent to the destination page in the usual way.

The disabled attribute is significantly different from readonly. The HTML

```
<input type=text" name="forename" value="John" disabled>
```

causes the forename box to be 'greyed out', i.e. its contents will appear faint as well as being unchangeable. Most importantly, when Submit is pressed no value for forename will be sent to the destination page.

[2] If both are specified, disabled takes priority.

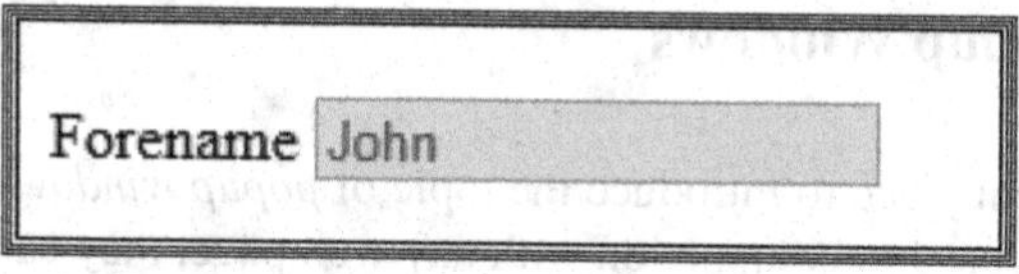

In cases where it is important for the value of a disabled attribute to be sent to the destination page this can be achieved by adding a hidden field such as

```
<input type="hidden" name="forename" value="John">
```

Text boxes, password boxes, textareas, radio groups, checkboxes, file boxes and select boxes can all be disabled, but only the first three can be made readonly.

Here are examples of the HTML needed to disable each of the various types of box.

```
<input type="text" name="forename" size=20 maxlength=50 disabled>
<input type="password" name="name2" size="20" value="secret123" disabled>
<textarea name="address" rows=2 cols=24 disabled >Hello World!</textarea>

<input type="radio" name="agegroup" value="group1"> under 20
<input type="radio" name="agegroup" value="group2"> 20 to 40
<input type="radio" name="agegroup" value="group3" disabled> 40 to 60
<input type="radio" name="agegroup" value="group4" disabled> 60+

<input type="checkbox" name="tsandcs" value="terms" checked disabled>

<select name="nationality" disabled>
<option value="GB">British</option>
<option value="FR">French</option>
<option value="US">United States</option>
<option value="CN">Chinese</option>
</select>

<input type="file" name="myproject file" disabled>
```

Note that each radio button can be disabled separately. In this example only the third and fourth of a 'radio group' of four buttons are disabled.

In case you are wondering why anyone would want to place a file box (which has no default value) on a web form and then disable it, it might be that the form object was generated automatically using a PHP script and that there are some circumstances when the box should be disabled and others when it should not be.

In the case of the text, password and textarea form objects the attribute *disabled* may be replaced by *readonly*. Incidentally if a file box is given a readonly attribute it is treated in the same way as disabled.

9.5 Using Popup Windows

This is a convenient place to introduce the topic of *popup windows*. Although they can potentially be used in conjunction with any web page, they can be particularly helpful when used to clarify the meaning of one or more of the questions in a web form.

Here is a typical example. The user is asked to agree to terms and conditions, but what are they? A link is provided so that he or she can find out.

Enter your details below

Forename * Surname *

Address *

Age Group under 20 20 to 40 40 to 60 60+

Nationality British

I agree to the terms and conditions What are they?

Submit Reset

Press the Submit button to send us your form

The system implementer needs to create a webpage containing the terms and conditions. We will assume that its relative address is "whatarethey.htm". Then a link has to be added to the HTML forming the web form next to the checkbox form object. This is likely to be

```
<a href="whatarethey.htm" target=_blank>What are they?</a>
```

The target=_blank part of this indicates that clicking on the link will open a new webpage of the same size as the original window. Having read the information the user then needs to close the new page and continue completing the web form. This is potentially confusing and a distraction (generally of little practical value) from the user's main focus – completing the form.

An alternative is to arrange for a small window known as a *popup window* or just as a *popup* to appear, superimposed on the webpage with the necessary information. The effect looks like this:

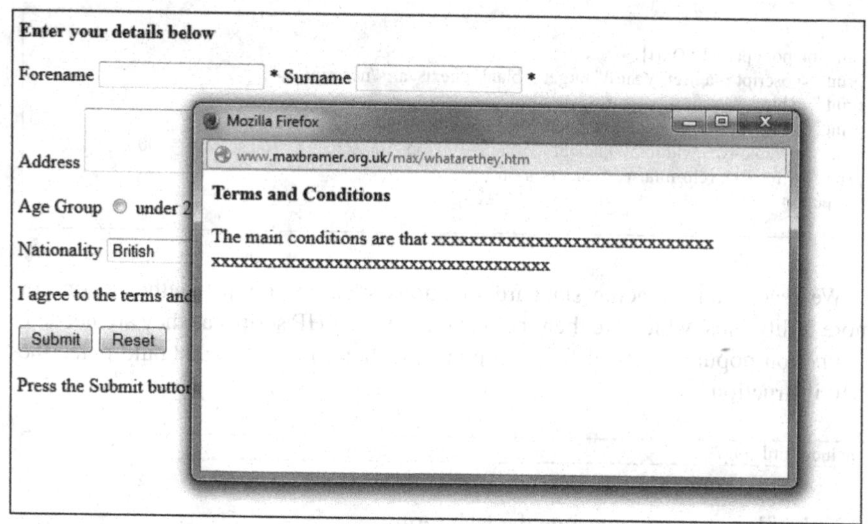

Having read (or perhaps just glanced at) the terms and conditions, it is natural for the user to close the popup window, to clear it out of the way, and continue filling in the form.

There is no facility in HTML to create a popup window but we can do it using JavaScript.[3]

Where the <a href="whatarethey.htm" target=_blank> What are they? </a> line would otherwise appear we place this complicated expression:

```
<noscript><a href="whatarethey.htm" target=_blank>What are they?</a></noscript>
<a href=# onClick="var nw=window.open('whatarethey.htm','moreinfowindow','scrollbars=yes,
resizable=yes,width=500,height=250,left=100,top=100,screenX=100,screenY=100');nw.focus();
return false;">What are they?</a>
```

This is a JavaScript statement written as part of a HTML <a href> tag. Making this replacement has no effect on what the user sees on the web form, but clicking on the link now produces the new page as a popup.

Unfortunately the JavaScript used to generate the popup is far from intuitively obvious to write and is likely to prove hard to remember. This is where using a PHP function is helpful. We can place the JavaScript inside a PHP function with two arguments, the first being the address of the new page and the second being the text of the link. A suitable PHP function would be the following:

---

[3] JavaScript is a scripting language with some similarities to PHP. However it is generally used very differently, for example to check that a value entered in a web form is numeric, before it is sent to the destination page, or to change the colour of a link when the user's mouse moves over it. There are many books devoted to JavaScript (not to be confused with the programming language Java, which is entirely different). Our only use of JavaScript in this book will be in connection with popups.

```
<?php
function popup($url,$text){
print "<noscript><a href=\"$url\" target=_blank>$text</a></noscript>\n";
print "<a href=# ";
print "onClick=\"var nw=window.open('$url','moreinfowindow','scrollbars=yes,";
print "resizable=yes,width=500,height=250,left=100,top=100,screenX=100,screenY=100');";
print "nw.focus(); return false;\">$text</a>\n";
} // popup
?>
```

We recommend placing standard functions such as popup together in one or more utility files, which are then included into your PHP scripts as they are needed. If function popup is part of file utils.php, say, then to use it you should place the PHP instruction

```
include "utils.php";
```

in the file you use to generate the web form.

To create the popup from within the web form you need to put the PHP function call

```
popup("whatarethey.htm","What are they?");
```

at the appropriate place.

The extension of the page used to generate the web form will now need to be php, not htm or html, even if the rest of the lines in the files are HTML.

If there is no other PHP in the file the above two lines will need to be enclosed in PHP tags, e.g.

```
<?php include "utils.php"; ?>
```

and

```
<?php popup("whatarethey.htm","What are they?"); ?>
```

Now we have the popup function we can embellish it. For example we might make the width and height values into parameters which default to 500 and 250 respectively. A suitable revised version of the popup function would be like this:

```
<?php
function popup($url,$text,$width=500,$height=250){
print "<noscript><a href=\"$url\" target=_blank>$text</a></noscript>\n";
print "<a href=# ";
print "onClick=\"var nw=window.open('$url','moreinfowindow','scrollbars=yes,";
print "resizable=yes,width=$width,height=$height,left=100,top=100,screenX=100,screenY=100');";
print "nw.focus(); return false;\">$text</a>\n";
} // popup
?>
```

Chapter Summary

This chapter gives a detailed explanation of webforms as a means by which the user of a web browser can send information to a PHP script known as a *destination page*. It is shown how to specify form objects on a webform in HTML and how this process can often be simplified using functions written in PHP.

Practical Exercise 9

(1) Convert the HTML used to create the webforms shown in Sects. 9.2 and 9.4 so that all the form objects are generated using PHP functions stored in 'utility' file wfutils.php.

(2) What effect does making the above change have on the names of the files needed to store the webforms?

Chapter 10
Passing Variables to a PHP Script II

Chapter Aims
After reading this chapter you should be able to:

- write the PHP statements that enable values sent by any of the form objects described in Chap. 9 to be used in a destination page
- send variable values to a destination page using an extended URL and write PHP statements to use the values sent in the destination page
- use session variables to pass values around the PHP scripts in a large website.

10.1 Introduction

In the last chapter we looked at the most common way of passing the values of variables into a PHP script: the use of a webform to send values from a *sending page* to a *destination page* written in PHP.

In this chapter we discuss the PHP statements needed in a destination page to make use of the values passed from a webform. We also discuss two other ways in which values can be passed into a PHP script.

10.2 Destination Pages

When the user completes a form and presses the submit button, the values entered in the various fields are sent to the web page (PHP script) specified in the action field of the <form> tag. This will generally cause some action to be taken and may

M. Bramer, *Web Programming with PHP and MySQL*,
DOI 10.1007/978-3-319-22659-0_10

involve the creation or updating of an entry in a database or a text file. To start our explanation of how to construct a PHP script for the destination page we will not attempt to do anything useful with the values received and will instead concentrate on establishing what exactly has been sent to the destination page and in what form.

For convenience we will repeat the web form shown at the start of Chap. 9.

Enter your details below

Forename * Surname *

Address *

Age Group ○ under 20 ○ 20 to 40 ○ 40 to 60 ○ 60+

Nationality British

I agree to the terms and conditions ☐

Submit Reset

Press the Submit button to send us your form

In all our examples the destination page has been named destin1.php. However it can potentially be any PHP file on the server where the sending page is located, referred to by a relative address such as ../mydir/update.php.

Pressing the Submit button causes the values entered by the user to be sent to the destination file, as 'key and value' pairs in the associative array $_POST (or in some cases a different associative array, as will be seen later).

Please note that the name $_POST is case sensitive. So are the names of the other system associative arrays introduced later in this chapter.

We give below a very short PHP script that will enable us to discover what the values sent to $_POST are.

```
<?php
foreach ($_POST as $var=>$value)
print "Next item: ".$var."=>".$value."<br>";
?>
```

The script extracts each of the key/value pairs from the array $_POST and outputs them in the form key=>value.

Suppose that now we complete the form with the following values and press Submit.

Enter your details below

Forename Erin * Surname Bryce *

Address Long Street Longtown *

Age Group ◉ under 20 ○ 20 to 40 ○ 40 to 60 ○ 60+

Nationality British

I agree to the terms and conditions

Submit Reset

Press the Submit button to send us your form

The outputs from the script destin1.php will be as follows.

```
Next item: forename=>Erin
Next item: surname=>Bryce
Next item: address=>Long Street Longtown
Next item: agegroup=>group1
Next item: nationality=>GB
Next item: tsandcs=>terms
Next item: Submit=>Submit
```

There are several points to note:

- The key part of each key/value pair is the name of the field on the web form. The 'value' part is the value entered by the user in the case of the first three fields and a value corresponding to the user's input (including values set by default) for the next three.
- The first two lines show the values entered by the user in the forename and surname text boxes. In a real destination page script we could refer to these values as $_POST['forename'] and $_POST['surname']. They are (just) the values of two elements in the associative array $_POST. In practice it would probably be more convenient to assign each value to a variable for use later in the script. The natural choice of variable names for this would be $forename and $surname, although this is not obligatory. So in practice the first few lines of the script of a destination page are likely to be assignments such as

```
$forename=$_POST['forename'];
$surname=$_POST['surname'];
```

- The value displayed for address is the text entered by the user, but run together with a space between the two lines. The web form would in fact have transmitted the values 'carriage return' and 'linefeed' to indicate the line break. These are the characters that would be represented in a PHP string as \r and \n. However web browsers replace any sequence of such characters, as well as tabs, spaces etc. by just a single space and it is this that has caused the effect seen here. If we particularly want to display the value passed with the original line breaks intact we can do this by replacing the 'carrriage return and linefeed' combination by HTML break characters, i.e.
. To do that we can use the PHP str_replace function, e.g.

```
$address=str_replace("\r\n","<br>",$_POST['address']);
```

- The values of agegroup and nationality are the values specified in the HTML of the web page corresponding to the choices made by the user. The same applies to the checkbox, where the name value is tsandcs.
- Perhaps surprisingly the Submit button has sent the name/value pair Submit/Submit. This can be avoided if the name field for the Submit button in the webform is set to "", i.e. an empty string, but there is no benefit to be achieved from doing this. Having the name/value pair sent is also a useful reminder that there can be more than one submit button on a form.

We will now change the form so that the Select box for nationality has size=2 and also the attribute 'multiple' specified, thus ensuring that it no longer has a default value. We will avoid filling in any values or making any selections and simply press the Submit button. The output is shown below:

```
Next item: forename=>
Next item: surname=>
Next item: address=>
Next item: Submit=>Submit
```

We can see that null values (i.e. empty strings "") have been sent from the web form to the destination page, whereas the array elements corresponding to agegroup, nationality and tsandcs (i.e. the checkbox) have vanished altogether. It makes little difference whether nothing is sent to the destination form or an empty string is sent. If we try to print the non-existent value of $_POST['nationality'] we will get an empty string. If we test the value of $_POST['nationality'] by say if ($_POST['nationality']=="") the system will act as if the corresponding value exists and is an empty string. This is a consequence of the way PHP deals with variables that have not previously been assigned any values, i.e. it assumes that they have an empty string as their value.

One difference that may be significant is if we use the isset function to test whether a value has been sent. The four lines of PHP

```
$forename=$_POST['forename'];
$agegroup=$_POST['agegroup'];
if (isset($forename)) print "forename set<br>"; else print "forename not set<br>";
if (isset($agegroup)) print "agegroup set<br>"; else print "agegroup not set<br>";
```

will produce the output

```
forename set
agegroup not set
```

even though both have null values (i.e. they are empty strings). When it is applied to values sent to a destination page the value returned by the isset function is always TRUE for text boxes, password boxes and textareas whether the field has been left empty or not. The conclusion to draw from this is that isset should not be used for those kinds of field. However it is useful for testing whether a selection has been made for other fields in a web form such as radio boxes and selection boxes.

We will now go back to the second example of a web form given in Chap. 9. The HTML is repeated below for convenience.

```
<b>Enter your details below</b><p>
<form name="form2" method="post" action="destin1.php" enctype="multipart/form-data">
Student Number
<input type="text" name="snumber" size=6 maxlength=6> *<p>
Password
<input type="password" name="spassword" size=20 maxlength=20> * </p>
<input type="hidden" name="projectRef" value="COMP102-3">
Upload your project report (maximum 1MB)<br>
<input type="hidden" name="MAX_FILE_SIZE" value="1048576">
<input type="file" name="report"> * </p>
<p></p>
<input type="submit" name="Submit" value="Submit">
</form>
```

The corresponding web form looks like this.

Enter your details below

Student Number [ ] *

Password [ ] *

Upload your project report (maximum 1MB)

[ ] Browse... *

Submit

Entering Student Number stud99, password mysecret, choosing file myreport.pdf, then pressing Submit will produce the following output from destin1.php.

```
Next item: snumber=>stud99
Next item: spassword=>mysecret
Next item: projectRef=>COMP102-3
Next item: Submit=>Submit
```

The value in the password box is reflected as plain text, rather than black dots. The value of the hidden field (COMP102-3) is also displayed.

No information about the uploaded file is displayed, although strangely if we had omitted the enctype="multipart/form-data" attribute in the <form> tag the additional line

```
Next item: report=>myreport.pdf
```

would be displayed.

The correct way of finding out about the name and other properties of an uploaded file is to use the system associative array $_FILES. There needs to be additional PHP coding in the destination page to use this information to save the uploaded file, as we will illustrate later in this chapter.

If we leave the form blank and then press Submit the output will be like this.

```
Next item: snumber=>
Next item: spassword=>
Next item: projectRef=>COMP102-3
Next item: Submit=>Submit
```

We can see that a key/value pair is sent to the destination page for a password field even when the field is empty, as is the case for text fields and textareas.

10.2.1 Checking for Compulsory Values

Although it a common practice to include an asterisk on a web form to indicate that entering a value is compulsory there is nothing in the form objects themselves to enforce this and it is necessary for it to be tested in the destination page. So a typical script might be like this:

```
$forename=$_POST['forename'];
$surname=$_POST['surname'];
$address=$_POST['address'];

if ($forename=="" || $surname=="" || $address=="")
  print "Error - you have not completed a compulsory field."
    ." Press the back button on your browser to go back and correct your entry";
else {
// other lines here
}
```

10.2.2 Checking for Numeric Values and Integers

There are sometimes other requirements, e.g. that a value entered must be numeric. Although there are several PHP functions that can be used for this, it is more complicated than it may appear and it is important to bear in mind that all values are received by the destination page as strings not numbers.

We recommend using the function is_numeric. For example, if a form has a field named 'price' which is meant to contain the price of a purchase, the destination page script might include

```
$price=$_POST['price'];
print "price=".$price."<br>";
if (is_numeric($price)) print "Value ".$price." is numeric<br>";
else print "Value ".$price. " is non-numeric<br>";
```

The definition PHP uses of a numeric field is one that contains an optional sign, any number of digits, an optional decimal part and an optional exponential part. So a value such as −84.37E-2 is considered numeric. Leading spaces are accepted but trailing spaces will make any value be treated as non-numeric. For this and other reasons it is generally a good idea to trim all values entered by the user. Changing the first line of the script to

```
$price=trim($_POST['price']);
```

will solve the problem of trailing spaces.

It may also be a requirement that an integer value is entered. There is a function is_int that will test for an integer value but if it is applied to a value that was sent to the destination page from a web form the test will invariably fail. This is because the value sent is always held as a string not a number.

```
$price=trim($_POST['price']);
print "price=".$price."<br>";
if (is_numeric($price)) print "Value ".$price." is numeric<br>";
else print "Value ".$price. " is non-numeric<br>";
if (is_int($price)) print "Value ".$price." is an integer<br>";
else print "Value ".$price." is not an integer<br>";
```

Entering a value such as 89 will then produce the output

```
price=89
Value 89 is numeric
Value 89 is not an integer
```

Fortunately PHP is very flexible in converting between strings and numbers. Performing an arithmetic operation on $price, even just multiplying it by 1 will convert the value into an integer.

If we add some additional lines to the script to make it

```
$price=trim($_POST['price']);
print "price=".$price."<br>";
if (is_numeric($price)) print "Value ".$price." is numeric<br>";
    else print "Value ".$price. " is non-numeric<br>";
if (is_int($price)) print "Value ".$price." is an integer<br>";
    else print "Value ".$price." is not an integer<br>";
$new=$price*1;
if (is_int($new)) print "New value ".$new." is an integer<br>";
    else print "New value ".$new." is not an integer<br>";
```

and then send the value 89, the output will be

```
price=89
Value 89 is numeric
Value 89 is not an integer
New value 89 is an integer
```

10.2.3 Multiple Selections

We will now return to the case of a selection box from which multiple selections can be made. Suitable HTML for this is shown below.

```
Please send me information about (select all that apply)<p>
<select name="interests[]" size=4 multiple>
<option value="1">Sport</option>
<option value="2">Films</option>
<option value="3">Drama</option>
<option value="4">Local Events</option>
<option value="5">Services</option>
<option value="6">Education</option>
<option value="7">Transport</option>
</select>
```

This will generate a web form of the following kind.

Please send me information about (select all that apply)

Sport
Films
Drama
Local Events

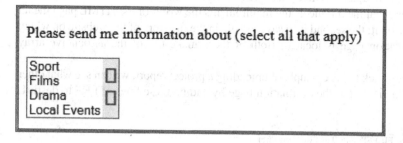

If we now select, say, Local Events followed by Education and press Submit, the foreach statement in the original version of destin1.php will produce the output line

```
Next item: interests=>Array
```

which is not very helpful. To go further we need to examine the array of values sent with the name *interests*. We can do this with the following lines of HTML. Note that we start by testing whether the value is an empty string. This is because if nothing is selected the form will not be sent anything at all as the value of *interests*, rather than an array, and in that case the foreach statement will cause a serious error to occur. In the case where $select has a non-null value the foreach statement will produce each of the values selected in turn.

```
$selected=$_POST['interests'];
if ($selected!="") {
  foreach($selected as $key=>$value)
  print "next option is: ".$key."=>".$value."<br>";
}
```

In our example the output from these extra lines of PHP will be

```
next option is: 0=>4
next option is: 1=>6
```

Note that although we said earlier that the two choices were made in the order Education then Local Events, they are extracted by foreach in the order in which they appear in the list of <option> tags in the HTML that generated the selection box.

10.2.4 File Fields

We now come to probably the most awkward part of writing a destination page: how to deal with an uploaded file. There are two parts to this: the first (which is optional) is to ensure that the file meets the requirements the writer of the HTML page meant to impose on it; the second is to save the file in the file store of the website on which the destination page is located. Both of these make use of the associative array $_FILES.

If we go back to the example of uploading a project report, we can see what other information is sent to the destination page by adding these lines of PHP to destin1.php

```
foreach ($_FILES['report'] as $var=>$value)
print "file item: ".$var."=>".$value."<p>";
```

If we upload a PDF field named myreport.pdf the output produced by the foreach statement will be something like this:

```
file item: name=>myreport.pdf
file item: type=>application/pdf
file item: tmp_name=>/tmp/phpJY2iNm
file item: error=>0
file item: size=>280951
```

These can be referred to in a PHP script by the names $_FILES['report']['tmp_name'] etc.

You may want to verify that the file size is less than your required maximum. You can also check that the file type is what you were expecting. In this case it is shown as application/pdf. However it is important to realise that this simply indicates that the file extension was pdf, not that the contents are in PDF format. Allowing a user to upload a file to your website inherently poses a potential security risk. How much you need to worry about this (or take steps to avoid it) probably depends mainly on your application.

Some common file extensions and the corresponding values returned as the 'type' value are given below:

doc	application/msword
docx	application/vnd.openxmlformats-officedocument.wordprocessingml.document
xls	application/vnd.ms-excel
xlsx	application/vnd.openxmlformats-officedocument.spreadsheetml.sheet
ppt	application/vnd.ms-powerpoint
pptx	application/vnd.openxmlformats-officedocument.presentationml.presentation
pdf	application/pdf
txt	text/plain
php	text/plain
gif	image/gif
jpg	image/jpeg
jpeg	image/jpeg

To determine whether an uploaded file is genuinely of the type indicated by its file extension is a difficult task. One PHP function that attempts to do so is the PHP function mime_content_type. For example if files abc.gif and def.php are what their extensions suggest the two lines

```
print mime_content_type('abc.gif') ."<br>";
print mime_content_type('def.php');
```

will produce the output

```
image/gif
text/plain
```

A determined hacker who knew how mime_content_type uses various indicators of a file's content to determine its type could no doubt work out a way to fool it. Computer security is a big topic, far outside the scope of this book. As with all security, keeping out even the most determined and skilled hacker is an endless struggle, but it is easy to take some basic precautions such as using mime_content_type to verify that an uploaded file is (probably) of the type you expect. Regrettably the function is not available with all versions of PHP.

Once a copy of a file has been uploaded it is held as a temporary file, possibly in a directory named /tmp with an obscure name such as phpJY2iNm. The next step is to move it into a permanent location on your website's file store with its permanent name, which we will assume will normally be the name of the original file on your hard disc. We will also assume that you wish the file to be stored in a folder with the name 'uploads'. Then we can use the function move_uploaded_file, which as its name suggests moves the uploaded file to its new permanent location. It is desirable to check that this has been done successfully. We can do so by:

```
$filename=$_FILES["report"]["name"];
if (move_uploaded_file($_FILES["report"]["tmp_name"], "uploads/".$filename))
  print "The file has been uploaded.";
else print "Sorry, there was an error uploading your file.";
```

There are a number of reasons why a file upload may fail. If this happens you should check that the <form> tag includes the attribute settings method="post" and enctype="multipart/form-data". Another possibility is that a system-wide file size restriction may have been violated. These often seem to apply to files larger than either 2MB or 5MB. Finally it may be that the file system has protections set that prevent the uploaded file being written to the target directory. The last of these possibilities can be checked using the is_writable function. In the above example the test would be

```
if (is_writable('uploads')) xxxxxxx
```

10.2.5 Quotes in Text Fields and Textareas

We will return once again to our original web form

Enter your details below

Forename * Surname *

Address *

Age Group ○ under 20 ○ 20 to 40 ○ 40 to 60 ○ 60+

Nationality British

I agree to the terms and conditions ☐

Submit Reset

Press the Submit button to send us your form

This time we will try entering values in the text fields and textarea that include double and/or single quotes. For example:

Enter your details below

Forename James "Jimmy" * Surname O'Brien *

Address
```
"The Laurels"
St. Michael's Way
Long Town
```
*

Age Group under 20 20 to 40 40 to 60 60+

Nationality British

I agree to the terms and conditions

Submit Reset

Press the Submit button to send us your form

The output generated by destin1.php will then include

```
Next item: forename=>James \"Jimmy\"
Next item: surname=>O\'Brien
Next item: address=>\"The Laurels\" St. Michael\'s Way Long Town
```

Each double and single quote has been 'escaped', i.e. preceded by a backslash character, when the values are printed.

The use of quotes in text fields (i.e. text boxes and password boxes) and textareas is generally a nuisance, but as we can see there are often legitimate reasons why they may be needed. If the script goes on to store the values in a database (as will be illustrated in the MySQL chapters of this book), there is also a potential security risk where a hacker may be able to follow a quote sign in a text field or textarea by some malicious text in order to send unwanted commands to your database. Rather than explain this potential problem (known as *code injection*) in detail we will give a possible solution to it which also avoids the irritation of having every quote symbol escaped by a backslash character. We suggest that the destination script should replace all double and single quotes by the innocuous 'slanting quote' character, correctly known as a *backtick*. We can do this for each field, say forename, by the lines

```
$forename=str_replace("\"","`",$forename);
$forename=str_replace("'","`",$forename);
```

The first argument in the second line may be difficult to read. It is a double quote, then a single quote, then a double quote. (Single quotes enclosed in double quotes do not need to be escaped with a backslash character.)

After the replacements to the forename, surname and address values given above, printing the three values separated by commas will produce

```
James `Jimmy`,O`Brien,`The Laurels` St. Michael`s Way Long Town
```

This approach avoids a number of problems and the difference between a slanted quote and the original double and single quotes is unlikely to be of any concern to users.

10.3 Passing Variables to a PHP Script as Part of a URL

Although the most common way to pass variables and their values to a PHP script is using a web form, another possibility is to pass variable/value pairs to a web address, e.g.

http://www.xxxx.com/admin/update.php?x=2&y=JamesWilliamson&mode=edit

Such an *extended URL* may be

- given in a link the user clicks on
- the value of the action parameter in a web form
- the target of an automatic jump using the *header* function (see Chap. 5)

or simply typed into the address bar of a web browser.

In the first three cases an address relative to that of the current page may be specified, e.g.

```
"../../admin/update.php?x=2&y=James Williamson&mode=edit"
```

This example illustrates the key points about this extended form of URL:

- The name of the destination PHP file is followed by a? symbol, followed by one or more variable=value pairs, separated by & characters.
- Variable names should generally be chosen to follow the same rules as PHP variable names without an initial $ sign (as they are not PHP variables). However they may contain certain special characters but not=signs.
- Values may contain embedded spaces and special characters such as – */% ! and _ (underscore), but must not contain any ampersands. They should not be enclosed in quotes. If any double or single quotes are used they are regarded as significant characters. The same comments apply as for quotes in web forms.

In all cases the destination page must be a PHP script, as for a web form. However, unlike for a web form, the variable=value pairs are passed as values of the system associative array $_GET. So the three values passed to http://www.xxxx.com/admin/update.php by the URL http://www.xxxx.com/admin/update.php?x=2&y=JamesWilliamson&mode=edit can be referred to as $_GET['x'], $_GET['y'] and $_GET['mode'].

It frequently makes scripts easier to write (and read) if we start by assigning the value of each of the elements of $_GET to a variable, e.g.

```
$x=$_GET['x'];
$y=$_GET['y'];
$mode=$_GET['mode'];
```

It is not essential for the names of the PHP variables to match the variable names used in the URL as they do in this example.

The following simple PHP script, named destin2.php, can be used to check what is passed to a PHP script from an extended URL.

```
<?php
foreach ($_GET as $var=>$value)
print "Next GET item: ".$var."=>".$value."<br>";
?>
```

Now a jump to

```
destin2.php?name=James Darwin&age=47&type=&status=Assistant Consultant
```

will give the output

```
Next GET item: name=>James Darwin
Next GET item: age=>47
Next GET item: type=>
Next GET item: status=>Assistant Consultant
```

(Note that null values are permitted, as for variable *type* above.)

Sometimes it is helpful for a page to link to itself, probably with some new variable/value settings. To do this the address to jump to can be specified as just, e.g.

```
?name=Louise Austen&age=31
```

with the absence of a file name before the ? symbol indicating the current web page.

In some complex websites it may happen that on some occasions a particular variable may be passed to a destination page by being set in a web form, whereas on other occasions it is passed to the same page as part of an extended URL. In such cases it may be worthwhile to use the associative system array $_REQUEST. This contains the combination of all the variable/value pairs currently set in either $_POST or $_GET, as the following example illustrates.

Enter your details below

Student Number *

Password *

Upload your project report (maximum 1MB)

Browse... *

Submit

This is the HTML corresponding to the above web form.

```
<b>Enter your details below</b><p>
<form name="form2" method="post" action="destin3.php?x=1&z=25&lect=Henry Carter"
  enctype="multipart/form-data">
Student Number
<input type="text" name="snumber" size=6 maxlength=6> *<p>
Password
<input type="password" name="spassword" size=20 maxlength=20> * </p>
<input type="hidden" name="projectRef" value="COMP102-3">
Upload your project report (maximum 1MB)<br>
<input type="hidden" name="MAX_FILE_SIZE" value="1048576">
<input type="file" name="report"> * </p>
<p></p>
<input type="submit" name="Submit" value="Submit">
</form>
```

In this case the value of the action parameter of the <form> tag is the extended URL

destin3.php?x=1&z=25&lect=Henry Carter

This script displays the values in the three arrays $_POST, $_GET and $_REQUEST. Using the web form with typical input will produce the following output.

```
Next POST item: snumber=>14827
Next POST item: spassword=>mysecret
Next POST item: projectRef=>COMP102-3
Next POST item: MAX_FILE_SIZE=>1048576
Next POST item: Submit=>Submit

Next GET item: x=>1
Next GET item: z=>25
Next GET item: lect=>Henry Carter

Next REQUEST item: x=>1
Next REQUEST item: z=>25
Next REQUEST item: lect=>Henry Carter
Next REQUEST item: snumber=>14827
Next REQUEST item: spassword=>mysecret
Next REQUEST item: projectRef=>COMP102-3
Next REQUEST item: MAX_FILE_SIZE=>1048576
Next REQUEST item: Submit=>Submit
```

If we now change the value of the action attribute to
"destin3.php?snumber=100&spassword=abcdefg&lect=Henry Carter"
the output changes to

```
Next POST item: snumber=>14827
Next POST item: spassword=>mysecret
Next POST item: projectRef=>COMP102-3
Next POST item: MAX_FILE_SIZE=>1048576
Next POST item: Submit=>Submit

Next GET item: snumber=>100
Next GET item: spassword=>abcdefg
Next GET item: lect=>Henry Carter

Next REQUEST item: snumber=>14827
Next REQUEST item: spassword=>mysecret
Next REQUEST item: lect=>Henry Carter
Next REQUEST item: projectRef=>COMP102-3
Next REQUEST item: MAX_FILE_SIZE=>1048576
Next REQUEST item: Submit=>Submit
```

We can see that if there are conflicting values for a variable set in $_POST and $_GET the value stored in $_REQUEST is the one in $_POST.

10.4 Passing Values to PHP Scripts Using Session Variables

Although textbooks on PHP necessarily illustrate the language's facilities using small-scale examples it is important to bear in mind that many large commercial sites will have many pages and as the user proceeds to (say) make a purchase he or she may move from one to another, to a third, back to the second, then to a fifth and so on.

Sometimes one PHP generated web page will include a link to another or a web form that will jump to another page when Submit is pressed. Sometimes a page will jump to itself with different values or even invisibly jump to another page using the header function described in Chap. 5. In order for the site to 'keep track' of what is going on a great deal of information may need to be transmitted from one page to the other, most of it meaningless to the user. This can be done using hidden values in a web form or by values passed in URLs but when the number of variables is at all large these methods can become very cumbersome to use.

Many sites get round this by storing data values, known as *cookies* on the user's PC. PHP does it by using *session variables* held on the server. This involves storing just one meaningless value on the user's PC, which many may find a more acceptable approach than using cookies. The first PHP script creates a session and then generally writes some values to a PHP system associative array named $_SESSION. The next page can then use the values in $_SESSION even though it did not create it. It can also change values, delete them or add new ones. The final page destroys the session. It is all a little more complex than this but not much.

To illustrate the process in detail we have created some small test scripts named sess1.php, sess2.php etc. They are listed below. We will go through a possible sequence of events step by step.

Script sess1.php

```
<?php
session_start();
print "<b>Information about Session Variables</b><br>";
$_SESSION['staffname']="John Smith";
$_SESSION['staffage']=47;
$_SESSION['stafftitle']="Lecturer";

 if ($_SESSION!="") foreach ($_SESSION as $var=>$val) print $var."=>".$val."<br>";

print "Click <a href=\"sess2.php\">here</a> to go on";
?>
```

The user points his/her web browser to sess1.php. As the script is executed PHP comes to the instruction session_start(). This has to be placed before any HTML and before any output is generated using PHP print statements. This is most important. The PHP system now checks if there is a session value stored on the user's PC. At this point there is not so it writes one with an obscure value such as

b7cdfg12ab7802dfg. Next the assignment statements in the script place values in the $_SESSION array, just as if it were any other associative array. This and all our later scripts go on to use a *foreach* statement to display the contents of $_SESSION so we can see exactly what has been stored. (Incidentally, the reason for the test 'if ($_SESSION!="")' is that if nothing is stored PHP treats $_SESSION as an uninitialised variable not an array, so the foreach instruction will lead to a fatal error.) For sess1.php the output produced is as follows:

Information about Session Variables
staffname=>John Smith
staffage=>47
stafftitle=>Lecturer

In practice the script will no doubt perform many other (more valuable) operations, but these are of no concern to us for this example. Eventually it gives the user a link which they press to move to sess2.php. Or perhaps the script simply comes to an end and the user opens a second web browser and points it to sess2.php, it makes no difference which. Script sess2.php now comes into operation.

Script sess2.php

```
<?php
session_start();
print "Age is: ".$_SESSION['staffage']."<br>";
print "Title is: ".$_SESSION['stafftitle']."<br>";
$_SESSION['compref']="worldcorp";
print "<b>Information about Session Variables</b><p>";
if ($_SESSION!="") foreach ($_SESSION as $var=>$val) print $var."=>".$val."<br>";

print "Click <a href=\"sess3.php\">here</a> to go on";
?>
```

The script comes to the session_start() instruction (which, as always, must be before any HTML or PHP print instructions have been sent to the browser). This time the browser checks and finds that there is already a session value such as b7cd-fg12ab7802dfg stored on the user's hard disc. It therefore gives the PHP script access to the values in the $_SESSION array. It now uses two of the values already set: staffage and stafftitle, and sets a new one: compref. The foreach instruction shows the values that are now stored and of course accessible to the script.

staffage=>47
stafftitle=>Lecturer
Information about Session Variables
staffname=>John Smith
staffage=>47
stafftitle=>Lecturer
compref=>worldcorp

Next the user clicks on a link which opens a replacement browser window, pointing at sess3.php.

Script sess3.php

```
<?php
session_start();
print "<b>Information about Session Variables</b><p>";
$_SESSION['staffcode']="Sci387";
unset($_SESSION['stafftitle']);
if ($_SESSION!="") foreach ($_SESSION as $var=>$val) print $var."=>".$val."<br>";
// webform follows here
?>
```

The script now sets a further variable staffcode to "Sci387" and unsets stafftitle. The foreach instruction now gives this output.

```
Information about Session Variables
staffname=>John Smith
staffage=>47
compref=>worldcorp
staffcode=>Sci387
```

After more processing the script displays a web form. The user completes it and presses the Submit button. A new script sess4.php opens in the same browser window.

Script sess4.php

This script shuts the session down. We do this in two steps: first unset all the variables and then destroy the session. (The first of these is not needed in this case, but is included to illustrate how to do it.) The session_destroy() instruction causes the stored value b7cdfg12ab7802dfg to be removed from the user's hard disc.

```
<?php
session_start();
print "<b>Information about Session Variables</b><p>";

// remove all session variables
session_unset();
// destroy the session
session_destroy();

if ($_SESSION!="") foreach ($_SESSION as $var=>$val) print $var."=>".$val."<br>";
?>
```

Finally the foreach statement produces no output, showing that the session has ended.

```
Information about Session Variables
```

Chapter Summary
This chapter describes how to implement a destination page which receives values sent to it by a webform, as described in Chap. 9. The use of system associative array $_POST is explained. The values sent by a webform if a form element is given no value (and has no default value) are also considered. It is next shown how to check for compulsory values and to test whether values entered are numbers or integers.

Complications which arise in connection with multiple selections from a webform selection box are described, followed by the potentially difficult issue of dealing with an uploaded file. This leads to a description of system associative file $_FILES, the 'type' values associated with common file extensions such as doc, docx and xls, and how to establish the file type of an uploaded file.

Quote symbols in text fields and textareas can present security problems and it is shown how these can be handled. The chapter goes on to illustrate another way of sending the values of variables to a destination script, using an extended URL, and the use of the system associative arrays $_GET and $_REQUEST in the destination page.

The chapter ends with a description of a method of passing variables around PHP scripts that is often used with larger websites: using session variables.

Practical Exercise 10
Write a PHP script to serve as a destination page for the webform shown towards the end of Sect. 10.2. If all the compulsory fields have been completed and the uploaded file is in PDF format the script should save the file to folder 'projects' with a name that includes the project reference and the student number. (For the purpose of this exercise it is not necessary to check that the password entered matches the student number or that the maximum file size restriction has been met.)

Chapter 11
PHP in Action: Managing a Members' Area

Chapter Aims
After reading this chapter you should be able to:

- use the material introduced earlier in the book to write useful PHP scripts, especially to deal with information sent from a webform and to create, read and analyse the content of text files.

This chapter is designed to reinforce the material in Chaps. 7 and 9 about text files and webforms as well as illustrating a number of programming techniques and the use of several of the functions described earlier.

Like many other organisations the Erewhon Society has a members' area on its website. This is a password-protected area containing information about Society events, plus possibly pictures and video clips for downloading, technical or professional advice particularly relevant to Society members etc. Having access to this area is seen as a major benefit of Society membership. So it needs to be protected from prying eyes.

A members' area is a feature of many organisations' websites but it is desirable not to keep the whole of your website secret (unless you are representing an international criminal organisation or a secret government agency perhaps) as the publicly accessible pages are your organisation's 'shop window', a place to attract new members to join, so the members' area should not normally be the whole of the site.

M. Bramer, *Web Programming with PHP and MySQL*,
DOI 10.1007/978-3-319-22659-0_11

11.1 Entering Passwords

To gain access to the members' area the member has to enter a secret password on the Erewhon Society home page and press a button labelled 'Submit'. We will temporarily assume that the home page is named erewhon.htm. We will also assume that the home page begins like this, with information for the general public lower down.

The Erewhon Society

Welcome to our home page

Members' Area

Enter your password and click on Submit

Submit

Most readers will probably have seen webforms like this (frequently several boxes not just one) on websites they have used for purchasing goods, booking holidays etc.

The HTML needed to create the simple form above (everything below the line "Members' Area") is as follows

```
<FORM ACTION="memarea1.php" name="form1" METHOD="POST">
<INPUT TYPE="TEXT" NAME="verifier" SIZE=20>
   Enter your password and click on Submit<p>
<INPUT TYPE="SUBMIT" VALUE="Submit">
</FORM>
```

- The <FORM> tag signifies the start of the webform and specifies that the destination page for the form is memarea1.php. This does not begin with http:// or https:// which indicates that the destination page is a file with the name memarea1.php relative to the calling page (the one on which the webform is located).
- The first <INPUT> tag specifies that a text field named verifier, 20 characters wide, should be displayed.
- This should be followed by three spaces and then the text 'Enter your password and click on Submit' (without the quotes).[1]
- The second <INPUT> tag signifies that a Submit button should be displayed.
- The </FORM> tag signifies the end of the form.

[1] The combination   (six characters) indicates a space. If we had simply entered three spaces by using the space bar three times the web browser would display all three of them as just a single space.

When the user enters a value, say mypass, in the password box and presses Submit the variable/value pair 'verifier=mypass' is sent to the destination page memarea1.php.

In the destination page we generally start by telling the PHP interpreter that we wish to use the values sent to it from the webform. In this case there is only one value, i.e. the password entered in the text box named 'verifier'. We can access this value by using the PHP statement

```
$verifier=$_POST["verifier"];
```

Having done this the destination page script can refer to a variable $verifier which has the value entered by the user in the webform. (Note that the PHP variable does not have to be named $verifier. Any valid PHP variable name can be used.)

If we simply wanted to print the value entered by the user, the complete contents of file memarea1.php might be as follows.

```
<?php
$verifier=$_POST["verifier"];
print "You entered the password: ".$verifier;
?>
```

This would output to the user's web browser the one line

```
You entered the password: mypass
```

We can make a small improvement to the webform before going further. When the user types the password into the text box on the webform the characters typed are visible to anyone going past, coming into the room etc. This is not a big problem, but it is customary to arrange for the entry of passwords to be a little more secure. If the line

```
<INPUT TYPE="TEXT" NAME="verifier" SIZE=20>
```

in the HTML of the webform is replaced by

```
<INPUT TYPE="PASSWORD" NAME="verifier" SIZE=20>
```

when the user enters a password each character typed is displayed as a black dot, thus making the password unreadable by any unwanted observer.

So far all our PHP script does is to output the password entered by the user from a webform. Of course we do not really want to output the value entered by the user. We want to compare the value he or she entered with the true value of the password and take action accordingly.

Let us assume that the correct password is butler (all lower case letters), in homage to the English author Samuel Butler who wrote the novel *Erewhon*. This is a poor choice of password (it is short, completely alphabetic and not too hard to guess), but it will suffice for the present purpose.

The PHP script below shows a simple 'if' statement used to check whether or not the password entered is correct.

```
<?php
$verifier=$_POST["verifier"];
if ($verifier=="butler") print "Correct password";
else print "Invalid password - go back and try again";
?>
```

Of course, this is of very little use. If the user enters the correct password we want to display the contents of the members' area in his or her browser, not just confirm that the password is correct. Before going on to this we will first consider the possibility that the user enters a password similar to the correct one, such as Butler or BUTLER. We may decide that any use of upper and lower case letters in the spelling of butler will be accepted. If so, we can achieve this by taking the user's input and replacing all upper case letters by the corresponding lower case ones, a process known as *forcing the user's input into lower case*. To do this we use the strtolower function, introduced in Chap. 5.

```
<?php
$verifier=$_POST["verifier"];
$verifier=strtolower($verifier);
if ($verifier=="butler") print "Correct password";
else print "Invalid password - go back and try again";
?>
```

Another possibility is that the member inadvertently types one or more spaces before the password butler, or possibly after it, or even both. We may wish to treat this as just demonstrating a lack of familiarity with using webforms and accept it as valid. We can achieve this by 'trimming' the user's input to remove any leading or trailing spaces using the trim function described in Chap. 5. The trim function takes a string as its argument and returns the same string with any initial or final spaces, tabs, 'newline' and 'carriage return' characters removed. We add the following as the fourth line of the file.

```
$verifier=trim($verifier);
```

We now need to replace the statement

```
print "Correct password";
```

by a statement group that gives the information for members which is the reason for the page existing.

The revised form of the PHP file would be something like this.

```
<?php
$verifier=$_POST["verifier"];
$verifier=strtolower($verifier);
$verifier=trim($verifier);
if ($verifier=="butler"){
  // first line of information
  // second line
  // third line
}
else print "Invalid password - go back and try again";
?>
```

11.2 Turning PHP On and Off

The part between the opening and closing braces for the statement group may be very substantial and is likely to involve the outputting of many lines of HTML. We can do this using a succession of PHP print statements such as this:

```
<?php
$verifier=$_POST["verifier"];
$verifier=strtolower($verifier);
$verifier=trim($verifier);
if ($verifier=="butler"){
  print "<html>";
  print "<head></head>";
  print "<body>";
  print "<h3>Here is the secret information for members</h3>";
  print "More information here!";
  print "</body>";
  print "</html>";
}
else print "Invalid password - go back and try again";
?>
```

Although possible, this method of outputting lines of HTML would be very tedious to write. Instead we can use one of the most helpful (and time-saving) features of PHP.

Instead of enclosing each line of HTML in a print statement, we simply 'turn off' PHP (with a closing PHP tag) after the opening brace of the statement group following the 'if' condition, then write the lines of HTML, then 'turn on' PHP (with an opening PHP tag) just before the closing brace of the statement group. The result looks like this.

```
<?php
$verifier=$_POST["verifier"];
$verifier=strtolower($verifier);
$verifier=trim($verifier);
if ($verifier=="butler"){
?>
<html>
<head></head>
<body>
<h3>Here is the secret information for members</h3>
More information here!
</body>
</html>
<?php
}
else print "Invalid password - go back and try again";
?>
```

The webpage displayed in the user's browser will look like this.

Here is the secret information for members

More information here!

11.3 A Note on Security

It is important to keep website security in perspective. There is a large difference between information aimed at club members only and classified military secrets and the measures taken to protect the information should reflect this. (Our advice is to make sure that the latter type of information is nowhere near your website, as 100 % reliable protection is virtually impossible.)

However there is one common 'security hole' which definitely is worth plugging and easily can be. Supposing the Erewhon Society's web domain is www.erewhonsoc.org and to access the home page we point our web browser to http://www.erewhonsoc.org/erewhon.htm. What happens if someone enters the address http://www.erewhonsoc.org/ (ending with a slash character) instead?

We might prefer it if this gave an error message but unfortunately many browsers will instead give a listing of all the files in the home directory. This may be helpful to a malevolent person wishing to find weaknesses/errors in the scripts that can be used to damage the website, perhaps by deleting or corrupting important records. There are still many people who would regard this as a good afternoon's 'sport' rather than malicious damage and it is important to take this risk seriously. Fortunately it is easy to plug this particular security hole. If no file name is explicitly given, as in the example above, the web browser searches for any file in the specified directory that is named index.php, index.htm or index.html (there are also a few other possibilities). If one of them is present the corresponding webpage is displayed. If more than one is present the browser displays one of them in order of preference index.html, then index.htm, then index.php.

It is important to make sure that in every directory or sub-directory you use there is a file with one of these three names. In the case of the Erewhon Society, the home page erewhon.htm (the one with the members' area form) is pure HTML. It would be much better if it were renamed index.htm or index.html. Either would allow the Society to quote its web address in the short form http://www.erewhonsoc.org/ or just www.erewhonsoc.org.

11.4 Writing a Log File

We will next assume that the Secretary of the Erewhon Society wishes to keep records of all accesses of the members' area, including failed attempts. To do this, additional lines need to be added to the file memarea1.php to write information about each attempted access to a text file named (say) "login.txt", stored in the home directory of the website.

We first need to decide what format this text file should take. It seems sensible to store information about one access of the members' area per line, giving details of the date, the password entered and whether or not it was successful. For example a small version of the login.txt file might look like this.

```
Jan 07 2011 11.07 a.m. butler succeeded
Jan 07 2011 9.16 p.m. xyz failed
Feb 04 2012 6.14 p.m. Butler succeeded
Mar 18 2012 4.23 a.m. butler succeeded
```

However it is usually better to store dates not in text form but as a six-digit number, with two digits for each of the year, month and day (we will assume that there are no dates before 2000 recorded).

We do this by storing, say, Christmas Day 2016 as 161225. This is a six-figure number: the first pair of digits represents the year (counting from 2000), the next pair represents the month and the third pair represents the day. Numbers less than 10 are 'padded out' to two digits with an initial zero, so September 3rd 2001 would be 010903.

The benefit of this approach is that if one date A is after another date B, the six digit number corresponding to A will be larger than the six digit number corresponding to B. If we write a line of text to the login.txt file every time the members' area is accessed the dates (in six digit form) will be in ascending numerical order.

We can obtain a date in this format using the PHP function call date("ymd") described in Chap. 5.

We can gain a similar effect for times by forming a four-digit number with the first pair of digits representing the hour (using the 24-hour clock) and the second pair representing the minutes, both pairs being padded out with a leading zero if less than 10. This can be achieved using the function call date("Hi"). If the time were 3.15 a.m., it would be stored as 0315 and 6.07 p.m. would be stored as 1807. This again has the merit that if a time X is after a time Y the four-digit number corresponding to X will be greater than the four-digit number corresponding to Y.

The four lines of content previously shown for the login.txt file would be better stored as

```
110107,1107,butler,succeeded
110107,2116,xyz,failed
120204,1814,Butler,succeeded
120318,1623,butler,succeeded
```

Note that there are now four values per line. They are separated by commas and all spaces have been removed. The four values to be output to each line of the login.txt file are date("ymd"), date("Hi"), $verifier and the string "succeeded" or "failed", depending on whether or not the password was accepted.

If we wanted to output this information to the web browser rather than writing it to a text file (which is most unlikely), we could change memarea1.php to the following:

```
<?php
$verifier=$_POST["verifier"];
print date("ymd").",".date("Hi").",".$verifier.",";
$verifier=strtolower($verifier);
$verifier=trim($verifier);
if ($verifier=="butler"){
print "succeeded\n";
?>
<html>
<head></head>
<body>
<h3>Here is the secret information for members</h3>
More information here!
</body>
</html>
<?php
}
else print "Invalid password - go back and try again";
print "failed\n";
?>
```

The lines that have been added are printed in **bold**.

11.5 Storing Data in Text Files

Although the topic of storing information in and retrieving it from a mySQL database will be covered in detail later in this book, the use of plain text files (i.e. files organised as lines of text, each line representing a 'unit of information') on the server to store data of a fairly basic kind is also well worth knowing about. It is described in Chap. 7. For newcomers to PHP using text files has the advantage of avoiding the need to learn another language (mySQL or something similar) at the same time as learning PHP.

Before we can write to a file, we first have to 'open' it, i.e. establish a 'link' to the file from a PHP script. We do this using the system function *fopen*, which takes two arguments. The first argument is the name of the file, login.txt, the second is a string constant indicating how we intend to use the file, in this case "a" indicating that we intend to *append* to it, i.e. write additional records (lines of text) to it, which are to be placed after those already there, assuming the file already exists. If no file of the given name exists, an empty file with the specified name but no contents will first be created.

We can write the statement

```
$fp=fopen("login.txt","a");
```

to open file login.txt for 'appending' with file pointer $fp.

Having opened the login.txt file for appending, we can then write lines of text to it using the *fwrite* system function, for example:

```
fwrite($fp,"This is an example line\r\n");
```

The two 'escape sequences' \r and \n signify that we want the output string to end with the characters 'carriage return' and 'newline'. (This is important if we want the file to be human-readable or if we intend to read it using the *file* function described in Chap. 7.)

Once we have finished writing to an open file we should close it again, i.e. make it unavailable for use (until and unless it is opened again). We can do this using the *fclose* function, which takes the file pointer as its only argument and does not return a value.

```
fclose($fp);
```

Returning to the Erewhon Society example, all that is needed to write a new record to the login.txt file every time the web browser points to the memarea1.php page is to change the script given previously, replacing each of the print statements highlighted in bold by a fwrite statement, and then to add fopen and fclose statements. This gives the following new version of memarea1.php.

```
<?php
$verifier=$_POST["verifier"];
$fp=fopen("login.txt","a");
fwrite($fp,date("ymd").",".date("Hi").",".$verifier.",");
$verifier=strtolower($verifier);
$verifier=trim($verifier);
if ($verifier=="butler"){
fwrite($fp,"succeeded\r\n");
?>
<html>
<head></head>
<body>
<h3>Here is the secret information for members</h3>
More information here!
</body>
</html>
<?php
}
else {
print "Invalid password - go back and try again";
fwrite($fp,"failed\r\n");
}
fclose($fp);
?>
```

(The lines that have been inserted or changed are printed in **bold**.)

11.6 Multiple Passwords

The committee members of the Erewhon Society all use a special password, samuel, which gives them access to more information in the members' area than ordinary members of the Society. To deal with this we first need to adjust the test on the value of $verifier:

```
if ($verifier=="butler") {
// other lines here
}
```

to test whether the value is either butler or samuel. We can do this using the logical operator || which represents 'or'. The first of the lines given above needs to be replaced by

```
if ($verifier=="butler" || $verifier=="samuel") {
```

The || operator links two conditional expressions, in this case $verifier=="butler" and $verifier=="samuel". The compound conditional expression is true if either of the two constituent conditional expressions is true, i.e. if the password entered is either butler or samuel. Note that it would not be correct to write

```
if ($verifier=="butler" || "samuel"){
```

This would not be linking two conditional expressions ("samuel" on its own is not a conditional expression). This is a common source of errors.

Making this change to memarea1.php enables both committee members and ordinary Society members to access the members' area. The next stage is to adjust the lines of HTML in memarea1.php that cause information to be displayed for those that log into the members' area. The current version of this is as follows.

```
<html>
<head></head>
<body>
<h3>Here is the secret information for members</h3>
More information here!
</body>
</html>
```

We can give more information to committee members by adding two small PHP scripting blocks, as shown below.

```
<html>
<head></head>
<body>
<h3>Here is the secret information for members</h3>
More information here!
<?php
if ($verifier=="samuel") {
?>
Information for committee members only<p>
Special information here!
<?php
}
?>
</body>
</html>
```

(The lines that have been inserted or changed are printed in **bold**.)

11.7 Reading a Log File

We will now develop a script named readlog.php which can be used to read the members' area access log and summarise the number of accesses for a chosen year. We will assume that there is a simple webform for doing this with a Select Box that allows a choice of four possible years: 2016–2019.

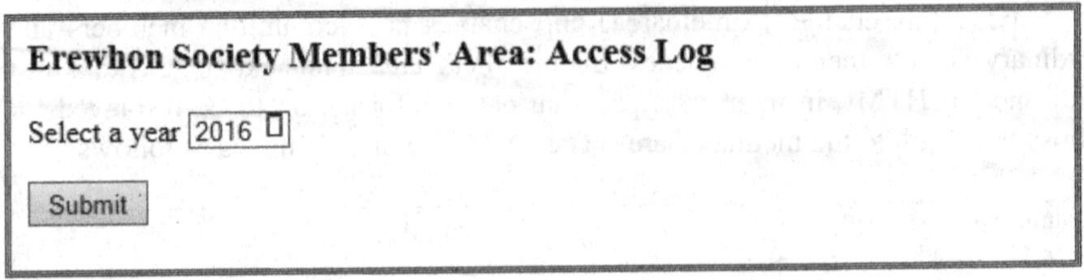

If we select 2017 and press Submit the output will be a table such as this

Breakdown of login accesses for year: 2017

Month	Successes	Failures	Total
1	19	5	24
2	13	8	21
3	17	2	19
4	15	3	18
5	15	4	19
6	22	4	26
7	21	6	27
8	10	4	14
9	20	3	23
10	17	2	19
11	17	1	18
12	11	3	14
Total	**197**	**45**	**242**

The number of accesses, both successes and failures plus the total number are displayed for each month of the chosen year.

We start by giving the HTML for the webform shown above which uses a Select Box.

```
<h3>Erewhon Society Members' Area: Access Log</h3>
<form name="form1" action="" method="post">
Select a year
<select name="selyear">
<option value="16">2016</option>
<option value="17">2017</option>
<option value="18">2018</option>
<option value="19">2019</option>
</select>
<p>
<input type="submit" name="Submit" value="Submit">
</form>
```

For ease of reference we will call the lines of HTML above by the name 'HTML1'.

Note that if a year such as 2017 is selected, the value given to webform variable selyear is the string "17" not "2017". This will be useful later.

The action parameter of the <form> tag is given as action="" rather than something like action="destpage.php" as might be expected. This is because we are going to use readlog.php as its own destination page, rather than having separate calling and destination pages as we did for the Members' Area login page at the beginning of the chapter.

The figure below shows the overall structure of readlog.php. It starts by checking whether a value of the webform variable selyear has been passed from the webform to the same page. If the value is an empty string we display the webform with the 'Select a year' box. If not we generate the table of accesses for the chosen year.

```
<?php
$selyear=$_POST['selyear'];
if ($selyear==""){
?>
[INSERT HTML1 HERE]
<?php
}
else{
// insert statements to generate table for chosen year
} //else
?>
```

11.7.1 Generating the Access Table

In order to generate the access table we will work through the lines of text in file login.txt in turn. For each one we will extract the year and the month and then increment a suitable counter. We will use array elements such as $succeed[10] and $fail[10] to hold the number of successful and unsuccessful accesses in month 10 of the chosen year. This gives an initial version of 'statements to generate table for chosen year'.

```
$arr=file("login.txt");
$i=0;
while ($i<count($arr)){
  $next=trim($arr[$i]);
  $parts=explode(",",$next);
  // extract year, month and result from $parts
  // if the year is the same as $selyear increase the value of
  // array $succeed or $fail by one, as appropriate

  $i++;
} //while
// display results in tabular form
```

Note that the value of $arr[$i] is trimmed. This is necessary to remove the end of line characters from each line of login.txt.

A typical line of the login file looks like this

160829,1912,Butler,succeeded

Dividing this into its separate components using the explode function gives array $parts with four elements like this:

$parts[0]	$parts[1]	$parts[2]	$parts[3]
160829	1912	Butler	Succeeded

$parts[0] holds the date, in this case August 29th 2016, in coded form. $parts[3] holds either the word 'succeeded' or the word 'failed'. $parts[1] and $parts[2] hold the time and the password entered, respectively. These are irrelevant as far as this script is concerned.

We need to decompose the date to find the values of the year and the month. We can store the value of the date in a variable $date which will always hold a string of six characters. The characters in each string are automatically numbered starting at zero, for example:

Character					
0	1	2	3	4	5
1	6	0	8	2	9
Year		Month		Day	

We can extract the two digit values for year and month using the substr (substring) function by the PHP statements

```
$year=substr($date,0,2);
$month=substr($date,2,2);
```

The second argument of the function is the index number of the first character on the substring. The third argument is the number of characters in the substring (two in each case here).

We need to test whether the value of $selyear is the same as the value of $year for the current line of login.txt. If it is we increase the value in either array $succeed or array $fail for the month by one, as appropriate, and also increase the value of array $total (which records the total number of attempted accesses) for that month by one. We also increase the value of either variable $successful or variable $failure by one. These variables record the total number of successful and unsuccessful accesses for the chosen year.

We can now replace the comments 'extract year, month and result from $parts' and 'if the year is the same as $selyear increase the value of array $succeed or $fail by one, as appropriate' by the following. *Note that there is a subtle error in this, which will be explained later.*

```
$date=$parts[0];
$year=substr($date,0,2);
if ($year==$selyear){
  $month=substr($date,2,2); // from 01 to 12
  $res=$parts[3];
  if ($res=="succeeded"){
    $succeed[$month]++;
    $successful++;
  } //if
  else{
    $fail[$month]++;
    $failure++;
  } //else
    $total[$month]++;
} //if
```

Before going on to generate the table of access values we can make an improvement to the script as developed so far. The file login.txt records the date and time when each person attempted to log in to the Members' Area, so it is inherently stored in date and time order. This means that once we find a value of $year that is greater than the selected year $selyear, all the other dates in the file must be greater than $selyear too, so we do not need to consider those records.

We can reduce the amount of processing required by changing the *while* condition

```
while ($i<count($arr)){
```

to the compound condition

```
while ($i<count($arr) && $more=="yes"){
```

We then set $more to "yes" outside the while loop and change its value to "no" as soon as we encounter a value of $year greater than $selyear. The (partial) PHP script for generating the access table becomes the following (which still contains the error mentioned earlier):

```
$arr=file("login.txt");
$more="yes";
$i=0;
while ($i<count($arr) && $more=="yes"){
  $next=trim($arr[$i]);
  $parts=explode(",",$next);
  $date=$parts[0];
  $year=substr($date,0,2);
  if ($year==$selyear){
    $month=substr($date,2,2); // from 01 to 12
    $res=$parts[3];
    if ($res=="succeeded"){
      $succeed[$month]++;
      $successful++;
    } //if
    else{
      $fail[$month]++;
      $failure++;
    } //else
    $total[$month]++;
  } //if
  else if ($year>$selyear) $more="no";
  $i++;
} //while
// display results in tabular form
```

Lines that have been added or changed are shown in bold.

11.7.2 Displaying the Results in Tabular Form

We now need to display the values in the arrays $succeed, $fail and $total for each of the months from 1 to 12.

If we were displaying constant values rather than the contents of array elements the HTML would be like this

```
<tr>
<td>1</td>
<td>19</td>
<td>5</td>
<td>24</td>
</tr>
<tr><td>2</td>
<td>13</td>
<td>8</td>
<td>21</td>
</tr>
```

We need to write a loop for values of $i from 1 to 12 (one per month) to print out the corresponding values of arrays $succeed, $fail and $total for each value of $i, with the correct use of HTML <tr>, </tr>, <td> and </td> tags.

This leads to the following partial script to replace the comment 'display results in tabular form' given earlier:

```
print "<h3>Breakdown of login accesses for year: 20".$selyear."</h3>\n";
print "<table border=1>\n";
print "<tr><td>Month</td><td>Successes</td><td>Failures</td><td>Total</td></tr>\n";
for ($i=1;$i<=12;$i++){
  print "<tr>\n";
  print "<td>".$i."</td>\n";
  print "<td>".$succeed[$i]."</td>\n";
  print "<td>".$fail[$i]."</td>\n";
  print "<td>".$total[$i]."</td>\n";
  print "</tr>\n";
} //for
print "<tr><td><b>Total</b></td><td><b>".$successful."</b></td><td><b>".$failure
  ."</b></td><td><b>".($successful+$failure)."</b></td></tr>\n";
print "</table>\n";
```

Now if we put all the pieces of PHP script together, point our web browser to readlog.php and select the year 2017 we get the following:

Breakdown of login accesses for year: 2017

Month	Successes	Failures	Total
1			
2			
3			
4			
5			
6			
7			
8			
9			
10	17	2	19
11	17	1	18
12	11	3	14
Total	**197**	**45**	**242**

This is definitely not what we were expecting! The values for months 1–9 have vanished, even though the overall totals are correct. This brings us to the rather subtle error in Sect. 11.7.1 mentioned earlier. The problem is with the line

```
$month=substr($date,2,2);
```

followed by the lines

```
$succeed[$month]++;
```

```
$fail[$month]++;
```

```
$total[$month]++;
```

The value of a month earlier than October, say March, extracted by the first statement is the two-character string "03", with a leading 0 character, not the number 3. So the other three statements increment the value of $succeed["03"] etc.

The loop to print out the value of $succeed[$i] when $i has the value 3 prints the value of $succeed[3]. This is an uninitialized value and therefore an empty string. To get the value we require we needed to print $succeed["03"] and similarly for the other two arrays. (In view of this explanation it may seem remarkable that the correct values are output for months 10, 11 and 12. It seems that PHP treats the string "12" as if it were the number 12 but "01" as different from the number 1.

The easiest way to deal with this problem is to convert the value of $month from a string to a number before the assignment statements

```
$succeed[$month]++;
```

etc. are reached.

There are several ways this can be done. A simple one is to replace

```
$month=substr($date,2,2);
```

by the two lines

```
$month=substr($date,2,2);
$month=$month*1;
```

Multiplying $month by one in this way makes PHP convert a string such as "03" to a number 3 and this solves the problem.

11.7.3 Adding HTML Tags Using Include

HTML experts will no doubt have noticed that the script so far developed only produces the content of the <BODY> section of an HTML page. There are no <HTML>, <HEAD>, </HEAD>, <BODY>, </BODY> or </HTML> tags. To save space in this book we often leave all that part of the HTML for our pages out. It is also a (possibly regrettable) fact that most web browsers seem to display web pages correctly even without such apparently vital elements. However for this example we will put them in.

We will assume that we have the two files start.php and end.php defined in Chap. 3 (when the INCLUDE statement was introduced) and that these are in the same directory as readlog.php.

We then need to place

```
include "start.php";
```

near the beginning of the script and

```
include "end.php";
```

near the end.

Putting all these pieces together we obtain the following final version of the script.

```
<?php
include "start.php";
$selyear=$_POST['selyear'];
if ($selyear==""){
?>
<h3>Erewhon Society Members' Area: Access Log</h3>
<form name="form1" action="" method="post">
Select a year
<select name="selyear">
<option value="16">2016</option>
<option value="17">2017</option>
<option value="18">2018</option>
<option value="19">2019</option>
</select>
<p>
<input type="submit" name="Submit" value="Submit">
</form>
<?php
}
else{
$arr=file("login.txt");
$more="yes";
$i=0;
while ($i<count($arr) && $more=="yes"){
  $next=trim($arr[$i]);
  $parts=explode(",",$next);
  $date=$parts[0];
  $year=substr($date,0,2);
  if ($year==$selyear){
    $month=substr($date,2,2); // from 01 to 12
    $month=$month*1;
    $res=$parts[3];
    if ($res=="succeeded"){
      $succeed[$month]++;
      $successful++;
    } //if
    else{
      $fail[$month]++;
      $failure++;
    } //else
    $total[$month]++;
  } //if
  else if ($year>$selyear) $more="no";
  $i++;
} //while
print "<h3>Breakdown of login accesses for year: 20".$selyear."</h3>";
print "<table border=1>\n";
print "<tr><td>Month</td><td>Successes</td><td>Failures</td><td>Total</td></tr>\n";
for ($i=1;$i<=12;$i++){
  print "<tr>\n";
  print "<td>".$i."</td>\n";
  print "<td>".$succeed[$i]."</td>\n";
  print "<td>".$fail[$i]."</td>\n";
  print "<td>".$total[$i]."</td>\n";
  print "</tr>\n";
} //for
print "<tr><td><b>Total</b></td><td><b>".$successful."</b></td><td><b>".$failure
  ."</b></td><td><b>".($successful+$failure)."</b></td></tr>\n";
print "</table>\n";
} //else
include "end.php";
?>
```

Chapter Summary

This chapter reinforces the material in Chaps. 7 and 9 about text files and webforms as well as illustrating a number of programming techniques and the use of several functions introduced earlier in the book.

Practical Exercise 11

Write a PHP script to read file login.txt (assumed to be in the format shown at the end of Sect. 11.4) and tabulate the number of times each incorrect attempt at a password has been made. (Treat upper and lower case letters as equivalent.)

Chapter 12
Using a MySQL Database I

Chapter Aims
After reading this chapter you should be able to:

- understand the principal features of a MySQL database and database management system
- use the MySQL commands needed to create a MySQL database, insert a record into a table, delete and update records and change the structure of a table.

A very valuable feature of PHP is that it provides straightforward facilities for managing databases of a certain very widely-used kind known as *MySQL databases*. These facilities are fully integrated with the other standard features of the language, which means that full advantage can be taken of the availability of loops, variables etc. to provide very powerful facilities from inside an executing PHP script.

In this and the next two chapters we will describe the principal facilities available in the MySQL language, independently of PHP. In Chap. 15 we will show how to execute MySQL commands to manage a database from within an executing PHP script. The following chapters will illustrate the power of the combination of PHP and MySQL in a number of applications.

12.1 MySQL Databases

The kinds of database that can be accessed using PHP are known as *relational databases*. In a relational database information is stored in a number of two-dimensional structures called *tables*. These can be represented in pictorial form in a natural way

M. Bramer, *Web Programming with PHP and MySQL*,
DOI 10.1007/978-3-319-22659-0_12

as tables on a flat surface such as a sheet of paper or a screen. Each table contains information about a related set of *entities*, such as the people in a company, the cities in Paris, the trains that leave from Vienna station, mammals that live in Australia etc. There is just one value (or sometimes none) in each cell of the table. The tables in a database will often be related, e.g., information about different departments in a business, but they may also be entirely independent.

Each relational database table can be represented by a two-dimensional display such as this:

241	John	Smith	45	male
151	Mary	Jones	23	female
299	Jane	Smith	19	female
45	Henry	Pearson	56	male

Here we have a table with four rows and five columns. Each row gives a reference number followed by the forename, surname, age and sex for one employee of a small business. We call each row a *record* or sometimes a *tuple*.

Each column is called a *field*. It corresponds to one of the attributes of each entity represented in the table (e.g., the forename of each employee). This tabular form is clearly a very natural way of storing data in many cases. As well as the data itself the relational database will hold information about each table, such as the names of all the fields and also their types (integer, text etc.).

A type of relational database that is widely used in conjunction with PHP scripts is called a *MySQL database*. This is an open-source version of a relational database management system called SQL (standing for Structured Query Language) which was originally developed for large commercial mainframe computers back in the 1970s.[1] MySQL is very popular for web programming applications and most PHP systems now come with an associated MySQL database management system.

As well as denoting the overall system that manages a set of relational databases, the term MySQL is (perhaps confusingly) used to describe a relational database managed by such a system and also the 'query language' used to maintain such a database. So we can say that the MySQL language is used to maintain one or more MySQL databases in a MySQL relational database management system. The aim of this and the remaining chapters of this book is to show you how to use the MySQL language to maintain a MySQL database. MySQL is called a *query language*, indicating that it comprises a set of queries that are sent to a relational database to ask it questions or to give it instructions such as to add a record or to change the contents of an existing record. In this book we will generally use the term 'commands' rather than 'queries'.[2]

[1] A note on pronunciation: SQL is pronounced (for historical reasons) as 'sequel'. However MySQL is not usually pronounced as 'my sequel', but in the obvious way as 'my-ess-queue-ell'.

[2] Another term used is MySQL statements. We prefer to use the word 'commands', which correctly describes the cycle: we tell the computer what to do, it responds, we tell it what to do next and so on.

A relational database can contain many tables and, depending on the specific system used, it may be possible for a user to have several databases. For example a company may have an employee database with tables for, say, the marketing department, the finance department, the manufacturing department etc. It may also have databases on many other matters, for example cities in the United States, airline schedules, car parts and so on, including ones that were originally collected for entirely separate purposes. Database specialists often link together information stored in several databases and/or tables.

The aim of this book is not to teach database design. For basic applications driven from web pages a great deal can be achieved with a single database with just one table.

12.2 Creating a Database

To create a new database is straightforward. To create an empty database named *mydb1* containing no tables we use the command:

CREATE DATABASE mydb1

Depending on the PHP system you use there may be restrictions on the number of databases you can create, possibly only one.

12.2.1 Specifying the Current Database

We next need to tell the system that our MySQL commands will always refer to database *mydb1*, unless we explicitly say otherwise. A database can be specified as being the *current database* by the command:

USE mydb1

When MySQL commands are issued via a PHP script there is a different way of specifying a current database. We will explain how this is done in Chap. 15.

12.3 Creating a Table

Creating a table in a database is considerably more complicated than creating the database itself and we will defer a discussion of how to do it until Chap. 14. At present we will assume that we already have a database, named (not very imaginatively) *mydb1* with a single table named (even less imaginatively) *mytable1*. The case of multiple tables (possibly in different databases) will be considered in Chap. 13.

The original state of database table *mytable1* is, of course, empty. We will show this as a (paper) table as follows:

refnum	**Forename**	**Surname**	**sex**	**occupation**	**cityBorn**	**yearBorn**	**number_of_children**

The table has zero rows, each comprising eight fields: refnum, Forename etc., the meaning of which should be self-explanatory.

Note that the heading row shown above is not part of the content of the table. It is included in most of the figures in this chapter, printed in bold, for the convenience of the reader (and the author). The above is a table with zero rows.

As well as a name, each field has a type: integer, text etc. which was specified when the table was created. More details of this will be given in Chap. 14. At present we will just assume that there are different types of field, each with a 'MySQL type' as shown in the table below.

Field Name	MySQL type	Notes
refnum	integer	Integer field
Forename	varchar(30)	Variable length text field – up to 30 characters
Surname	varchar(30)	Variable length text field – up to 30 characters
sex	enum('M', 'F')	'Enumeration field' – possible values M and F
occupation	varchar(30)	Variable length text field – up to 30 characters
cityBorn	varchar(30)	Variable length text field – up to 30 characters
yearBorn	year	A four digit integer from 1901 to 2155
number_of_children	integer	Integer field

12.4 Issuing MySQL Commands

The intention is to issue MySQL commands from within an executing PHP script and we will show how to do that in Chap. 15. However it is much easier to illustrate the features of the language if we (temporarily) separate it out from PHP and assume that we have a system which enables us to type in MySQL commands one-by-one at our keyboard, with the system responding by displaying the current contents of the table on our screen after executing each one.

Many MySQL systems come with a software package called phpMyAdmin which is designed to facilitate the management of a MySQL database using a web browser.[3] Some versions of phpMyAdmin provide a visual way of entering commands that avoids the user needing to learn the MySQL language. As we wish to learn the MySQL language we will ignore any such facility that may be available to you and concentrate on the simple (but imaginary) keyboard input and visual display output system described above.

However, it is important always to bear in mind that whereas a PHP script can send a string of characters (i.e., a MySQL command) to a MySQL server it cannot

[3] The name is misleading, as the PHP language is in no way involved.

receive a two-dimensional image back, merely a series of characters. How to process that output to give a visual form of display for a webpage or to use it in some other way will be considered in Chap. 15.

12.5 Naming Databases, Tables and Fields

The names of databases, tables and fields all follow the same convention. Names that are any combination of upper and lower case letters, digits, underscores and dollar signs can be written as they are without any surrounding quotes but may also be written enclosed in quotes. Other names, including those with embedded spaces or hyphens, must be enclosed in quotes. Note that the quote symbols that are used are not the customary straight quote character ' but the slanted quote character ` which is also known as a backtick. With the slanted quotes in a larger than normal font size a quoted name looks like this:

` this is a name that includes a space `

In this book we will generally avoid using names that need to be enclosed in slanted quotes and strongly recommend that you do the same. We will therefore avoid using the slanted quotes except in a few of the early examples.

The eight field names used for mytable1 show a number of different naming conventions: an initial lower case letter, an initial upper case letter, an embedded capital letter in cityBorn and yearBorn showing where a new word starts (known as 'camel case') and an embedded underscore in the name number_of_children. All of these are valid and there is no need for them to be enclosed in slanted quotes.

12.5.1 Case Sensitivity of Database, Table and Field Names

Whether or not database and table names are case sensitive depends on the operating system (Windows, Linux etc.) used by the server that holds the database. Hence MySQL commands which work correctly with one server may fail with another. *In this book we will make the conservative assumption that database and table names are always case sensitive and act accordingly.*

Field names are never case sensitive, so the field Forename can also be written as foreNAME etc.

12.6 Setting a Primary Key

There is one more step to take before we finally get to the stage of entering some data in our table. It does not have to be done immediately and in some systems it is not compulsory to do it, but we strongly recommend that you always do. This is to set what is called a *primary key* for your table.

The primary key of a table is a field or combination of fields that uniquely identifies each record in the table. We might choose Surname as the primary key, but of course it is possible for more than one person in our table to have the same surname.

Instead we will choose to make the combination of Forename and Surname our primary key. We do this by entering the MySQL command:

ALTER TABLE mytable1 ADD PRIMARY KEY(Forename, Surname)

On reflection, this is also an unwise choice. It is not likely that two or more people with the same forename and surname will ever need to be entered in the database, but if they are the system will not be able to handle it properly. A primary key needs to be unique and a much safer choice is to use field refnum, a four-digit reference number.

We will remove the previous primary key using the command

ALTER TABLE mytable1 DROP PRIMARY KEY

and then set a replacement by the command

ALTER TABLE mytable1 ADD PRIMARY KEY (refnum)

12.7 Adding a Record to the mytable1 Table

Finally we come to the question of adding some data to our empty table.

We can do this using an INSERT command, such as the following:

INSERT INTO `mydb1`.`mytable1` (`refnum`, `Forename`, `Surname`, `sex`,`occupation`, `cityBorn`,`yearBorn`,`number_of_children`) VALUES ('2461', 'Ann', 'Williams', 'F', 'doctor','Paris','1997', '2')

Executing this command will produce the updated table with one record:

refnum	Forename	Surname	sex	occupation	cityBorn	yearBorn	number_of_children
2461	Ann	Williams	F	doctor	Paris	1997	2

Before we say more about the INSERT INTO command there are some general points to make that also apply to other MySQL commands.

1. The keyword INSERT INTO, like other MySQL keywords, is not case sensitive, so it might also be written as insert INTO, insert into etc. However in this book we will generally write keywords in upper case.

2. Field values (as opposed to field names) are case sensitive, so Williams is not the same as williams.
3. The database, table and field names do not require the use of slanted quotes, so the command could be written as just

INSERT INTO mydb1.mytable1 (refnum, Forename, Surname, sex, occupation, cityBorn,yearBorn,number_of_children) VALUES ('2461', 'Ann', 'Williams', 'F', 'doctor','Paris','1997', '2')

4. We will assume that we have previously told the system that *mydb1* is the current database. So we can drop the database name and the following dot, giving just

INSERT INTO mytable1 (refnum, Forename, Surname, sex, occupation, cityBorn,yearBorn,number_of_children) VALUES ('2461', 'Ann', 'Williams', 'F', 'doctor','Paris','1997', '2')

5. The quote symbols to use around field values are straight quotes, e.g. 'Williams'. This is most important and potentially a considerable source of errors. If the quotes are omitted the field value is taken to be the name of a field not a constant. For example

INSERT INTO mytable1 (refnum, Forename, Surname, sex, occupation, cityBorn,yearBorn,number_of_children) VALUES ('2461', 'Ann', Williams, 'F', 'doctor','Paris','1997', '2')

With no quotes around the surname Williams the system interprets the command as an instruction to set the value of the Surname field to the value in a field called Williams. There is no such field of course, so the command will fail.

However the command

INSERT INTO mytable1 (refnum, Forename, Surname, sex, occupation, cityBorn,yearBorn,number_of_children) VALUES ('2461', 'Ann', Forename, 'F', 'doctor','Paris','1997', '2')

would be valid (although pointless). It tells the system to set the value of the Surname field to the value in the Forename field, giving a record with the distinctly unusual full name Ann Ann. It is hard to think of any practical use for this facility when using the INSERT INTO command but it can be useful in other situations, such as when copying a value from one field to another (see Sect. 12.10).

6. Field values that are purely numerical need not be enclosed in quotes. It is best to omit the quotes if the field is of a numerical type, but for efficiency reasons we recommend that the quotes are retained in the case of a text field even when the value itself is purely numerical.

By removing the unnecessary quotes the INSERT command can be further simplified to:

INSERT INTO mytable1 (refnum, Forename, Surname, sex, occupation, cityBorn, yearBorn, number_of_children) VALUES (2461, 'Ann', 'Williams', 'F', 'doctor','Paris',1997, 2)

7. If the list of field names before the VALUES keyword includes all the fields in the correct 'left-to-right' order we can omit it and it will be assumed by the MySQL system as a default. Thus the command can be further reduced to:

INSERT INTO mytable1 VALUES (2461, 'Ann', 'Williams', 'F', 'doctor','Paris',1997, 2)

8. If you read other books on MySQL you will probably see that when entering MySQL commands at a keyboard it is possible to enter more than one command at a time if they are separated by semicolons. However this is not applicable when executing MySQL commands using PHP, so we will ignore this possibility in this book and assume that commands are always entered one by one.
9. Some MySQL systems require a semicolon at the end of each command but this too is not applicable when executing MySQL commands using PHP and so we will not adopt this convention in this book.

12.7.1 The INSERT INTO Command

Returning to the INSERT INTO command, not all the field values need to be entered, and the field names can be placed in any order so for example just

INSERT INTO mytable1 (Forename, Surname, occupation, refnum, cityBorn) VALUES ('Martin', 'Johnson', 'plumber',1851,'London')

would be valid with the table now looking like this.

refnum	Forename	Surname	sex	occupation	cityBorn	yearBorn	number_of_children
2461	Ann	Williams	F	doctor	Paris	1997	2
1851	Martin	Johnson		plumber	London		

Note that the records do not have to be entered into the table in ascending order of the primary key.

We now enter five more commands to add additional rows into the table

INSERT INTO mytable1 VALUES (2547, 'Mary', 'Johnson', 'F', 'technician','Paris',1989, 3)

INSERT INTO mytable1 VALUES (634, 'James', 'Robinson', 'M', 'none','Geneva',2007, 0)

INSERT INTO mytable1 VALUES (1927, 'Bryan', 'Brown', 'M', 'engineer','Toronto',1987, 2)

INSERT INTO mytable1 VALUES (4821, 'Sarah', 'Green', 'F', 'engineer','Paris',1981, 1)

INSERT INTO mytable1 VALUES (3842, 'Frances', 'Bryce', 'F', 'translator','Northampton',1980, 2)

giving a table with seven records.

refnum	Forename	Surname	sex	occupation	cityBorn	yearBorn	number_of_children
2461	Ann	Williams	F	doctor	Paris	1997	2
1851	Martin	Johnson		plumber	London		
2547	Mary	Johnson	F	technician	Paris	1989	3
634	James	Robinson	M	none	Geneva	2007	0
1927	Bryan	Brown	M	engineer	Toronto	1987	2
4821	Sarah	Green	F	engineer	Paris	1981	1
3842	Frances	Bryce	F	translator	Northampton	1980	2

Before going on we will change the name of the field *number_of_children* to the simpler form *numchild*. We will also take the opportunity to change the field type from INTEGER to TINYINT, which is sometimes used when the numbers stored are certain to be small. (The difference between different types of integer field will be explained in Chap. 14.) We can make both changes by a single command:

ALTER TABLE mytable1 CHANGE number_of_children numchild tinyint

Note that this command can be used to change either the name of the field, its field type or (as here) both.

Now the command

INSERT INTO mytable1 VALUES (2947, 'Jane', 'Wilson', 'F', 'unemployed','Dresden',1972, 10)

gives a revised table:

refnum	Forename	Surname	sex	occupation	cityBorn	yearBorn	numchild
2461	Ann	Williams	F	doctor	Paris	1997	2
1851	Martin	Johnson		plumber	London		
2547	Mary	Johnson	F	technician	Paris	1989	3
634	James	Robinson	M	None	Geneva	2007	0
1927	Bryan	Brown	M	engineer	Toronto	1987	2
4821	Sarah	Green	F	engineer	Paris	1981	1
3842	Frances	Bryce	F	translator	Northampton	1980	2
2947	Jane	Wilson	F	unemployed	Dresden	1972	10

One of the values that can be inserted into a field in NULL. This is not to be confused with zero for a numerical field or '' (an empty string) for a character field. These are both specific values, whereas NULL indicates a non-existent value, i.e., that there is no value. It is possible to test whether a field has (or does not have) a NULL value using a WHERE clause, which will be introduced in Sect. 12.8.

12.7.2 The REPLACE INTO Command

The REPLACE INTO or REPLACE command (the word INTO is optional) is the same as INSERT INTO except that if an existing row has the same primary key value as a new row to be inserted, the existing row is deleted. In that situation an INSERT INTO command would fail.

12.8 Deleting a Record

We next decide to delete the record for Bryan Brown. We can do this with the command

DELETE FROM mytable1 WHERE refnum=1927

giving the table

refnum	**Forename**	**Surname**	**sex**	**occupation**	**cityBorn**	**yearBorn**	**numchild**
2461	Ann	Williams	F	Doctor	Paris	1997	2
1851	Martin	Johnson		plumber	London		
2547	Mary	Johnson	F	technician	Paris	1989	3
634	James	Robinson	M	None	Geneva	2007	0
4821	Sarah	Green	F	engineer	Paris	1981	1
3842	Frances	Bryce	F	translator	Northampton	1980	2
2947	Jane	Wilson	F	unemployed	Dresden	1972	10

The part of this command from WHERE onwards is called a 'WHERE clause'. *If it were not present the effect would be to delete all records in the table.* An alternative in this case would have been the command

DELETE FROM mytable1 WHERE occupation='engineer' AND yearBorn=1987

but this would have deleted all the engineers born in 1987, if there had been more than one, not just Bryan Brown. This illustrates the value of having a primary key (the refnum field). We can write the clause 'WHERE refnum=1927' and be certain that only one record will be affected.

A useful additional clause, which can be placed at the end of a DELETE command, is a LIMIT *clause*. This takes the form LIMIT *integer*, most commonly LIMIT 1 and restricts the number of records that can be deleted by the command. For example

DELETE FROM mytable1 WHERE refnum=1927 LIMIT 1

ensures that the system does not waste time trying to delete more than one person with refnum value 1927 (which in any case is not possible as it is a primary key). As soon as that record is deleted the system does not attempt to find more.

12.9 Changing a Table

We will now make some more (entirely unnecessary) changes to table mytable1 simply to illustrate some other facilities.

First we decide that we would like to add a field passportRef, a varchar(12) field between occupation and cityBorn. We can do this by the command

ALTER TABLE mytable1 ADD passportRef VARCHAR(12) AFTER occupation

refnum	Forename	Surname	sex	occupation	passportRef	cityBorn	yearBorn	numchild
2461	Ann	Williams	F	Doctor		Paris	1997	2
1851	Martin	Johnson		plumber		London		
2547	Mary	Johnson	F	technician		Paris	1989	3
634	James	Robinson	M	None		Geneva	2007	0
4821	Sarah	Green	F	engineer		Paris	1981	1
3842	Frances	Bryce	F	translator		Northampton	1980	2
2947	Jane	Wilson	F	unemployed		Dresden	1972	10

If we had instead entered

ALTER TABLE mytable1 ADD passportRef VARCHAR(12)

the new column would have been placed at the end, i.e., as the right-most column. Entering

ALTER TABLE mytable1 ADD passportRef VARCHAR(12) FIRST

instead would have caused passportRef to be placed as the first (i.e., the left-most) column.

Having inserted passportRef immediately after occupation, we change our mind and decide to remove the passportRef field. We do this by:

ALTER TABLE mytable1 DROP passportRef

thus restoring the table to its previous state.

The word COLUMN is optional in a command to delete a column, so the last command could have been written as

ALTER TABLE mytable1 DROP COLUMN passportRef

If we had wanted to delete more than one column we could have done this with a command such as

ALTER TABLE mytable1 DROP COLUMN passportRef, DROP occupation, DROP Forename

(The word COLUMN after DROP is optional each time.)

We will now empty the table of all its records and start again, entering the same eight records in a more efficient way than the first time.

The most efficient way to delete all the records in the table is to use the command

TRUNCATE mytable1

This removes all the records but most importantly it preserves the structure of the table, i.e., the field names, field types etc., which is what we want to do. If instead we had entered the command

DROP TABLE mytable1

It would have deleted the table altogether, rather than just the contents.

We are now back to having an empty table and can restore the eight records present at the end of Sect. 12.7 in the same order as before, either by eight separate INSERT INTO commands or more efficiently like this.

As before we start with two INSERT INTO commands:

INSERT INTO mytable1 VALUES (2461, 'Ann', 'Williams', 'F', 'doctor','Paris',1997, 2)

INSERT INTO mytable1 (Forename,Surname,occupation,refnum,cityBorn) VALUES ('Martin', 'Johnson', 'plumber',1851,'London')

(The field names in the second command are deliberately presented in a different order from the other commands as a reminder that this is possible. This command also shows that not all fields need to be included.)

The remaining six insertions all use the same eight fields so we can combine them into a much more compact form as a single INSERT INTO command as follows:

INSERT INTO mytable1
VALUES (2547, 'Mary', 'Johnson', 'F', 'technician','Paris',1989, 3),
(634, 'James', 'Robinson', 'M', 'none','Geneva',2007, 0),
(1927, 'Bryan', 'Brown', 'M', 'engineer','Toronto',1987, 2),
(4821, 'Sarah', 'Green', 'F', 'engineer','Paris',1981, 1),
(3842, 'Frances', 'Bryce', 'F', 'translator','Northampton',1980, 2),
(2947, 'Jane', 'Wilson', 'F', 'unemployed','Dresden',1972, 10)

We are now back to the previous form of the table with eight records:

refnum	**Forename**	**Surname**	**sex**	**occupation**	**cityBorn**	**yearBorn**	**numchild**
2461	Ann	Williams	F	doctor	Paris	1997	2
1851	Martin	Johnson		plumber	London		
2547	Mary	Johnson	F	technician	Paris	1989	3
634	James	Robinson	M	None	Geneva	2007	0
1927	Bryan	Brown	M	engineer	Toronto	1987	2
4821	Sarah	Green	F	engineer	Paris	1981	1
3842	Frances	Bryce	F	translator	Northampton	1980	2
2947	Jane	Wilson	F	unemployed	Dresden	1972	10

12.10 Updating a Table

The next job is to fill in the missing values in the entry for Martin Johnson. While we are doing it we will correct his occupation, which we know recently changed to butcher. To do this we use the UPDATE command, as follows:

UPDATE mytable1 SET sex='M', occupation='butcher',yearBorn=1970, numchild= 99 WHERE refnum= 1851 LIMIT 1

(We are using the code 99 in the numchild field to indicate 'unknown'.) This gives an updated table:

refnum	Forename	Surname	sex	occupation	cityBorn	yearBorn	numchild
2461	Ann	Williams	F	doctor	Paris	1997	2
1851	Martin	Johnson	M	butcher	London	1970	99
2547	Mary	Johnson	F	technician	Paris	1989	3
634	James	Robinson	M	None	Geneva	2007	0
1927	Bryan	Brown	M	engineer	Toronto	1987	2
4821	Sarah	Green	F	engineer	Paris	1981	1
3842	Frances	Bryce	F	translator	Northampton	1980	2
2947	Jane	Wilson	F	unemployed	Dresden	1972	10

The SET keyword in the UPDATE command can be followed by any number of *fieldname=value* pairs separated by commas. As before, numbers are not enclosed in quotes.

A very important part of the UPDATE command is the WHERE clause at the end. If it had been omitted all the table entries would have been changed not just one.

Although this example shows a simple test on the value of the primary key, WHERE clauses can be considerably more complex. To illustrate this we will first add an additional field at the end of the table, with name *extra* and type varchar(10).

We do this using the command

ALTER TABLE mytable1 ADD extra varchar(10)

This gives an augmented table

refnum	Forename	Surname	sex	occupation	cityBorn	yearBorn	numchild	extra
2461	Ann	Williams	F	doctor	Paris	1997	2	
1851	Martin	Johnson	M	butcher	London	1970	99	
2547	Mary	Johnson	F	technician	Paris	1989	3	
634	James	Robinson	M	None	Geneva	2007	0	
1927	Bryan	Brown	M	engineer	Toronto	1987	2	
4821	Sarah	Green	F	engineer	Paris	1981	1	
3842	Frances	Bryce	F	translator	Northampton	1980	2	
2947	Jane	Wilson	F	unemployed	Dresden	1972	10	

We can set all the values in the *extra* column to the value 'no' by the simple command

UPDATE mytable1 SET extra='no'

giving a revised table

refnum	Forename	Surname	sex	occupation	cityBorn	yearBorn	numchild	extra
2461	Ann	Williams	F	doctor	Paris	1997	2	no
1851	Martin	Johnson	M	butcher	London	1970	99	no
2547	Mary	Johnson	F	technician	Paris	1989	3	no
634	James	Robinson	M	None	Geneva	2007	0	no
1927	Bryan	Brown	M	engineer	Toronto	1987	2	no
4821	Sarah	Green	F	engineer	Paris	1981	1	no
3842	Frances	Bryce	F	translator	Northampton	1980	2	no
2947	Jane	Wilson	F	unemployed	Dresden	1972	10	no

We will now set the value in the *extra* field to 'yes' for all women with more than two children using the command

UPDATE mytable1 SET extra='yes' WHERE sex='F' AND (numchild>2 AND numchild!=99)

giving the updated table

refnum	Forename	Surname	sex	occupation	cityBorn	yearBorn	numchild	extra
2461	Ann	Williams	F	doctor	Paris	1997	2	no
1851	Martin	Johnson	M	butcher	London	1970	99	no
2547	Mary	Johnson	F	technician	Paris	1989	3	yes
634	James	Robinson	M	None	Geneva	2007	0	no
1927	Bryan	Brown	M	engineer	Toronto	1987	2	no
4821	Sarah	Green	F	engineer	Paris	1981	1	no
3842	Frances	Bryce	F	translator	Northampton	1980	2	no
2947	Jane	Wilson	F	unemployed	Dresden	1972	10	yes

Note that the condition numchild!=99 was added to guard against the possibility of a woman with an unknown number of children (coded as 99) being given a value of 'yes'. There were no such people in this particular case.

We will now change the value of field *extra* for Martin Johnson to the value '5734', which as the field is of type varchar(10) is a string of four digits not a number. The reason for doing so will soon become apparent. We enter the command

UPDATE mytable1 SET extra='5734' WHERE refnum=1851

and the table becomes:

refnum	Forename	Surname	sex	occupation	cityBorn	yearBorn	numchild	extra
2461	Ann	Williams	F	doctor	Paris	1997	2	no
1851	Martin	Johnson	M	butcher	London	1970	99	5734
2547	Mary	Johnson	F	technician	Paris	1989	3	yes
634	James	Robinson	M	None	Geneva	2007	0	no
1927	Bryan	Brown	M	engineer	Toronto	1987	2	no
4821	Sarah	Green	F	engineer	Paris	1981	1	no
3842	Frances	Bryce	F	translator	Northampton	1980	2	no
2947	Jane	Wilson	F	unemployed	Dresden	1972	10	yes

To illustrate some further points about the use of the UPDATE statement we will first change the *extra* field to be of type int(6). We enter the command

ALTER TABLE mytable1 CHANGE extra extra int(6)

The table now looks like this.

refnum	Forename	Surname	sex	occupation	cityBorn	yearBorn	numchild	extra
2461	Ann	Williams	F	doctor	Paris	1997	2	0
1851	Martin	Johnson	M	butcher	London	1970	99	5734
2547	Mary	Johnson	F	technician	Paris	1989	3	0
634	James	Robinson	M	None	Geneva	2007	0	0
1927	Bryan	Brown	M	engineer	Toronto	1987	2	0
4821	Sarah	Green	F	engineer	Paris	1981	1	0
3842	Frances	Bryce	F	translator	Northampton	1980	2	0
2947	Jane	Wilson	F	unemployed	Dresden	1972	10	0

Note that as the previous contents were all text values (yes and no) rather than numbers, they were automatically destroyed by the type conversion and replaced by a default integer value of zero. The one exception is the entry for Martin Johnson which was a text string comprising solely digits, i.e., '5734'. This has been replaced by the integer value 5734.

We can now show some possible uses for a value in a *field=value* pair that is not a constant. We will set the value of the *extra* field to the year after each person was born. The command to do this is

UPDATE mytable1 SET extra=yearBorn+1

refnum	Forename	Surname	sex	occupation	cityBorn	yearBorn	numchild	extra
2461	Ann	Williams	F	doctor	Paris	1997	2	1998
1851	Martin	Johnson	M	butcher	London	1970	99	1971
2547	Mary	Johnson	F	technician	Paris	1989	3	1990
634	James	Robinson	M	None	Geneva	2007	0	2008
1927	Bryan	Brown	M	engineer	Toronto	1987	2	1988
4821	Sarah	Green	F	engineer	Paris	1981	1	1982
3842	Frances	Bryce	F	translator	Northampton	1980	2	1981
2947	Jane	Wilson	F	unemployed	Dresden	1972	10	1973

If we want to calculate the age of each person in the year 2020 (assuming they are still alive, of course) and store the values in field *extra*, we enter the command:

UPDATE mytable1 SET extra = 2020-yearBorn

Table *mytable1* is now:

refnum	Forename	Surname	sex	occupation	cityBorn	yearBorn	numchild	extra
2461	Ann	Williams	F	doctor	Paris	1997	2	23
1851	Martin	Johnson	M	butcher	London	1970	99	50
2547	Mary	Johnson	F	technician	Paris	1989	3	31
634	James	Robinson	M	None	Geneva	2007	0	13
1927	Bryan	Brown	M	engineer	Toronto	1987	2	33
4821	Sarah	Green	F	engineer	Paris	1981	1	39
3842	Frances	Bryce	F	translator	Northampton	1980	2	40
2947	Jane	Wilson	F	unemployed	Dresden	1972	10	48

For the next example we first have to change the type of field *extra* again to varchar(50). We can do this by the command

ALTER TABLE mytable1 CHANGE extra extra varchar(50)

The table appears to be unaltered but *extra* values that display as, say, 23 are now the character strings '23' etc. not the numbers 23 etc.

We can now update the table so that the *extra* field contains the full name of each person by

UPDATE mytable1 SET extra=concat(Forename,' ',Surname)

This gives a revised table:

refnum	Forename	Surname	sex	occupation	cityBorn	yearBorn	numchild	extra
2461	Ann	Williams	F	doctor	Paris	1997	2	Ann Williams
1851	Martin	Johnson	M	butcher	London	1970	99	Martin Johnson
2547	Mary	Johnson	F	technician	Paris	1989	3	Mary Johnson
634	James	Robinson	M	None	Geneva	2007	0	James Robinson
1927	Bryan	Brown	M	engineer	Toronto	1987	2	Bryan Brown
4821	Sarah	Green	F	engineer	Paris	1981	1	Sarah Green
3842	Frances	Bryce	F	translator	Northampton	1980	2	Frances Bryce
2947	Jane	Wilson	F	unemployed	Dresden	1972	10	Jane Wilson

This illustrates the use of the MySQL function *concat*, which takes any number of character strings and joins them together (i.e., *concatenates* them). To avoid possible confusion we will point out here that if the value in the Forename or Surname field subsequently changes, the value of *extra* will not change. This is a database table, not a spreadsheet!

Before leaving the UPDATE command, we will also point out that (as for the DELETE command) a LIMIT clause, generally LIMIT 1, can be placed at the end of an UPDATE command to restrict the number of records changed by the command. This is particularly useful when a table is updated using its primary key. For example

UPDATE mytable1 SET extra='yes' WHERE refnum=4821 LIMIT 1

will ensure that once the system has updated the (one and only) record with refnum 4821 it does not spend time searching for another one, a search which is inevitably doomed to fail.

As with the INSERT INTO command, one of the values that can be given to one or more fields is NULL, denoting that there is no value. For example

UPDATE mytable1 SET extra=NULL WHERE yearBorn<1980

We can test whether a field is or is not null by a WHERE clause, e.g.,

WHERE yearBorn IS NULL

or

WHERE yearBorn IS NOT NULL

Field *extra* has now outlived its usefulness so we will delete it using

ALTER TABLE mytable1 DROP extra

The table is restored to:

refnum	Forename	Surname	sex	occupation	cityBorn	yearBorn	numchild
2461	Ann	Williams	F	doctor	Paris	1997	2
1851	Martin	Johnson	M	butcher	London	1970	99
2547	Mary	Johnson	F	technician	Paris	1989	3
634	James	Robinson	M	None	Geneva	2007	0
1927	Bryan	Brown	M	engineer	Toronto	1987	2
4821	Sarah	Green	F	engineer	Paris	1981	1
3842	Frances	Bryce	F	translator	Northampton	1980	2
2947	Jane	Wilson	F	unemployed	Dresden	1972	10

12.11 Summary of MySQL Commands

Here is a summary of all the MySQL commands used in this chapter. In all cases *tablename* can optionally be preceded by the name of a database followed by a dot. A complete list of the MySQL commands used in this book is given in Sect. 19.3.

ALTER TABLE *tablename*	ADD *fieldname field-specification* AFTER *fieldname*	Add a field to a table after a specified column
ALTER TABLE *tablename*	ADD *fieldname field-specification* FIRST	Add a field to a table as the first column
ALTER TABLE *tablename*	ADD *fieldname field-specification*	Add a field to a table as the last column
ALTER TABLE *tablename*	ADD PRIMARY KEY (*fieldname*)	To set a primary key for a table, when none already set. May also be a sequence of field names separated by commas
ALTER TABLE *tablename*	CHANGE *oldfieldname newfieldname field-specification*	Change a field name and/or specification in a table
ALTER TABLE *tablename*	DROP *fieldname1* ,DROP *fieldname2* ,DROP *fieldname3* etc. [DROP may optionally be followed by COLUMN each time]	Delete one or more fields from a table
ALTER TABLE *tablename*	DROP PRIMARY KEY	To remove an existing primary key from a table
CREATE DATABASE *databasename*		Create an empty database with the given name

(continued)

DELETE FROM *tablename*	WHERE *condition* [optionally followed by LIMIT *number*]	Delete one or more records from a table. See Sect. 12.8 for more information about conditions
DROP TABLE *tablename*		Delete a table
INSERT INTO *tablename*	(*fieldnames separated by commas)* VALUES (*field values, separated by commas*)	Create a new record. The field values must be in the same order as the field names
REPLACE INTO *tablename*	(same as for INSERT INTO)	Same as INSERT INTO except that if an existing row has the same primary key value as a new row to be inserted, the existing row is deleted
TRUNCATE *tablename*		Empty a table, but retain structure (field names, field types etc.)
UPDATE *tablename*	SET *field=value* WHERE *condition* [optionally followed by LIMIT *number*] Can also be a succession of *field=value* pairs, separated by commas	Change the value of one or more fields in one or more records in the specified table. If the WHERE clause and the LIMIT clause are omitted all the records in the table are changed
USE *databasename*		Make *databasename* the current database

Chapter Summary

This chapter introduces the MySQL language for managing relational databases, which will form the topic of the remainder of the book. It is shown how to create a database, insert a record into a table, delete and update records and also how to change the structure of a table. (The topic of creating a table is deferred until a later chapter.)

Practical Exercise 12

(1) Which of the following are not valid MySQL field names? Explain why.

2700xyz
abc-def
_xyz68ABC
\`abc\`
\`abc-def\`
\`your title\`
father's_name
$26ABxy_$

(2) Write a MySQL command to replace record 1927 in the table shown at the end of Sect. 12.10 by a new record for Bryony McTavish who is a doctor born in 1988 in New York.

(3) Given a table such as mytable1 shown at the end of Sect. 12.10 write MySQL commands to do the following:

   (a) Delete anyone with the surname Johnson

   (b) Create a new integer field immediately after yearBorn that contains the number of years each person was born after the year 1960.

Chapter 13
Using a MySQL Database II

Chapter Aims

After reading this chapter you should be able to:

- use the MySQL commands needed to extract information from a database table, combine information from different tables, rename a table and delete either a table or a database
- understand the different types of 'join' operation available in MySQL
- find the version of MySQL that you are using.

In this chapter we continue the description of the principal features available in the MySQL language which was begun in Chap. 12. In Chap. 15 we will show how to execute MySQL commands to manage a database from within an executing PHP script.

As in Chap. 12 we will assume that we have a database named *mydb1* with a single table named *mytable1*. We will further assume that the contents are as they were at the end of Sect. 12.10. A copy of the table is reproduced below.

M. Bramer, *Web Programming with PHP and MySQL*,
DOI 10.1007/978-3-319-22659-0_13

refnum	Forename	Surname	sex	occupation	cityBorn	yearBorn	numchild
2461	Ann	Williams	F	doctor	Paris	1997	2
1851	Martin	Johnson	M	butcher	London	1970	99
2547	Mary	Johnson	F	technician	Paris	1989	3
634	James	Robinson	M	None	Geneva	2007	0
1927	Bryan	Brown	M	engineer	Toronto	1987	2
4821	Sarah	Green	F	engineer	Paris	1981	1
3842	Frances	Bryce	F	translator	Northampton	1980	2
2947	Jane	Wilson	F	unemployed	Dresden	1972	10

13.1 The Select Command

We now come to one of the most widely used of all the MySQL commands. The whole point of storing information in a database is to be able to retrieve it again and then use it. The SELECT command produces a table showing the values of some or all of the fields in a table for some or all of the records. To display the complete contents of table *mytable1* we can simply enter

SELECT * FROM mytable1

The * character here represents all fields.

Frequently we do not want to see all the fields in our table, but just a few of them. The command

SELECT Forename,Surname,sex,numchild FROM mytable1

will display

Forename	Surname	sex	numchild
Ann	Williams	F	2
Martin	Johnson	M	99
Mary	Johnson	F	3
James	Robinson	M	0
Bryan	Brown	M	2
Sarah	Green	F	1
Frances	Bryce	F	2
Jane	Wilson	F	10

Warning – although in these examples the MySQL SELECT command produces a two-dimensional tabular display on the user's screen it is important to appreciate that when we issue MySQL commands via PHP all that is returned for most commands apart from SELECT is a logical value that is either 1 indicating 'command succeeded' or an empty string indicating 'command failed'.

In the case of a (valid) SELECT command an object is returned from which the row and column values can be extracted and (if we wish) displayed in a two-dimensional table. Although this sounds cumbersome it has one important advantage: we do not necessarily have to display the values in a table, we can use them in any way we wish. For example if we imagine a similar table to mytable1 but including email addresses, we might send an email to all the people selected which included their name and occupation.

13.1.1 Order by Clauses

An important factor to consider when using a SELECT command is that it may produce a table in an arbitrary order determined by the system. So far in this book all tables have shown the records in the order in which they were entered into the table but this may or may not be the order in which they would actually be displayed and in any case such an order is not likely to be very helpful. A better choice will often be ascending order of the primary key. To achieve that for the mytable1 table we use an ORDER BY clause, giving the command

SELECT * FROM mytable1 ORDER BY refnum

Applying this to our example table gives this output.

refnum	Forename	Surname	sex	occupation	cityBorn	yearBorn	numchild
634	James	Robinson	M	none	Geneva	2007	0
1851	Martin	Johnson	M	butcher	London	1970	99
1927	Bryan	Brown	M	engineer	Toronto	1987	2
2461	Ann	Williams	F	doctor	Paris	1997	2
2547	Mary	Johnson	F	technician	Paris	1989	3
2947	Jane	Wilson	F	unemployed	Dresden	1972	10
3842	Frances	Bryce	F	translator	Northampton	1980	2
4821	Sarah	Green	F	engineer	Paris	1981	1

The rows are the same as before but now they are arranged in ascending order of refnum.

The command

SELECT * FROM mytable1 ORDER BY refnum ASC

would give the same effect (ASC stands for 'ascending'), whereas

SELECT * FROM mytable1 ORDER BY refnum DESC

produces a table in descending order of refnum (DESC standing for 'descending'). Many other orders are also possible. For example if we want a table in ascending order of surname with any 'ties' arranged in descending order of forename, we can use the command

SELECT * FROM mytable1 ORDER BY surname, forename DESC

This gives the following output.

refnum	Forename	Surname	sex	occupation	cityBorn	yearBorn	numchild
1927	Bryan	Brown	M	engineer	Toronto	1987	2
3842	Frances	Bryce	F	translator	Northampton	1980	2
4821	Sarah	Green	F	engineer	Paris	1981	1
2547	Mary	Johnson	F	technician	Paris	1989	3
1851	Martin	Johnson	M	butcher	London	1970	99
634	James	Robinson	M	none	Geneva	2007	0
2461	Ann	Williams	F	doctor	Paris	1997	2
2947	Jane	Wilson	F	unemployed	Dresden	1972	10

The command

SELECT Forename,Surname,sex,numchild FROM mytable1 ORDER BY Surname,Forename

will give

Forename	Surname	sex	numchild
Bryan	Brown	M	2
Frances	Bryce	F	2
Sarah	Green	F	1
Martin	Johnson	M	99
Mary	Johnson	F	3
James	Robinson	M	0
Ann	Williams	F	2
Jane	Wilson	F	10

Sometimes we may want to use an ORDER BY clause with a field for which alphabetical (or numerical) order would not be appropriate. For example we may have a field named *size* with values 'very small', 'small', 'average', 'large' or 'very large'. Generating rows in alphabetical order of this field would hardly be very helpful. Instead we can use an ORDER BY FIELD clause, for example

ORDER BY FIELD(size, 'very small', 'small', 'average', 'large', 'very large')

Other possible examples, which should be self-explanatory, include

ORDER BY FIELD(season,'Spring', 'Summer', 'Autumn', 'Winter')

ORDER BY FIELD(degreeClass,'First', 'Second', 'Third', 'Unclassified', 'Fail')

A (slightly artificial) example using the *mytable1* table would be if we wished to order the output by the *numchild* field, i.e. the number of children, but with the numbers 0 and 99 (indicating 'unknown') in the last two places.

We can do this by the command

SELECT * FROM mytable1 ORDER BY FIELD(numchild,1,2,3,4,5,6,7,8,9,10,0,99),refnum ASC

which generates the output

refnum	Forename	Surname	sex	occupation	cityBorn	yearBorn	numchild
4821	Sarah	Green	F	engineer	Paris	1981	1
1927	Bryan	Brown	M	engineer	Toronto	1987	2
2461	Ann	Williams	F	doctor	Paris	1997	2
3842	Henrietta	Bryce	F	translator	Northampton	1980	2
2547	Mary	Johnson	F	technician	Paris	1989	3
2947	Jane	Wilson	F	unemployed	Dresden	1972	10
634	James	Robinson	M	none	Geneva	2007	0
1851	Martin	Johnson	M	butcher	London	1970	99

We can also sort in the reverse order, e.g. the command
SELECT * FROM mytable1 ORDER BY FIELD
(numchild,1,2,3,4,5,6,7,8,9,10,0,99) DESC,Surname

produces the output

refnum	Forename	Surname	sex	occupation	cityBorn	yearBorn	numchild
1851	Martin	Johnson	M	butcher	London	1970	99
634	James	Robinson	M	none	Geneva	2007	0
2947	Jane	Wilson	F	unemployed	Dresden	1972	10
2547	Mary	Johnson	F	technician	Paris	1989	3
1927	Bryan	Brown	M	engineer	Toronto	1987	2
3842	Henrietta	Bryce	F	translator	Northampton	1980	2
2461	Ann	Williams	F	doctor	Paris	1997	2
4821	Sarah	Green	F	engineer	Paris	1981	1

13.1.2 Where Clauses

We will often wish to see only those records that satisfy a WHERE condition such as those previously used with the DELETE and UPDATE commands. For example:

SELECT Surname,Forename,yearBorn FROM mytable1 WHERE sex='M' and numchild>0 AND numchild!=99 ORDER BY Surname,Forename

gives a table showing the name and year of birth of all the men with children (there is only one).

Surname	Forename	yearBorn
Brown	Bryan	1987

In general, the WHERE clause comprises a test on the values of one or more fields. This can be a *simple condition* such as

sex='F'

or a more complex one constructed from simple conditions using the logical operators AND, OR and NOT. Parentheses can also be used to avoid ambiguity and to construct more complex conditions. For example:

sex='F' AND (yearBorn>1980 OR numchild!=99) AND NOT (occupation='doctor' OR occupation='engineer')

Each simple condition is of the form *field operator value*. These operators are called *comparison operators*. They return a result that is either true or false. There are several comparison operators available in MYSQL. The main ones are given in this table.

=	is equal to
!=	does not equal
<>	does not equal
<	is less than
<=	is less than or equal to
>	is greater than
>=	is greater than or equal to

Conditions can also make use of the arithmetic operators including + − * and /. It is also possible to include functions such as *GREATEST* and *LEAST*. These can appear on either side of the comparison operator. For example if i1, i2, i3, i4 and i5 are all integer fields, possible conditions include

WHERE i1+i2 < i3-i4*i5

WHERE GREATEST(i1,i2,i3)>99

WHERE LEAST(i2,i5) > LEAST(i1,i3,i4).

The GREATEST and LEAST functions take the values of two or more numerical fields and return the largest and the smallest values, respectively.

Other functions available include the CONCAT function, illustrated in Sect. 12.10, which takes two or more character fields or string constants such as '...' and ' ' (space) and joins them together.

So CONCAT(Forename,'...',Surname) would give the values of the Forename and Surname fields for a particular record joined together by three dots. This function can be particularly useful as part of a SELECT command.

A further operator that can be used with either numerical or character fields is BETWEEN. Unlike the other operators this one takes two values after the operator, joined by AND. For example:

SELECT * FROM mytable1 WHERE yearBorn BETWEEN 1982 AND 2000 ORDER BY yearBorn

gives the output

refnum	Forename	Surname	sex	occupation	cityBorn	yearBorn	numchild
1927	Bryan	Brown	M	engineer	Toronto	1987	2
2547	Mary	Johnson	F	technician	Paris	1989	3
2461	Ann	Williams	F	doctor	Paris	1997	2

and the command

SELECT * FROM mytable1 WHERE Surname BETWEEN 'Bryce' AND 'Johnson' ORDER BY Surname

gives the output

refnum	Forename	Surname	sex	occupation	cityBorn	yearBorn	numchild
3842	Frances	Bryce	F	translator	Northampton	1980	2
4821	Sarah	Green	F	engineer	Paris	1981	1
1851	Martin	Johnson	M	butcher	London	1970	99
2547	Mary	Johnson	F	technician	Paris	1989	3

Note that if there is a WHERE clause it must come before any ORDER BY clause.

13.1.3 Displaying Values that are not Fields

Using a SELECT command we can display values that are not explicitly given as fields in the table. For example, using the CONCAT function, entering

SELECT CONCAT(Forename,' ',Surname), sex FROM mytable1 WHERE numchild>1 AND numchild!=99 ORDER BY Surname,Forename

will give

Bryan Brown	M
Frances Bryce	F
Mary Johnson	F
Ann Williams	F
Jane Wilson	F

13.1.4 Limit Clauses

A further facility available with the SELECT command is to limit the number of rows output. We can do this by placing a LIMIT clause at the end of the SELECT command, e.g.

SELECT * FROM mytable1 ORDER BY yearBorn DESC LIMIT 4

will give

refnum	Forename	Surname	sex	occupation	cityBorn	yearBorn	numchild
634	James	Robinson	M	none	Geneva	2007	0
2461	Ann	Williams	F	doctor	Paris	1997	2
2547	Mary	Johnson	F	technician	Paris	1989	3
1927	Bryan	Brown	M	engineer	Toronto	1987	2

i.e. the four youngest people in the table. There is little value in doing this for our small example, but if we imagine a selection from a table with hundreds of thousands of employee records arranged in descending order of salary the potential value for identifying (e.g.) the highest 20 earners is clear.

There is another reason for using a LIMIT clause. Say we have a command such as

SELECT Forename,Surname,yearBorn FROM mytable1 WHERE refnum=2461

and we have a table with 100,000 records they will all have to be checked even though there is only one possible record satisfying the condition (or conceivably none if there is no record with such a value of refnum). If there is no such record all 100,000 records will unavoidably have to be searched to ascertain that. On the other hand once you have found the one record that matches the WHERE condition, there is no point at all in checking the remainder of the 100,000 records. We can prevent that happening by adding a LIMIT 1 clause, making the command:

SELECT Forename,Surname,yearBorn FROM mytable1 WHERE refnum=2461 LIMIT 1

An extended form of the LIMIT clause is also available with two numbers after the keyword LIMIT separated by a comma. To illustrate this we will first consider the command

SELECT * FROM mytable1 ORDER BY yearBorn DESC

which produces this output:

refnum	Forename	Surname	sex	occupation	cityBorn	yearBorn	numchild
634	James	Robinson	M	none	Geneva	2007	0
2461	Ann	Williams	F	doctor	Paris	1997	2
2547	Mary	Johnson	F	technician	Paris	1989	3
1927	Bryan	Brown	M	engineer	Toronto	1987	2
4821	Sarah	Green	F	engineer	Paris	1981	1
3842	Frances	Bryce	F	translator	Northampton	1980	2
2947	Jane	Wilson	F	unemployed	Dresden	1972	10
1851	Martin	Johnson	M	butcher	London	1970	99

Supposing (rather unrealistically) that instead we want to ignore the two youngest people and display only the third, four, fifth and sixth youngest people in the table (i.e. those with refnum values 2547, 1927, 4821 and 3842). We can do that by starting the display at what would otherwise be the third row of the table, which (confusingly) we refer to as row number 2. (Row zero has refnum 634, so row 2 has refnum 2547.) Starting from that point we want to restrict the display to four rows only. Hence we enter the command:

SELECT * FROM mytable1 ORDER BY yearBorn DESC LIMIT 2,4

which produces the output

refnum	Forename	Surname	sex	occupation	cityBorn	yearBorn	numchild
2547	Mary	Johnson	F	technician	Paris	1989	3
1927	Bryan	Brown	M	engineer	Toronto	1987	2
4821	Sarah	Green	F	engineer	Paris	1981	1
3842	Frances	Bryce	F	translator	Northampton	1980	2

In this form of the LIMIT clause, the first number is referred to as the *offset*.

Another use of an offset occurs when, for example, we have previously found the 20 highest-earning employees using a LIMIT 20 clause and we now want to list the 21st to 50th highest. We can do this with the same command, replacing LIMIT 20 by LIMIT 20,30.

13.1.5 Applying Functions to the Values of a Field

As well as a list of fields in a SELECT command, we can use one or more functions that apply to the values of the field. The main ones of these are *max*, *min* and *avg*, giving respectively the largest, smallest and average values of a field. Thus the command:

SELECT min(yearBorn),max(yearBorn),min(Surname),max(Surname), min(numchild), max(numchild), avg(numchild) FROM mytable1

gives the single-row table

1970	2007	Brown	Wilson	0	99	14.8750

Note that *min* and *max* not only give the smallest and largest numbers for numerical fields but also the lowest and highest values in alphabetical order for text fields. The suspiciously high average number of children is explained by the fact that we are using a value of 99 to mean 'unknown'. To take such records out of the calculations we can use a WHERE clause:

SELECT min(yearBorn),max(yearBorn),min(Surname),max(Surname), min(numchild), max(numchild), avg(numchild) FROM mytable1 WHERE numchild!=99

giving the output

1972	2007	Brown	Wilson	0	10	2.8571

13.1.6 Finding the Number of Records in a Table

We can do this with the command

SELECT COUNT(*) FROM mytable1

which returns an object from which the number of records can be extracted.

We can also find the number of records where a specified field has a non-null value by, e.g.

SELECT COUNT(cityBorn) FROM mytable1

We can also find how many records satisfy a specified property. For example

SELECT COUNT(if(yearBorn>1985 AND sex='F',1,NULL)) FROM mytable1

The *if(yearBorn > 1985 AND sex = 'F',1,NULL)* part signifies that if the condition yearBorn > 1985 AND sex = 'F' is satisfied the value will be treated as 1 (meaning true) and the record will thus be counted; if not the value will be treated as NULL and so will not be counted.

13.1.7 Finding All the Distinct Values of a Field

It is sometimes useful to be able to find only the distinct values that are taken by a field. For our example table the command

SELECT sex FROM mytable1

will return eight values (one for each record in the table), five of them being F and the other three being M. By contrast

SELECT DISTINCT sex FROM mytable1

will return just the two values M and F.

This can be very helpful when exploring the contents of a large table. For example we might have a table of say 10,000 customer records in which the titles the customers use have not been standardised. For example it may be that one title has been entered in three ways: Mrs, Mrs. and in one case even MRs. Another may have been entered as Dr, Dr., Doctor or even Doc. Once we know which values have been used it is straightforward using UPDATE commands to standardise the values and then using an ALTER TABLE command to change the title field to an enumeration field so that entries remain standardised.

It is also possible to find all the distinct combinations of the values of two or more fields, e.g. by

SELECT DISTINCT sex,numChild FROM mytable1

13.2 Complex Select/Update Commands

It is possible to construct very elaborate commands in MySQL often combining the SELECT command with the UPDATE command or the INSERT INTO command. For example if we had a second table called *mytable2* with a varchar(50) field named Fullname, then the command

UPDATE mytable2 SET Fullname = (SELECT CONCAT(Forename, ' ',Surname) FROM mytable1 WHERE cityBorn = 'paris' ORDER BY refnum LIMIT 1)

would set the Fullname field for all records in table *mytable2* to the value 'Ann Williams'. It would be equivalent to entering

UPDATE mytable2 SET Fullname = 'Ann Williams'

With the flexibility of PHP at our disposal we can often perform such operations with much simpler MySQL commands.

MySQL has no way of storing the output from a SELECT command in a variable such as $X and then using $X in a later UPDATE command, but when MySQL commands are executed from within PHP this is straightforward to do. We will illustrate how to perform the above combined UPDATE/SELECT command in a simpler way using PHP in Chap. 15.

13.3 Combining Tables: Inner and Outer Joins

MySQL has many very powerful facilities beyond those shown in this book. One important facility that has not yet been illustrated is the use of a *join clause* to combine records from two or more tables.

Combining tables is called *making a join*. If we have two tables with a column in common, say a name field or a customer reference number, we can link the two tables together in a number of ways. To illustrate this, imagine that we have two new tables: *mytable4* and *mytable5*.

We will assume that table *mytable4* contains information we have assembled about a number of animals, large and small, that we have studied: the number of legs and wings they have and whether or not they can fly. Note that some animals appear more than once.

ind	Name	Legs	Wings	Canfly
1	dog	4	0	no
2	dove	2	2	yes
3	human	2	0	no
4	ostrich	2	2	no
5	eagle	2	2	yes
6	wasp	6	4	yes
7	human	2	0	no
8	ostrich	2	2	no
9	dove	2	2	yes
10	shark	0	0	no
11	vulture	2	2	yes
12	vulture	2	2	yes
13	salmon	0	0	no
14	magpie	2	2	yes
15	aardvark	4	0	no

Table *mytable5* gives information about the classification of a number of types of animal: mammal, bird, insect, reptile or fish.

Name2	AnimalType
dog	mammal
sparrow	bird
human	mammal
lion	mammal
ant	insect
tortoise	reptile
dove	bird
salmon	fish
wasp	insect

Some of the animal names appearing in the *Name* column in *mytable4* are not in the *Name2* column in table *mytable5* and *vice versa*. However five of the values occur in both columns, namely *dog*, *dove*, *human*, *salmon* and *wasp*.

By combining the tables we can produce a new table that has the five columns from *mytable4* followed (to their right) by the two columns from *mytable5*. This can be done in a number of ways.

There are three types of join command available in MySQL. The most important is probably the *inner join* command. We need to specify that we are joining *mytable4* and *mytable5* and that we are doing so on the basis of identical values in column *Name* (in *mytable4*) and column *Name2* (in *mytable5*). The command to do this is:

SELECT * FROM mytable4 INNER JOIN mytable5 ON mytable4.Name=mytable5.Name2 ORDER BY Name

(The ORDER BY clause is optional.)

Entering this command will give a combined table for the five animal names that appear in both *Name* and *Name2*:

ind	Name	Legs	Wings	Canfly	Name2	AnimalType
1	dog	4	0	no	dog	mammal
2	dove	2	2	yes	dove	bird
9	dove	2	2	yes	dove	bird
7	human	2	0	no	human	mammal
3	human	2	0	no	human	mammal
13	salmon	0	0	no	salmon	fish
6	wasp	6	4	yes	wasp	insect

Note that the values in *mytable5* are repeated for each occurrence of *dove* and *human* in column *Name*. We can now see the type of each animal, e.g. that a salmon is a fish.

The table names in the clause *ON mytable4.Name = mytable5.Name2* and the dots that follow them can be omitted as the two field names each occur in only one table. Otherwise, giving the table names explicitly would be essential.

The other two types of join available are called *outer joins*. The *left outer join* returns a row for each of the rows in the first table (*mytable4*), whether or not there is a corresponding row in the second table. The command:

SELECT * FROM mytable4 LEFT OUTER JOIN mytable5 ON mytable4.Name = mytable5.Name2 ORDER BY Name

returns the table:

ind	Name	Legs	Wings	Canfly	Name2	AnimalType
15	aardvark	4	0	no		
1	dog	4	0	no	dog	mammal
2	dove	2	2	yes	dove	bird
9	dove	2	2	yes	dove	bird
5	eagle	2	2	yes		
3	human	2	0	no	human	mammal
7	human	2	0	no	human	mammal
14	magpie	2	2	yes		
4	ostrich	2	2	no		
8	ostrich	2	2	no		
13	salmon	0	0	no	salmon	fish
10	shark	0	0	no		
11	vulture	2	2	yes		
12	vulture	2	2	yes		
6	wasp	6	4	yes	wasp	insect

Null values are used when a value in the *Name* field in the first table does not correspond to anything in the second table.

The *right outer join* returns a row for each of the rows in the second table (*mytable5*), whether or not there is a corresponding row in the first table. The command:

SELECT * FROM mytable4 RIGHT OUTER JOIN mytable5 ON mytable4.Name = mytable5.Name2 ORDER BY Name2

returns the table:

ind	Name	Legs	Wings	Canfly	Name2	AnimalType
					ant	insect
1	dog	4	0	no	dog	mammal
2	dove	2	2	yes	dove	bird
9	dove	2	2	yes	dove	bird
7	human	2	0	no	human	mammal
3	human	2	0	no	human	mammal
					lion	mammal
13	salmon	0	0	no	salmon	fish
					sparrow	bird
					tortoise	reptile
6	wasp	6	4	yes	wasp	insect

Null values are used when a value in the *Name2* field in the second table does not correspond to anything in the first table.

Although none of the *Name2* values in *mytable5* is duplicated, the entries in that table are duplicated in the table above where *Name2* is either *dove* or *human*. These are the values in common between the original fields *Name* and *Name2* for which there is more than one entry in *mytable4*. For those values there is a row in the combined table for each entry in *mytable4*.

13.4 Auto_Increment Fields

Although in the case of table *mytable1* we have a field, *refnum*, that can reasonably be used as a primary key this will not always be the case. Frequently there is no field that we can be sure will never be given the same value twice for different records.

The solution to this problem is to use an *auto_increment* field. This is a field (generally an integer type) which is automatically given a sequential number (generally starting at one and going up in steps of one) by MySQL whenever a new record is inserted into a table. This guarantees that each value will be different and means that the field can safely be used as a primary key. (It is not compulsory for an auto_increment field to be a primary key, but that is usually the reason for creating it.) It is not possible to have more than one auto_increment field in any table.

It would be best to set up an auto_increment field and make it the primary key when a table is created and we will illustrate how to do this in Chap. 14. However we can introduce an auto_increment field into our table *mytable1* as follows. First we remove the existing primary key (field *refnum*) by the command

ALTER TABLE mytable1 DROP PRIMARY KEY

Now we will create a new field called *auto1* of type int and specify that it is both a primary key and an auto_increment field. We can do this with the command:

ALTER TABLE mytable1 ADD auto1 int auto_increment PRIMARY KEY

This creates an integer field auto1 as the right-most field and makes it both the primary key and an auto_increment field.

We can now display our revised table in primary key order by

SELECT * FROM mytable1 ORDER BY auto1

with this result:

refnum	Forename	Surname	sex	occupation	cityBorn	yearBorn	numchild	auto1
634	James	Robinson	M	none	Geneva	2007	0	1
1851	Martin	Johnson	M	butcher	London	1970	99	2
1927	Bryan	Brown	M	engineer	Toronto	1987	2	3
2461	Ann	Williams	F	doctor	Paris	1997	2	4
2547	Mary	Johnson	F	technician	Paris	1989	3	5
2947	Jane	Wilson	F	unemployed	Dresden	1972	10	6
3842	Frances	Bryce	F	translator	Northampton	1980	2	7
4821	Sarah	Green	F	engineer	Paris	1981	1	8

The values of auto1, from 1 to 8 inclusive, have been added automatically to the records in the table (in the order of the previous primary key).

If we now add a ninth record by

INSERT INTO mytable1 (refnum,Forename, Surname,sex) VALUES (3001, 'John', 'Sanders', 'M')

the revised output becomes:

refnum	Forename	Surname	sex	occupation	cityBorn	yearBorn	numchild	auto1
634	James	Robinson	M	none	Geneva	2007	0	1
1851	Martin	Johnson	M	butcher	London	1970	99	2
1927	Bryan	Brown	M	engineer	Toronto	1987	2	3
2461	Ann	Williams	F	doctor	Paris	1997	2	4
2547	Mary	Johnson	F	technician	Paris	1989	3	5
2947	Jane	Wilson	F	unemployed	Dresden	1972	10	6
3842	Frances	Bryce	F	translator	Northampton	1980	2	7
4821	Sarah	Green	F	engineer	Paris	1981	1	8
3001	John	Sanders	M					9

Note that the user does not specify a value for auto1. It is supplied automatically by the MySQL system. If the auto_increment field is not in the right-most position the user should provide the dummy value '', i.e. an empty string.

By default, the starting value for auto_increment is 1, and it will increment by 1 for each new record. To change the starting value (or the next value to be used if some records have already been created) we can use a command such as:

ALTER TABLE mytable1 AUTO_INCREMENT=100

Having illustrated the use of an auto_increment field we will now restore our table to its previous state. We can do that with three commands, first to delete the field auto1, second to make refnum the primary key again and finally to delete the new record which we added with refnum value 3001.

ALTER TABLE mytable1 DROP auto1
ALTER TABLE mytable1 ADD PRIMARY KEY(refnum)
DELETE FROM mytable1 WHERE refnum=3001 LIMIT 1

13.5 The Show Command

The SHOW command is used to display in tabular form information about the names of the user's databases and tables and their structure, as opposed to the data values they hold. The same comment applies as for SELECT: when a MySQL command is executed via PHP, the response is not a table but an object from which the information can be extracted and used to generate a table as part of a webpage or for any other purpose we chose. We will show how we can make use of this in Chap. 15.

13.5.1 Show Databases

So far we have assumed that we have only one database *mydb1* and that it has just one table *mytable1*. If instead we had two databases the output from the command

SHOW DATABASES

would be a table such as

mydb1
database2

13.5.2 Show Tables

We will continue to assume that the currently selected database is mydb1, i.e. all MySQL commands relate to that database unless specified otherwise. If we temporarily assume that mydb1 has four tables not one, the output from the command

SHOW TABLES IN mydb1

which we can abbreviate to just

SHOW TABLES

will be similar to this

Tables_in_mydb1
mytable1
table2
next _table
fourth_table

13.5.3 Show Fields/ Show Columns/ Describe

We can find the names of the fields in a table *tablename* in database *databasename* and their properties by the command

SHOW FIELDS FROM *databasename.tablename*

(Note the dot between *databasename* and *tablename*.)

As mydb1 is the currently selected database we can examine table mytable1 by the simplified command

SHOW FIELDS FROM mytable1

Two alternative ways of writing this command are

SHOW COLUMNS FROM mytable1

and

DESCRIBE mytable1

These all give the same output:

Field	Type	Null	Key	Default	Extra
refnum	integer	NO	PRI	0	
Forename	varchar(30)	NO			
Surname	varchar(30)	NO			
sex	enum('M','F')	YES		NULL	
occupation	varchar(30)	YES		NULL	
cityBorn	varchar(30)	YES		NULL	
yearBorn	year	YES		NULL	
numchild	integer	YES		NULL	

For each of the eight fields in mytable1, the table shows the following

- Field – the name of the field (or column)
- Type – the data type for the field (those introduced in Chap. 12 were varchar, integer, enum and year).
- Null – whether the column can contain NULL values
- Key – whether the column is indexed (PRI indicates a primary key)
- Default – the field's default value
- Extra – additional information. In particular auto_ increment indicates that the field has been given the AUTO_INCREMENT option.

We will explain additional data types and the meanings of the other fields in Chap. 14 when we look at how tables can be created.

13.5.4 Show Variables

The command

SHOW VARIABLES

produces a display of the values of a large number of system variables, which are unlikely to be of much interest to most users. A more useful version of the command is

SHOW VARIABLES LIKE "version"

which will display the version of MySQL that you are using.

13.6 Some Further Commands and Adding Comments

To complete this chapter we will give a brief mention of three more MySQL commands which do not need detailed discussion and show how to include a comment in a MySQL Command.

13.6.1 Renaming a Table

To change the name of mytable1 to mytable99 there are two alternative commands available

ALTER TABLE mytable1 RENAME TO mytable99
RENAME TABLE mytable1 TO mytable99

13.6.2 Deleting a Table

To delete a table we use a command such as:

DROP TABLE mytable2

The tablename may be preceded by a database name followed by a dot if the table is not in the currently selected database.

13.6.3 Deleting a Database

The command

DROP DATABASE mydb2

deletes all the tables in the database and the database itself.

13.6.4 Including a Comment in a MySQL Command

Although we have not done so in this book it is possible to include a comment in a MySQL command. Any # sign or combination of two minus signs followed by a space and everything to the right of it is taken as a comment and ignored. Anything between /* and */ is also ignored. So the following commands are all equivalent:

DROP DATABASE mydb2
DROP DATABASE mydb2 # delete database
DROP DATABASE mydb2 -- delete database
DROP DATABASE /* delete database */ mydb2

13.7 Summary of MySQL Commands

Here is a summary of all the MySQL commands used in this chapter. In all cases *tablename* can optionally be preceded by the name of a database followed by a dot. A complete list of the MySQL commands used in this book is given in Sect. 19.3.

ALTER TABLE *tablename*	ADD *fieldname field-specification* May optionally be followed by PRIMARY KEY	Add a field to a table as the last column
ALTER TABLE *tablename*	ADD PRIMARY KEY (*fieldname*)	To set a primary key for a table, when none already set. May also be a sequence of field names separated by commas.
ALTER TABLE *tablename*	AUTO_INCREMENT=*unsigned integer*	Changes the starting value of an auto_increment field (or the next value to be used if some records have already been created)
ALTER TABLE *tablename*	DROP *fieldname1* ,DROP *fieldname2* ,DROP *fieldname3* *etc.* [DROP may optionally be followed by COLUMN each time]	Delete one or more fields from a table
ALTER TABLE *tablename*	DROP PRIMARY KEY	To remove an existing primary key from a table
ALTER TABLE *tablename*	RENAME TO *newtablename*	Change the name of a table
DELETE FROM *tablename*	WHERE *condition* [optionally followed by LIMIT *number*]	Delete one or more records from a table. See Sect. 12.8 for more information about conditions
DESCRIBE *tablename*		Equivalent to SHOW FIELDS FROM *tablename*
DROP DATABASE *databasename*		Delete a database
DROP TABLE *tablename*		Delete a table
RENAME TABLE *tablename*	TO *newtablename*	Rename a table

(continued)

SELECT * FROM *table1*	INNER JOIN *table2* ON *table1.field1=table2.field2* Can be followed by an optional ORDER BY clause. INNER JOIN can be replaced by LEFT OUTER JOIN or RIGHT OUTER JOIN	Combine tables (see Sect. 13.3)
SELECT * FROM *tablename*	WHERE *condition* ORDER BY *fieldnames separated by commas* [optional ASC or DESC after each one] LIMIT *number* Instead of a fieldname in the ORDER BY clause there can be the word FIELD followed by a fieldname and a list of values for the field, all separated by commas and enclosed in parentheses. See Sect. 13.1.1. Instead of any fieldname in the WHERE clause there can be a function (such as concat, greatest, least, min, max and avg) applied to one or more fieldnames. The WHERE, ORDER BY and LIMIT clauses are all optional. The LIMIT clause can also be LIMIT *offset,number*	Returns the values of all fields in some or all of the records in the table, possibly in a specified order and with a limit to the number returned
SELECT *fields separated by commas* FROM *tablename*	(As for SELECT * FROM *tablename)*	(As for SELECT * FROM *tablename)*
SELECT COUNT(*) FROM *tablename*		Returns the number of records in the table
SELECT COUNT (*fieldname*) FROM *tablename*		Returns the number of records in the table where the field has a non-null value
SELECT COUNT (IF (*condition,true value,falsevalue*)) FROM *tablename*		Returns the number of records in the table where a specified condition is met (see Sect. 13.1.6)
SELECT DISTINCT *fieldname* FROM *tablename*	May also be a sequence of field names, separated by commas.	Finds only the distinct values taken by a field or a combination of fields

(continued)

SHOW COLUMNS FROM *tablename*		Equivalent to SHOW FIELDS FROM *tablename*
SHOW DATABASES		Display a list of all the databases available to the user
SHOW FIELDS FROM *databasename.tablename*		Display information about the fields in the specified table in the specified database
SHOW FIELDS FROM *tablename*		Display information about the fields in the specified table in the current database
SHOW TABLES		Display a list of the tables in the currently selected database
SHOW TABLES IN *database*		Display a list of the tables in the specified database
SHOW VARIABLES		Display the values of a large number of system variables
SHOW VARIABLES	LIKE "version"	Display the version of MySQL that you are using

(continued)

UPDATE *tablename*	SET *field=value* WHERE *condition* [optionally followed by LIMIT *number*] Can also be a succession of *field=value* pairs, separated by commas. *value* can also be a SELECT command enclosed in parentheses (see Sect. 13.2)	Change the value of one or more fields in one or more records in the specified table. If the WHERE clause is omitted all the records in the table are changed.

Chapter Summary

This chapter continues to introduce the MySQL language for managing relational databases. It is shown how to extract information from a database table, how to combine information from different tables using join operations, how to create an 'auto increment' field as a primary key, how to rename a table, delete either a table or a database and how to find the version of MySQL that you are using

Practical Exercise 13

(1) Given a table such as the one shown in Sect. 13.1.4

(a) write a MySQL command to display all the details for the oldest person in the table (ignore the possibility of a tie).
(b) write a MySQL command to list all the cities in which the women in the table were born.
(c) write MySQL commands to change the primary key to a combination of cityBorn and yearBorn.

(2) Why would doing (1) (c) be unwise?
(3) Given tables mytable4 and mytable5 shown in Sect. 13.3 write a MySQL command that will display all types of animal that can fly.

Chapter 14
Creating and Updating MySQL Tables

Chapter Aims

After reading this chapter you should be able to:

- use a MySQL command to create a database table
- understand the various data types available in MySQL
- construct an appropriate column definition for each field in a table
- copy the structure and/or the contents of one table to another
- find the structure of a table
- change the structure, name and field specification of a table.

In this chapter we complete the description of the MySQL language which was begun in Chaps. 12 and 13. We come to the topic of creating a table with a given structure which was deferred from Chap. 12. We also show how to modify the structure of a table and how to copy a table.

14.1 Creating a Table

To create a table in a database that already exists we use the CREATE TABLE command. The command used to create table *mytable1* might have been the following.

M. Bramer, *Web Programming with PHP and MySQL*,
DOI 10.1007/978-3-319-22659-0_14

```
CREATE TABLE mytable1 (
refnum integer NOT NULL DEFAULT 0,
Forename varchar(30) NOT NULL,
Surname varchar(30) NOT NULL,
sex enum('M','F'),
occupation varchar(30),
cityBorn varchar(30),
yearBorn year,
numchild integer,
PRIMARY KEY (refnum)
)
```

The final component before the closing parenthesis specifies which field is the table's primary key. It is not essential to have such a field (or combination of fields) but it is highly recommended to do so.

The preceding lines comprise a specification of each of the table's eight fields, followed by commas. The entry for each field is the name of the field, followed by the *column definition*, which comprises the data type, followed (depending on the type selected) by some optional clauses such as NOT NULL or DEFAULT 0.

14.2 Data Types

The data type begins with a keyword such an INTEGER or VARCHAR and may be followed (depending on the type) by some additional keywords such as UNSIGNED.

MySQL has six main categories of data type, most of which comprise several individual types that are variations on a common theme. They are summarised below.

14.2.1 Integer Types

The principal member of this category is INTEGER, which can be abbreviated to INT. However there are four other members, which are mainly of interest to those who administer large databases where minimizing the amount of storage required for integer values is important or those who wish to use exceptionally large integer values.

Each of the integer types may optionally be followed by an unsigned integer in parentheses, e.g. INT(2). This number indicates a display width for integer types, which is entirely separate from the range of values that can be stored. For example an INT field may be specified as INT(4) signifying that integers with fewer than four significant digits will be displayed padded out to four characters by spaces to the left. However this does not prevent integers with more than four digits being both stored and displayed in full. If no display width is specified, a default value of 11 characters is assumed unless the UNSIGNED option is chosen (see below), in which case the default is 10 characters.

The main reason for specifying a display width is to use it in conjunction with the ZEROFILL clause described below.

All the members of this category can be followed by optional keywords:

- UNSIGNED which indicates that the values to be stored are restricted to positive and zero integers.
  If UNSIGNED is not specified negative integers may also be stored.
- ZEROFILL which indicates that when a value is displayed it is padded (if necessary) with zeroes up to the display width specified in the column definition. (Values that are longer than the display width are displayed in full.) If no display width is specified, the unsigned integer default value of 10 characters is assumed. If ZEROFILL is specified, MySQL automatically adds the UNSIGNED attribute to the column.

The six integer types available are given in the following table, which shows how many bits of storage each such value will occupy and the range of integer values that may be stored for a field of that type. The latter depends on whether the field is 'signed' or 'unsigned'.

Type	Number of bits	Range of values (signed)	Range of values (unsigned)
TINYINT	8	−128 to 127	0 to 255
SMALLINT	16	−32768 to 32767	0 to 65535
MEDIUMINT	24	−8388608 to 8388607	0 to 16777215
INT or INTEGER	32	−2147483648 to 2147483647	0 to 4294967295
BIGINT	64	−9223372036854775808 to 9223372036854775807	0 to 18446744073709551615

Clearly specifying type INT or INTEGER will be perfectly adequate for most purposes, unless storage space is a particular issue.

Some possible column definitions of integer type are:

```
SMALLINT
INTEGER UNSIGNED
SMALLINT(2) ZEROFILL
BIGINT(50) UNSIGNED ZEROFILL
```

14.2.2 *Fixed Point Types*

These are non-integer numerical values that are stored exactly. They are used when exact precision is important, which is particularly likely to be the case for monetary values. There are two fixed-point data types: DECIMAL and NUMERIC, which are equivalent. For these types two numbers are normally specified after the keyword. They are enclosed in parentheses and separated by a comma.

The first number, called the *precision*, indicates how many significant digits can be stored. The second number, called the *scale*, indicates the number of digits that can be stored after the decimal point. Thus for a field specified as DECIMAL(5,2) numbers from –999.99 to 999.99 can be stored.

As for integer types, members of this category can be followed by the optional keywords UNSIGNED and ZEROFILL. If ZEROFILL is specified, MySQL automatically adds the UNSIGNED attribute to the column.

14.2.3 Floating Point Types

These are numerical values that are stored in binary form, using either 32 bits (single-precision) or 64 bits (double-precision) and converted to approximate decimal values before they are displayed. There are two kinds:

- FLOAT and REAL are equivalent. They specify that single precision will be used (32 bits of storage)
- DOUBLE PRECISION and DOUBLE are equivalent. They specify that double precision will be used (64 bits of storage).

All of them can optionally be followed by precision and scale values in parentheses. For example, a field defined as FLOAT(7,4) will look like –999.9999 when displayed.

Precision values up to 23 are appropriate for single-precision (32 bits) storage. If a larger precision value is specified, double-precision (64 bits) storage is required.

As for integer and fixed point types, members of this category can be followed by the optional keywords UNSIGNED and ZEROFILL. If ZEROFILL is specified, MySQL automatically adds the UNSIGNED attribute to the column.

14.2.4 Character Types

There are ten types of field that can be used to hold strings of characters.

CHAR (length)	A fixed length string of from 1 to 255 characters. Strings of fewer characters are stored right-padded with spaces. The (length) part is optional. If omitted a value of one is assumed
VARCHAR (length)	A variable length string. The value of *length* must be specified as an integer from 1 to 255
BLOB or TEXT	A field with a maximum length of 65535 characters. (BLOB stands for 'Binary Large Object'.) Sorting or comparison of stored data is case sensitive for BLOB and case insensitive with TEXT

(continued)

TINYBLOB or TINYTEXT	As for BLOB and TEXT but with a maximum of 255 characters
MEDIUMBLOB or MEDIUMTEXT	As for BLOB and TEXT but with a maximum of 16777215 characters
LONGBLOB or LONGTEXT	As for BLOB and TEXT but with a maximum of 4294967295 characters

14.2.5 *Enumeration Types*

Here the field must take one of a specified set of values, which are separated by commas. For example

ENUM ('M','F')

or

ENUM('Excellent','Good','Average','Poor','Very Poor')

14.2.6 *Date and Time Types*

There are five of these, each comprising a single word. The table below shows how data of each type is stored.

Type	Format	Example
DATE	'YYYY-MM-DD'	'2020-02-28'
YEAR	'YYYY'	'2010'
TIME	'HH:MM:SS'	'17:08:57'
DATETIME	'YYYY-MM-DD HH:MM:SS'	'2001-11-30 22:08:06'
TIMESTAMP	'YYYY-MM-DD HH:MM:SS'	'2001-11-30 22:08:06'

TIMESTAMP is the same as DATETIME with the current date and time automatically converted to UTC (Co-ordinated Universal Time, also known as Greenwich Mean Time). It is automatically set when a record is inserted into a table and automatically updated when the record is updated. (It should not be included explicitly in the INSERT INTO and UPDATE commands.)

14.3 NOT NULL and DEFAULT Clauses

Each of the above data types can be followed by either or both of the keywords NOT NULL and DEFAULT

NOT NULL specifies that it is not permitted to give the field a value of NULL. If a field is specified as NOT NULL, any attempt to assign it a value of NULL by an INSERT INTO or an UPLOAD command will cause the DEFAULT value to be used (as explained below). A primary key field should always be specified as NOT NULL.

DEFAULT *value* specifies a value to be given to a field if no value (except NULL) is assigned by an INSERT INTO command or an UPDATE command.

[a] If the field is numeric, the default value must be a number, e.g.

INT (2) DEFAULT 0

or

FLOAT (7,4) DEFAULT 6.5

[b] If the field is a string the default must be a string value or NULL, e.g.

VARCHAR(10) DEFAULT 'yes'

or

CHAR(6) DEFAULT ''

or

VARCHAR (20) DEFAULT NULL

[c] In the case of an enumeration field the default value must be one of the specified values, e.g.

ENUM('Excellent','Good','Average','Poor','Very Poor') DEFAULT 'Average'

If it is not appropriate to make one of the specified values the default, the NOT NULL and DEFAULT clauses should not be used.

[d] BLOB and TEXT fields cannot be given a default value.

If no explicit default value is given for a field, it is possible for it to take a NULL value and it is not specified as NOT NULL, MySQL adds an explicit DEFAULT NULL clause to the field definition.

14.3.1 Implied Default Values

If a field is specified as NOT NULL, with no default value given, when any attempt is made to assign a NULL value to it, MySQL will assign an appropriate value where that is possible. (In other cases an error will occur.)

- For an auto_increment field, the next value in the sequence is used
- For a numeric field (that is not an auto_increment field) the value zero is used
- For a string field (that is not an auto_increment field) an empty string is used
- For an enumeration field the default will be taken to be the first of the specified values
- For a DATE field the default will be '0000-00-00'
- For a YEAR field the default will be '0000'
- For a TIME field the default will be '00:00:00'
- For a DATETIME field the default will be '0000-00-00 00:00:00'

– For a TIMESTAMP field the default will be taken to be the function CURRENT_TIMESTAMP, which will enter the current year, month, day and time into the field in the correct format (using Co-ordinated Universal Time).

Note that a DATETIME field can be given the function CURRENT_TIMESTAMP as its default, but this has to be done explicitly. (This and the TIMESTAMP field are the only exceptions to the principle that a default value must always be a constant.)

14.4 AUTO_INCREMENT Clause

If an auto_increment field is required it is specified here immediately after the DEFAULT clause (if there is one). There may be at most one auto_increment field for any table. It is normally desirable for an auto_increment field also to be specified as PRIMARY KEY.

14.5 Key Clauses

The most important of these is

PRIMARY KEY

It follows immediately after the AUTO_INCREMENT clause (if there is one).

Although it is not essential, it is recommended for efficiency reasons that a primary key field is always explicitly given a NOT NULL specification.

14.6 Copying a Table

If we want to create a new table mytable2 with the same structure and field definitions, etc. as mytable1 we can do it with a single command:

CREATE TABLE mytable2 LIKE mytable1

The two tables can be in different databases that are accessible to the user, in which case each table name should be preceded by the name of a database followed by a dot.

If we want the contents of mytable1 to be copied to mytable2, thus giving an identical copy of the original table, we can use the further command:

INSERT INTO mytable2 SELECT * FROM mytable1

Using the two commands together clearly provides a very simple way of making a backup copy of a table.

14.7 Changing the Structure, the Name and the Field Specifications of a Table

The structure of a table, its name and/or the specifications of its fields can be changed using the ALTER TABLE command. We have already seen several versions of this. This section brings together and extends what has already been discussed about this very powerful command.

14.7.1 Primary Keys

- To remove an existing primary key
  ALTER TABLE *tablename* DROP *fieldname*
- To create a new primary key from one field
  ALTER TABLE *tablename* ADD PRIMARY KEY(*fieldname*)
- To create a primary key from more than one field
  ALTER TABLE *tablename* ADD PRIMARY KEY(*field1,field2,...*)

14.7.2 Set the Starting Value for an AUTO_INCREMENT Field

ALTER TABLE *tablename* AUTO_INCREMENT= *unsigned integer*

14.7.3 Change the Name of a Table

ALTER TABLE *oldname* RENAME TO *newname*

14.7.4 Add a New Field

ALTER TABLE *tablename* ADD *fieldname field-specification*

The *field-specification* can include all the clauses illustrated earlier in this chapter, e.g.

ALTER TABLE mytable1 ADD surname VARCHAR(30) NOT NULL DEFAULT ''

ALTER TABLE mytable1 ADD numchild INT(4) UNSIGNED ZEROFILL NOT NULL DEFAULT 99

ALTER TABLE mytable1 ADD refnum INTEGER NOT NULL PRIMARY KEY

ALTER TABLE mytable1 ADD indexfield INTEGER NOT NULL AUTO_INCREMENT PRIMARY KEY

If there is nothing following the *field-specification* the new field is placed in the right-most position

Instead we can use a clause AFTER *fieldN* to place it after *fieldN* or FIRST to place it in the left-most position.

14.7.5 Change the Name and/or Structure of a Field

We can change the name of a field and its specification with a single command

ALTER TABLE *tablename* CHANGE old*fieldname newfieldname field-specification*

If the old fieldname is the same as the new field name it is simpler to use another form of the command:

ALTER TABLE *tablename* MODIFY *fieldname field-specification*

In both cases the *field-specification* can include all the clauses illustrated earlier in this chapter (and should include all those that are to remain in force). For example

ALTER TABLE mytable1 CHANGE numchild numchildren INTEGER(4) UNSIGNED ZEROFILL

ALTER TABLE mytable1 MODIFY numchildren INTEGER NOT NULL AFTER occupation

ALTER TABLE mytable1 CHANGE numchildren numchild INTEGER AFTER yearBorn

If we are altering the specification of the PRIMARY KEY field there is no need to include the PRIMARY KEY clause. Once this is set it remains in force until it is removed using an ALTER TABLE … DROP PRIMARY KEY command.

14.7.6 Changing a Default Value

We can change or set a default value of a field by including DEFAULT *default-value* in the field specification, e.g.

ALTER TABLE mytable1 MODIFY numchild INTEGER NOT NULL DEFAULT 99

However if the only change is to the default value we can change it using a simpler form of the ALTER TABLE command:

ALTER TABLE mytable1 ALTER numchild SET DEFAULT 99

To remove the default value we can use

ALTER TABLE mytable1 ALTER numchild DROP DEFAULT

14.8 Using the SHOW Command to Find the Structure of a Table

A further use of the SHOW command is to find the structure of a table. The output from the command

SHOW CREATE TABLE mytable1

is a listing of a CREATE TABLE command that could have been used to create the table, which may include elements added automatically by the MySQL system.

14.9 Summary of MySQL Commands

Here is a summary of all the MySQL commands used in this chapter. In all cases *tablename* can optionally be preceded by the name of a database followed by a dot. A complete list of the MySQL commands used in this book is given in Appendix 3.

ALTER TABLE *tablename*	ADD *fieldname field-specification* AFTER *fieldname* May optionally be followed by PRIMARY KEY	Add a field to a table after a specified column
ALTER TABLE *tablename*	ADD *fieldname field-specification* FIRST May optionally be followed by PRIMARY KEY	Add a field to a table as the first column
ALTER TABLE *tablename*	ADD *fieldname field-specification* May optionally be followed by PRIMARY KEY	Add a field to a table as the last column
ALTER TABLE *tablename*	ADD PRIMARY KEY (*fieldname*)	To set a primary key for a table, when none already set. May also be a sequence of field names separated by commas.
ALTER TABLE *tablename*	ALTER *fieldname* DROP DEFAULT	Cancel the default value of a field
ALTER TABLE *tablename*	ALTER *fieldname* SET DEFAULT *value*	Set the default value of a field
ALTER TABLE *tablename*	AUTO_INCREMENT = unsigned *integer*	Changes the starting value of an auto_increment field (or the next value to be used if some records have already been created)
ALTER TABLE *tablename*	CHANGE *oldfieldname newfieldname field-specification*	Change a field name and/or specification in a table

(continued)

ALTER TABLE *tablename*	DROP *fieldname1* ,DROP *fieldname2* ,DROP *fieldname3* *etc.* [DROP may optionally be followed by COLUMN each time]	Delete one or more fields from a table
ALTER TABLE *tablename*	DROP PRIMARY KEY	To remove an existing primary key from a table
ALTER TABLE *tablename*	MODIFY *fieldname field-specification*	Change a field specification in a table
ALTER TABLE *tablename*	RENAME TO *newtablename*	Change the name of a table
CREATE TABLE *tablename* (*specification*)		This is discussed in detail in Chapter 14
CREATE TABLE *tablename*	LIKE *oldtablename*	Create new table with same structure and field specifications as an existing one
INSERT INTO *table2*	SELECT * FROM *table1*	Copy contents of table1 into table2
SHOW CREATE TABLE *tablename*		Gives a listing of a CREATE TABLE command that could have been used to create the table

Chapter Summary
This chapter concludes the description of the MySQL language begun in Chaps. 12 and 13. It shows how to use a MySQL command to create a database table, explaining the various data types available and shows how to construct an appropriate column definition for each field in a table. It is then shown how to copy the structure and/or the contents of one table to another, how to find the structure of a table and how to change the structure, name and field specification of a table.

Practical Exercise 14
Give possible CREATE TABLE commands for tables mytable1 (shown in Sect. 12.10) and mytable4 and mytable5 (both shown in Sect. 13.3).

Chapter 15
Using a PHP Script to Manage a MySQL Database

Chapter Aims
After reading this chapter you should be able to:

- use PHP to manage a MySQL database
- use PHP to send MySQL commands to a MySQL server
- use PHP to display the results of a MySQL SELECT, SHOW or DESCRIBE command in tabular form
- use PHP to determine the number of rows of a table affected by a MySQL INSERT, UPDATE, REPLACE or DELETE command
- understand the difference between PHP functions with names prefixed with mysql_ and those prefixed with mysqli_
- display the version of MySQL you are using.

In Chaps. 12, 13 and 14 we have given a detailed description of the MySQL language. In this chapter we come on to the topic of using a PHP script to issue MySQL commands to manage a database.

We will start by assuming that we already have a database *mydb1* containing a table *mytable1*. We will illustrate how to execute the command:

SELECT * FROM mytable1 ORDER BY refnum

from a PHP script and how to process the output sent back from the MySQL server and display the output in the form of a table in a webpage. We will call the PHP script that does this *sqltest.php*

M. Bramer, *Web Programming with PHP and MySQL*,
DOI 10.1007/978-3-319-22659-0_15

15.1 Connecting to a Database

A PHP script to manage a MySQL database will first need to establish a connection to the database server. To do this we need to specify our username and password and the name of our 'host', i.e. the server where MySQL is installed. The host name is normally *localhost*, assuming that the database is located on the same server as the website. If not it will probably be a string of characters, such as mydbhost.mycompany.com.

The username and password determine the database permissions the user has, e.g. whether or not he or she can create and delete a database. Unless you have your own server you will probably find that you are able to create and modify tables within one or more databases already provided for you by your service provider. A fourth piece of information that needs to be provided is the name of the database that we would like to be treated as the current database. For our examples these four values will be *myusername*, *mypassword*, *myhost* and *mydb1*, respectively.

We can write these in our script, as string constants "mypassword", etc. However if we intend to use MySQL commands at many different places in a script it will save typing and be less error-prone if we start by assigning the four values to variables and then use those variables every time we connect to the MySQL server. It will also make our scripts more portable – if we move the script to run on a different server or change the password only those four assignment lines will need to be changed.

We recommend using memorable names for the four variables that are unlikely to be used for anything else by mistake. In this book we will use *$sys_dbusername*, *$sys_dbpassword*, *$sys_dblocalhost* and *$DBName*. So at some early part of our script we could place the assignment statements:

```
$sys_dbusername="myusername";
$sys_dbpassword="mypassword";
$sys_dblocalhost="myhost";
$DBName="mydb1";
```

A problem with this approach, as so far described, is that if we eventually build up to having a large number of PHP files with these values assigned as constants in each one and then decide to change the password or move the database to a different web server we will need to change the same four lines in each of the separate PHP files. There is also a security risk involved in having confidential information in so many places. If anyone sees a listing of one of the scripts that uses the database values they may be able to access the database and potentially overwrite or delete all the contents. A better way of proceeding is to use the PHP *include* facility. First create a small PHP file, which we will call *sql.php*, with the following contents:

```
<?php
$sys_dbusername="myusername";
$sys_dbpassword="mypassword";
$sys_dblocalhost="myhost";
$DBName="mydb1";
?>
```

and then place an *include* statement

```
include "mysql.php";
```

near the start of every script that accesses the database.

Having done this, the next step is to enter the PHP statement that makes a connection to the MySQL server. Using the first three of our variables the command is

```
$Link=mysql_connect($sys_dblocalhost,$sys_dbusername,$sys_dbpassword);
```

We assign the result of making the connection to variable $Link (any variable name can be used but in this book we will always use $Link for consistency).

Assuming the connection is made successfully $Link becomes what is called a *link identifier*. This is needed for the next step in our process.

Using the link identifier we can now issue a sequence of MySQL commands to manage our database. As soon as the connection to the database is no longer needed we use the PHP statement

```
mysql_close($Link);
```

to close the connection. This is not essential but it is good practice to close the connection when it is no longer needed. So far our embryonic PHP script looks like this.

```
<?php
include "sql.php";
$Link=mysql_connect($sys_dblocalhost,$sys_dbusername,$sys_dbpassword);
//
// Insert PHP statements to manage the database
//
mysql_close($Link);
?>
```

Function mysql_close is a logical function which returns the value true if the action succeeds and false otherwise. However it is generally used in 'standalone' mode.

Before going on to explain how to issue MySQL commands to manage the database, we will go back to the mysql_connect line. What happens if the connection to the MySQL server fails? This could happen for a variety of reasons, not least that an incorrect username, password or hostname has been entered. We are very unlikely to want the script to continue executing, possibly for many thousands of instructions, despite the server connection having failed.

To avoid this we can change the mysql_connect statement to

```
$Link=mysql_connect($sys_dblocalhost,$sys_dbusername,$sys_dbpassword) OR die('connection to
server failed');
```

This is an instruction of a kind not previously used in this book. The effect of it is that if the connection fails the *die* function is executed. This causes the execution of the PHP script to terminate immediately. Instead of a string for the system to display such as 'connection to server failed' an alternative is to use the PHP *mysql_error* function:

```
$Link=mysql_connect($sys_dblocalhost,$sys_dbusername,$sys_dbpassword) OR die(mysql_error());
```

This gives the actual error message generated by the PHP system.

Our PHP script is now:

```
<?php
include "sql.php";
$Link=mysql_connect($sys_dblocalhost,$sys_dbusername,$sys_dbpassword) OR die(mysql_error());
//
// Insert PHP statements to manage the database
//
mysql_close($Link);
?>
```

The next step is to issue a MySQL command. Although our aim is for this to be a SELECT command, we will start with something a little simpler, namely:

RENAME TABLE mytable1 TO mytable99

First we assign this value to a variable, which in this book will always be $query, by the PHP statement

```
$query="RENAME TABLE mytable1 TO mytable99";
```

Then to send the command to the MySQL server we use the PHP statement:

```
$result = mysql_db_query($DBName,$query,$Link);
```

The mysql_db_query function takes three arguments: the name of the database, the query (i.e. the MySQL command) and the link identifier. It returns a result which in this book we will always assign to variable $result. The value of $result is always an empty string "" (corresponding to false) if the MySQL command fails, for example because of a typing error, or because it refers to a non-existent database or table. If the command succeeds there are two cases:

1. For commands such as ALTER TABLE or INSERT INTO, UPDATE, DELETE or RENAME which tell the MySQL system to do something, $result will have a value of 1 (indicating true).
2. If the command is one such as SELECT and SHOW which asks the system to return a table of values, the value given to $result will be a more complex 'resource object' from which the values can be extracted. We will come back to this shortly.

Returning to the RENAME example, we could replace the comments in our partial PHP script *sqltest.php* by just the two lines:

```
$query="RENAME TABLE mytable1 TO mytable99";
$result = mysql_db_query($DBName,$query,$Link);
```

The weakness of doing this is that we have no way of knowing whether the command has succeeded or failed. We may be confident enough in our programming skills not to worry about checking this, but all experience suggests that even the most 'obviously correct' program code can have hidden problems, for example, in this case, if we had misspelt the name of the table or if we had forgotten that we had previously renamed it as something else. A more cautious approach is to test the value of $result and display the query if it failed.

```
<?php
include "sql.php";
$Link=mysql_connect($sys_dblocalhost,$sys_dbusername,$sys_dbpassword) OR die(mysql_error());
$query="RENAME TABLE mytable1 TO mytable99";
$result = mysql_db_query($DBName,$query,$Link);
if ($result=="") print "Renaming failed<br>The command was: ".$query."<p>\n";
else print "Renaming succeeded<p>\n";
mysql_close($Link);
?>
```

We will now imagine that the renaming has been reversed (so the table is again called *mytable1*) and will go on to show how to deal with the MySQL command

SELECT * FROM mytable1 ORDER BY refnum

Assuming the SELECT command succeeds there are two special integer-valued functions we can use to find out the number of rows and columns in the resulting table. They are *mysql_num_rows()* and *mysql_num_fields()* respectively. They can both also be applied to the results of a SHOW command.[1] The following updated script shows how to use them.

```
<?php
include "sql.php";
$Link=mysql_connect($sys_dblocalhost,$sys_dbusername,$sys_dbpassword) OR die(mysql_error());
$query=" SELECT * FROM mytable1 ORDER BY refnum";

$result = mysql_db_query($DBName,$query,$Link);
mysql_close($Link);

if ($result=="") print "SELECT failed<br>The command was: ".$query."<p>\n";
else {
  // SELECT succeeded
  $numrows = mysql_num_rows($result);
  $numcols=mysql_num_fields($result);
  print "Number of rows: ".$numrows."<br>";
  print "Number of columns: ".$numcols."<p>\n";
}
?>
```

[1] But not the commands INSERT INTO, UPDATE, REPLACE or DELETE, for which the function *mysql_affected_rows* is used (See Sect. 15.6).

Giving the output:

```
Number of rows: 8
Number of columns: 8
```

Note that we have placed the statement

```
mysql_close($Link);
```

to close the connection immediately after the mysql_db_query statement, as variable $result can be used even after the connection is broken. If we were intending to go on to issue other MySQL commands using mysql_db_query we would probably not have broken the connection at that point, to avoid having to reconnect later.

Assuming that the MySQL SELECT command succeeded, $result will have been assigned a value that makes it into a special kind of variable known as a *resource*. Attempting to print out its value using the PHP statement

```
print $result;
```

will produce unhelpful output such as:

```
Resource id #5
```

In the case of a SELECT command it is probably best to think of the resource $result as a two-dimensional table containing all the records produced by the command, but with the important restriction that they can only be accessed one row (record) at a time. We can do this by placing a call to the mysql_fetch_array() function inside a *while* statement such as this:

```
while ($row=mysql_fetch_array($result)){
  // process elements of this row
} //while
```

(Any variable can be used instead of $row, but we will use that name throughout this book for consistency.)

Looping terminates when the system runs out of rows, which causes *mysql_fetch_array()* to return the value false (i.e. "").

If we know that there is only one row (e.g. because the SELECT command had a LIMIT 1 clause) we do not need the while loop and can just write:

```
$row=mysql_fetch_array($result);
```

Each value of $row is an array that contains the values of all the selected fields in mytable1 for one record. This array can be used with either a numerical index such as $row[3] (with the names of the fields numbered 0, 1, etc. in the order in which they were returned), or an 'associative' index such as $row[Surname].

If we prefer to have only one of these methods of indexing (which will save some processing time) we can replace the function mysql_fetch_array by either mysql_fetch_row (for an indexed array only) or mysql_fetch_assoc (for an associative array only).

This was the final state of table mytable1, when we left it at the end of Sect. 12.10.

refnum	Forename	Surname	sex	occupation	cityBorn	yearBorn	numchild
634	James	Robinson	M	none	Geneva	2007	0
1851	Martin	Johnson	M	butcher	London	1970	99
1927	Bryan	Brown	M	engineer	Toronto	1987	2
2461	Ann	Williams	F	doctor	Paris	1997	2
2547	Mary	Johnson	F	technician	Paris	1989	3
2947	Jane	Wilson	F	unemployed	Dresden	1972	10
3842	Frances	Bryce	F	translator	Northampton	1980	2
4821	Sarah	Green	F	engineer	Paris	1981	1

The rows are arranged in ascending order of the primary key, refnum. As before, the column headings do not form part of the table but are provided for the reader's convenience.

As we go through the rows one-by-one, imagine that we have come to the third row (with refnum = 1927). The values in the row are numbered starting from zero, so for the third row $row[0] is 1927. If we now print $row[4] and $row[6] we will get the values engineer and 1987. We can also refer to $row[occupation] and $row[yearBorn] which give the same values.

We will next print out the entries in each row, row-by-row, using associative indexes such as $row[refnum] and with values separated by spaces.

The expanded version of sqltest.php looks like this.

```
<?php
include "sql.php";
$Link=mysql_connect($sys_dblocalhost,$sys_dbusername,$sys_dbpassword) OR die(mysql_error());
$query=" SELECT * FROM mytable1 ORDER BY refnum";

$result = mysql_db_query($DBName,$query,$Link);
mysql_close($Link);

if ($result=="") print "SELECT failed<br>The command was: ".$query."<p>\n";
else {
  // SELECT succeeded
  $numrows = mysql_num_rows($result);
  $numcols=mysql_num_fields($result);
  print "Number of rows: ".$numrows."<br>";
  print "Number of columns: ".$numcols."<p>\n";
  while ($row=mysql_fetch_array($result)){
    print $row[refnum]." ". $row[Forename]." ". $row[Surname]
      ." ". $row[sex]." ". $row[occupation]." ". $row[cityBorn]
      ." ". $row[yearBorn]." ". $row[numchild]."<br>";
  } //while
} //else
?>
```

which gives the output

```
634 James Robinson M none Geneva 2007 0
1851 Martin Johnson M butcher London 1970 99
1927 Bryan Brown M engineer Toronto 1987 2
2461 Ann Williams F doctor Paris 1997 2
2547 Mary Johnson F technician Paris 1989 3
2947 Jane Wilson F unemployed Dresden 1972 10
3842 Frances Bryce F translator Northampton 1980 2
4821 Sarah Green F engineer Paris 1981 1
```

Although being able to refer to a value as $row[yearBorn], say, can be very helpful and can greatly aid the readability of PHP scripts, if we are dealing with a whole row it is often simpler to refer to the values as $row[0], $row[1] up to $row[7] and use a *for* loop.

We can replace the lengthy print statement in the above script by the much simpler pair of statements:

```
for ($i=0;$i<$numcols;$i++) print $row[$i]." ";
print "<br>";
```

In this case we could have used the constant eight instead of $numcols as we know how many fields there are, but we are eventually aiming at a script we can use even when we do not know the number of fields.

We are now approaching the point where we can achieve our aim of displaying the result of the SELECT command in tabular form. The HTML code for a table with a border round it is similar to this

```
<table border=1>
<tr>
<td>value1</td><td>value2</td> //etc.
</tr>
// more rows
</table>
```

To put the output from a SELECT command into a table we place

```
print "<table border=1>";
```

before the while loop in our script and

```
print "</table>";
```

outside the loop, and then replace the two statements

```
for ($i=0;$i<$numcols;$i++) print $row[$i]." ";
print "<br>";
```

in the while loop, which deals with only one row at a time, by

```
print "<tr>";
for ($i=0;$i<$numcols;$i++) print "<td>".$row[$i]."</td>";
print "</tr>";
```

The extended version of script sqltest.php is now:

```
<?php
include "sql.php";
$Link=mysql_connect($sys_dblocalhost,$sys_dbusername,$sys_dbpassword) OR die(mysql_error());
$query="SELECT * FROM mytable1 ORDER BY refnum";

$result = mysql_db_query($DBName,$query,$Link);
mysql_close($Link);

if ($result=="") print "SELECT failed<br>The command was: ".$query."<p>\n";
else {
  // SELECT succeeded
  $numrows = mysql_num_rows($result);
  $numcols=mysql_num_fields($result);
  print "Number of rows: ".$numrows."<br>";
  print "Number of columns: ".$numcols."<p>\n";

  print "<table border=1>";
  while ($row=mysql_fetch_array($result)){
    print "<tr>";
    for ($i=0;$i<$numcols;$i++) print "<td>".$row[$i]."</td>";
    print "</tr>";
  } //while
    print "</table>";
} //else
?>
```

This gives the output

Number of rows: 8
Number of columns: 8

634	James	Robinson	M	none	Geneva	2007	0
1851	Martin	Johnson	M	butcher	London	1970	99
1927	Bryan	Brown	M	engineer	Toronto	1987	2
2461	Ann	Williams	F	doctor	Paris	1997	2
2547	Mary	Johnson	F	technician	Paris	1989	3
2947	Jane	Wilson	F	unemployed	Dresden	1972	10
3842	Frances	Bryce	F	translator	Northampton	1980	2
4821	Sarah	Green	F	engineer	Paris	1981	1

This is good but it would be better if we could add the column headings. We start by observing that if we replace the MySQL SELECT command in sqltest.php by

SHOW COLUMNS FROM mytable1 the output will be the same table we saw in Sect. 13.5 (but without any column headings):

Field	**Type**	**Null**	**Key**	**Default**	**Extra**
refnum	integer	NO	PRI	0	
Forename	varchar(30)	NO			
Surname	varchar(30)	NO			
sex	enum('M','F')	YES		NULL	
occupation	varchar(30)	YES		NULL	
cityBorn	varchar(30)	YES		NULL	
yearBorn	year	YES		NULL	
numchild	integer	YES		NULL	

If we want to produce a one-row table showing only the field names (currently in column zero) we can do that by changing the while loop to:

```
print "<tr>";
while ($row=mysql_fetch_array($result)){
  print "<td>".$row[0]."</td>";
} //while
print "</tr>";
```

This produces the one row table

refnum	Forename	Surname	sex	occupation	cityBorn	yearBorn	numchild

Now we can combine the PHP instructions that produce the mytable1 table with the instructions that produce a row of headings to give an augmented table with the values in mytable1 preceded by a row of headings.

```
<?php
include "sql.php";
$Link=mysql_connect($sys_dblocalhost,$sys_dbusername,$sys_dbpassword) OR die(mysql_error());

$query="SELECT * FROM mytable1 ORDER BY refnum";
$result = mysql_db_query($DBName,$query,$Link);

$query2="SHOW COLUMNS FROM mytable1";
$result2 = mysql_db_query($DBName,$query2,$Link);

mysql_close($Link);

if ($result=="" || $result2=="") print "Command failed<p>\n";
else {
  $numrows = mysql_num_rows($result);
  $numcols=mysql_num_fields($result);

  print "<table border=1>\n";
  print "<tr>";
  while ($row2=mysql_fetch_array($result2)){
    print "<td><b>".$row2[0]."</b></td>";
  } //while
  print "</tr>\n";

  while ($row=mysql_fetch_array($result)){
    print "<tr>";
    for ($i=0;$i<$numcols;$i++) print "<td>".$row[$i]."</td>";
    print "</tr>\n";
  } //while
  print "</table>\n";
} //else
?>
```

Here we have two versions of $query and $result, the second versions being named $query2 and $result2 respectively. Once $result2 had been created we closed the connection to the server. The table was then constructed by using both $result and $result2. Rows 'extracted' from $result are given the name $row as usual. For $result2 we use the name $row2.

The outcome from the above script is the familiar table:

refnum	**Forename**	**Surname**	**sex**	**occupation**	**cityBorn**	**yearBorn**	**numchild**
634	James	Robinson	M	none	Geneva	2007	0
1851	Martin	Johnson	M	butcher	London	1970	99
1927	Bryan	Brown	M	engineer	Toronto	1987	2
2461	Ann	Williams	F	doctor	Paris	1997	2
2547	Mary	Johnson	F	technician	Paris	1989	3
2947	Jane	Wilson	F	unemployed	Dresden	1972	10
3842	Frances	Bryce	F	translator	Northampton	1980	2
4821	Sarah	Green	F	engineer	Paris	1981	1

15.2 A PHP Function to Display the Result of a Selection

Displaying the output of a SELECT command, for either all fields or a selection, in tabular form is likely to be such a common requirement that we recommend creating a function to do it which takes $result as its argument. Adding the column headings is more difficult if only a partial selection of fields is made, so we will dispense with that and convert our earlier set of instructions, which generate the table without any headings, into a call to a function *displaySelections*.

```
<?php
include "sql.php";
$Link=mysql_connect($sys_dblocalhost,$sys_dbusername,$sys_dbpassword) OR die(mysql_error());

$query=" SELECT Forename,Surname,numchild,refnum FROM mytable1 ORDER BY refnum";
$result = mysql_db_query($DBName,$query,$Link);
displaySelections($result);
mysql_close($Link);

// *****************************
function displaySelections($result){
if ($result=="") print "SELECT failed<br>The command was: ".$query."<p>\n";
else {
  // SELECT succeeded
  $numcols=mysql_num_fields($result);
  print "<table border=1>";
  while ($row=mysql_fetch_array($result)){
    print "<tr>";
    for ($i=0;$i<$numcols;$i++) print "<td>".$row[$i]."</td>";
    print "</tr>";
  } //while
  print "</table>";
} //else
} // displaySelections
// *****************************
?>
```

Running this script produces the output:

James	Robinson	0	634
Martin	Johnson	99	1851
Bryan	Brown	2	1927
Ann	Williams	2	2461
Mary	Johnson	3	2547
Jane	Wilson	10	2947
Frances	Bryce	2	3842
Sarah	Green	1	4821

We recommend placing the function in a PHP file such as *sqlutils.php* which can be included in a script whenever it is needed.

The *displaySelections* function also works when used with a SHOW or a DESCRIBE command.

We can modify the function a little and pass it two arguments: $query and $result instead of just $result and change its name to *processResult* to give a function which, as its name suggests, can be used to process the $result variable produced by any MySQL command. Commands not beginning with SELECT, SHOW, DESCRIBE or their variants produce the output COMMAND SUCCEEDED or COMMAND FAILED. Valid commands beginning with SELECT, SHOW or DESCRIBE are treated separately.

In this example the function is applied to a SELECT command which specifies four fields.

```
<?php
include "sql.php";
$Link=mysql_connect($sys_dblocalhost,$sys_dbusername,$sys_dbpassword) OR die(mysql_error());
$query="SELect Forename, Surname, sex, refnum FROM mytable1 "
  ."ORDER BY Surname,Forename";
$result = mysql_db_query($DBName,$query,$Link);
processResult($query,$result);
mysql_close($Link);
// ******************************
function processResult($query,$result){

if ($result=="") print "COMMAND FAILED<br>The command was: ".$query."\n";
else if ($result==1) print "COMMAND SUCCEEDED<p>\n";
else {  // must be SELECT, SHOW or DESCRIBE
  $numcols=mysql_num_fields($result);
  print "<table border=1>";
  while ($row=mysql_fetch_array($result)){
    print "<tr>";
    for ($i=0;$i<$numcols;$i++) print "<td>".$row[$i]."</td>";
    print "</tr>";
  } //while
  print "</table>";
} //else
} // processResult
// ******************************
?>
```

which produces the output:

Bryan	Brown	M	1927
Frances	Bryce	F	3842
Sarah	Green	F	4821
Martin	Johnson	M	1851
Mary	Johnson	F	2547
James	Robinson	M	634
Ann	Williams	F	2461
Jane	Wilson	F	2947

15.2.1 Finding the Version of MySQL

The MySQL command

```
SHOW VARIABLES LIKE "version"
```

was described in Sect. 13.5.4. It returns a single row of which the second value (i.e. $row[1]) is the number of the version of MySQL you are using. The following script will extract that value and output it to the user's screen.

```
?php
include "sql.php";
$Link=mysql_connect($sys_dblocalhost,$sys_dbusername,$sys_dbpassword)
    OR die(mysql_error());
$query="SHOW VARIABLES LIKE \"version\"";
$result = mysql_db_query($DBName,$query,$Link);
$row=mysql_fetch_array($result);
print "Version of MySQL is: ".$row[1];
mysql_close($Link);
?>
```

15.3 Using Simpler MySQL Commands

In Sect. 13.2 we illustrated the relatively complex MySQL command needed to extract a forename and surname from one table, join them together with a space between them and then set all values of the 'Fullname' field in a different table to that value. The MYSQL command was

UPDATE mytable2 SET Fullname = (SELECT CONCAT(Forename, ' ',Surname) FROM mytable1 WHERE cityBorn = 'paris' ORDER BY refnum LIMIT 1)

This is quite a complex MySQL command but a glance at a MySQL manual will soon convince you that there are many far more complex commands than that.

We promised that "we will illustrate how to perform the above combined UPDATE/SELECT command in a simpler way using PHP in Chap. 15" and now we will redeem that promise.

First it is worth stressing that for those who have no trouble writing MySQL commands such as the above (and remembering the many MySQL functions of which CONCAT is only one), that is the best way of doing it. Those for whom maximum processing speed is not an overwhelming issue compared with ease of use (which is likely to be most of the readers of this book) will probably find it easier and less error prone to use two or even three 'basic' MySQL commands rather than a complex long one, taking advantage of PHP's ability to store information in variables between one MySQL command and another and using the PHP language's standard functions, operators and other facilities.

In this case we will first extract the (single) values of Forename and Surname from mytable1 using

SELECT Forename,Surname FROM mytable1 WHERE cityBorn = 'paris' ORDER BY refnum LIMIT 1

Then we will join them together separated by a space using a PHP assignment statement. Finally, we will set the value in the Fullname field to that value for all records in table mytable2 using a simple UPDATE command. The PHP script to do this is given below.

```
<?php
include "sql.php";
$Link=mysql_connect($sys_dblocalhost,$sys_dbusername,$sys_dbpassword) OR die(mysql_error());

$query="SELECT Forename,Surname FROM mytable1 WHERE cityBorn = 'paris' ORDER BY
refnum LIMIT 1";
$result = mysql_db_query($DBName,$query,$Link);
if ($result=="") print "SELECT failed<p>\n";
else {
  $row=mysql_fetch_array($result);
  $full=$row[Forename]." ".$row[Surname];

  $query="UPDATE mytable2 SET Fullname='".$full."'";
  $result = mysql_db_query($DBName,$query,$Link);
  if ($result=="") print "UPDATE failed. query is: ".$query."<p>\n";
  else print "UPDATE succeeded<p>\n";
} //else
mysql_close($Link);
?>
```

(The first '$query=' statement is spread over two lines in this book because of the width limitations of the printed page. It is just one fairly long statement in PHP.)

The two most important statements are

```
$full=$row[Forename]." ".$row[Surname];
$query="UPDATE mytable2 SET Fullname='".$full."'";
```

The former statement joins the two parts of the name together with a space between them, using the standard PHP dot operator to join the strings.

The second statement creates a new query by combining a fixed part "UPDATE mytable2 SET Fullname=" with a variable part, $full, the value of which was not known when the PHP script began executing. This use of variables in constructing queries dynamically is standard practice and shows the value of using a general-purpose language such as PHP with the large range of facilities it offers as a way of managing a database.

It should be noted that a single quote character has been placed on either side of $full. Field values must always be quoted in this way, so the combination of characters after the = symbol is a single quote followed by a double quote. After $full there is a dot then a single quote enclosed in double quotes.

15.4 Combining Tables

This next example shows how to combine three tables.

We will assume that we have taken over the role of administrator for a database with three tables, *mytableA, mytableB* and *mytableC*, all containing information about the same eight members of a club.

The figures below show the content of the three tables.

refnum	Forename	Surname	sex
634	James	Robinson	M
1851	Martin	Johnson	M
1927	Bryan	Brown	M
2461	Ann	Williams	F
2547	Mary	Johnson	F
2947	Jane	Wilson	F
3842	Frances	Bryce	F
4821	Sarah	Green	F

mytableA

ref1	occupation	numchild
634	none	0
1851	butcher	99
1927	engineer	2
2461	doctor	2
2547	technician	3
2947	unemployed	10
3842	translator	2
4821	engineer	1

mytableB

refvalue	cityBorn	yearBorn
634	Geneva	2007
1851	London	1970
1927	Toronto	1987
2461	Paris	1997
2547	Paris	1989
2947	Dresden	1972
3842	Northampton	1980
4821	Paris	1981

mytableC

mytableC

On inspection we see that

- mytableA gives the reference number plus Forename, Surname and sex for each club member
- mytableB gives the reference number, occupation and number of children for each one
- mytableC gives the reference number, city and year of birth for each one.

In each case the reference number is the primary key field, but it has a different field name for each table.

Having examined the three tables and observed that exactly the same members occur in each one, we decide to combine the three tables into a single table with eight fields.

We first create an empty new table mytableNEW with suitable field definitions. (They are of course those of table mytable1, which we have seen many times before.)

We can now either study the MySQL documentation to find a suitable (but probably quite complex) command to combine the three tables or we can write a short PHP script to do the job.

The idea is to issue three MySQL commands, each one performing a SELECT * command for one of the tables. We create a separate 'resource' for each one (called $result1, $result2 and $result3) and then extract a row from all three resources for each pass through a WHILE loop and store these in arrays $row1, $row2 and $row3.

We then have all the data for each record in the new table available to us at the same time, e.g. for the first record in each table $row1[Forename], $row2[occupation] and $row3[cityBorn] are James, none and Geneva, respectively.

The most difficult part is to work out how to write the data to the new table. We could do it by issuing a separate INSERT INTO command at each pass through the WHILE loop, but there is a better approach. We will build up a single command that inserts all the new records into mytableNEW when the WHILE loop ends. This command takes the form

INSERT INTO mytableNEW VALUES (xxx),(xxx),(xxx), ...

Here each of the bracketed values (xxx) is created by one pass through the WHILE loop and contains all the values for one record separated by commas, e.g.

(634,'James','Robinson','sex','occupation','Geneva',2007,0)

We omit the surrounding quote characters for those fields that we know are always numeric. Each bracketed set of values needs to be preceded by a comma, except the first.

This leads to the script shown below.[2]

[2] The combination "'" is a single quote enclosed in double quotes. The combination "'," is a single quote followed by a comma, both enclosed in double quotes.

```
<?php
include "sql.php";
$Link=mysql_connect($sys_dblocalhost,$sys_dbusername,$sys_dbpassword) OR die(mysql_error());

$query1="SELECT * FROM mytableA ORDER BY refnum";
$query2="SELECT * FROM mytableB ORDER BY ref1";
$query3="SELECT * FROM mytableC ORDER BY refvalue";

$result1 = mysql_db_query($DBName,$query1,$Link);
$result2 = mysql_db_query($DBName,$query2,$Link);
$result3 = mysql_db_query($DBName,$query3,$Link);

$first=0;
$query="INSERT INTO mytableNEW VALUES ";
while ($row1=mysql_fetch_array($result1)){
  $row2=mysql_fetch_array($result2);
  $row3=mysql_fetch_array($result3);

  $new="("
  .$row1[refnum].","
  ."'".$row1[Forename]."',"
  ."'".$row1[Surname]."',"
  ."'".$row1[sex]."',"
  ."'".$row2[occupation]."',"
  ."'".$row3[cityBorn]."',"
  .$row3[yearBorn].","
  .$row2[numchild]
  .")";

  if ($first==0) $query=$query.$new;
  else $query=$query.",".$new;
  $first=1;
} //while

$result = mysql_db_query($DBName,$query,$Link);
mysql_close($Link);

if ($result==1) print "Operation succeeded<p>\n";
else print "Operation failed<p>\n";
?>
```

Running this script gives table *mytableNEW* the (by now not unfamiliar) content:

refnum	Forename	Surname	sex	occupation	cityBorn	yearBorn	numchild
634	James	Robinson	M	none	Geneva	2007	0
1851	Martin	Johnson	M	butcher	London	1970	99
1927	Bryan	Brown	M	engineer	Toronto	1987	2
2461	Ann	Williams	F	doctor	Paris	1997	2
2547	Mary	Johnson	F	technician	Paris	1989	3
2947	Jane	Wilson	F	unemployed	Dresden	1972	10
3842	Frances	Bryce	F	translator	Northampton	1980	2
4821	Sarah	Green	F	engineer	Paris	1981	1

15.5 A Visual MySQL Command Processing Tool

In this section we describe a software tool, stored in file commands.php, written in PHP which enables any user of a web browser to enter a (single) MySQL command and receive either a message that it succeeded or failed or, in the case of a successful SELECT, SHOW or DESCRIBE command, the values returned by the MySQL system in tabular form.

Pointing a web browser to commands.php produces the following initial screen.

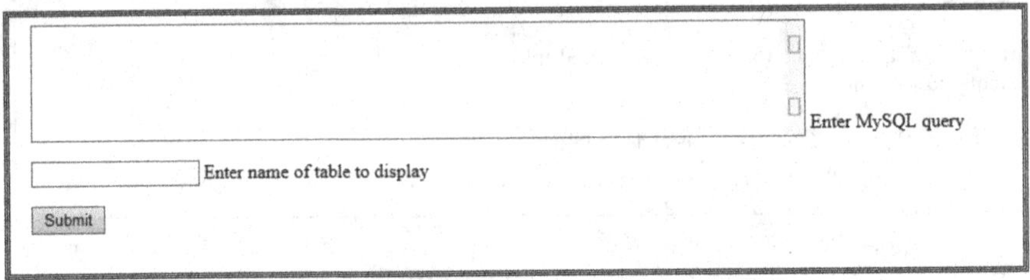

The user can now enter a single MySQL command, possibly extending over more than one line, into a textarea in a webform and also enter into a text box the name of a table to display.

As always in this book, the current database is specified as the value of variable $DBName in 'include' file sql.php. We will assume it is our usual database, named *mydb1*.

Entering the command

UPDATE mytable1 SET Forename='Henrietta' WHERE refnum=3842 LIMIT 1

and the table name mytable1 and pressing the Submit produces the following output:

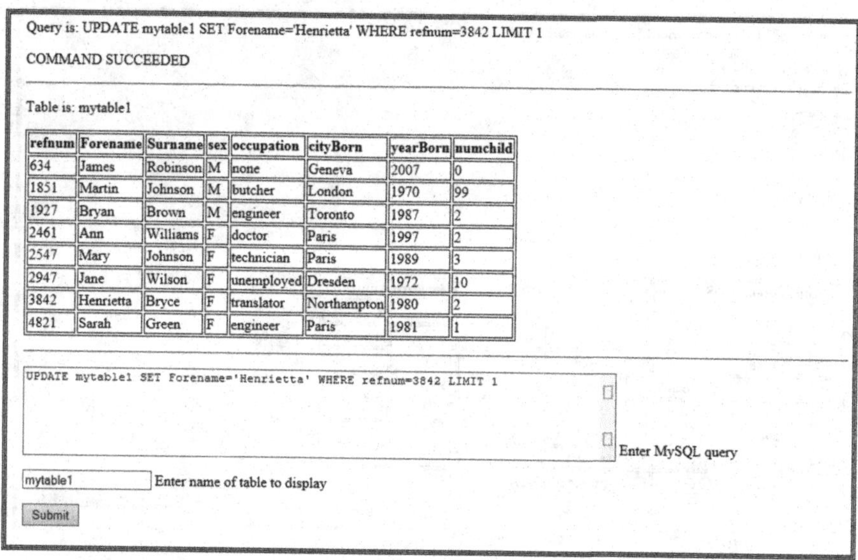

Query is: UPDATE mytable1 SET Forename='Henrietta' WHERE refnum=3842 LIMIT 1

COMMAND SUCCEEDED

Table is: mytable1

refnum	Forename	Surname	sex	occupation	cityBorn	yearBorn	numchild
634	James	Robinson	M	none	Geneva	2007	0
1851	Martin	Johnson	M	butcher	London	1970	99
1927	Bryan	Brown	M	engineer	Toronto	1987	2
2461	Ann	Williams	F	doctor	Paris	1997	2
2547	Mary	Johnson	F	technician	Paris	1989	3
2947	Jane	Wilson	F	unemployed	Dresden	1972	10
3842	Henrietta	Bryce	F	translator	Northampton	1980	2
4821	Sarah	Green	F	engineer	Paris	1981	1

```
UPDATE mytable1 SET Forename='Henrietta' WHERE refnum=3842 LIMIT 1
```

Enter MySQL query

mytable1 Enter name of table to display

Submit

The command has succeeded, as the display of table mytable1 confirms.

Note that the values previously entered in the webform, which is now in the bottom part of the display, are left there as default values for the next use of the webform.

If we now enter the command

SELECT sex,yearBorn FROM mytable1 WHERE refnum>2500

in the textarea, leave the contents of the table name box, i.e. mytable1, unchanged and press Submit, the following is displayed:

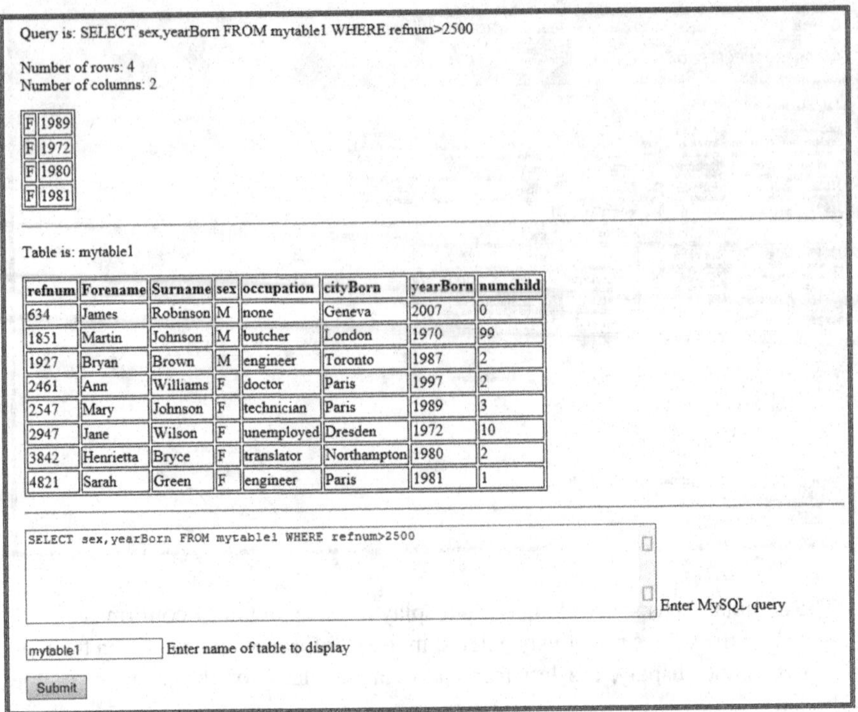

A listing of PHP script commands.php is shown below. It is complete except for two user-defined functions: processResult2 and showtable which are not (yet) listed. Line numbers have been added for ease of reference only but do not form part of the script itself.

```
1  <?php
2  include "sql.php";
3  $Link=mysql_connect($sys_dblocalhost,$sys_dbusername,$sys_dbpassword);
4  $query = trim($_POST['query']);
5  $query=str_replace('\\','',$query);
6  if ($query!=""){
7     print "Query is: ".$query."<p>\n";
8     $result = mysql_db_query($DBName,$query,$Link);
9     processResult2($query,$result);
10    print "<p><hr><p>\n";
11 } //query
12 //*************************************
13 // Display table, including headings
14 $table = $_POST['table']; // from form
15 if ($table!=""){
16 print "Table is: ".$table."<p>\n";
17 $query1="SHOW COLUMNS FROM ".$table;
18 $result1 = mysql_db_query($DBName,$query1,$Link);
19 $query2="SELECT * FROM ".$table;
20 $result2 = mysql_db_query($DBName,$query2,$Link);
21 showtable($result1,$result2);
22 print "<p><hr><p>\n";
23 } //table
24 // *************************************
25 mysql_close($Link);
26 ?>
27 <FORM name=submission action="?" method="post">
28 <textarea rows=6 cols=80 name=query><?php print $query;?></textarea> Enter mySQL query
29 <p></p>
30 <input type=textsize=20 maxlength=50 name=table value='<?php print $table?>'> Enter name
31 of table to display
32 <p></p>
33 <INPUT type=submit value="Submit" name=submit>
34 </FORM>
35 <?php
36 // ********************
37 // define function processResult2
38 // ********************
39 //define function showtable
40 // ********************
   ?>
```

- The HTML for the webform displayed on the initial screen (which will also appear as the bottom part of all subsequent screen displays) is given in lines 27–34. The <FORM> specifies action = "?" indicating that the destination page is the same page. Lines 28 and 30 take advantage of this to set the values passed to the script by the web form, now stored in variables $query and $table, as default values. (Both are empty strings for the initial screen.)
- Lines 2 and 3 include file sql.php as in the other examples and make the connection to the database. Line 25 closes the connection.
- In line 4 the value of the query variable sent by the webform (i.e. the MySQL command in the textarea) is trimmed and assigned to variable $query. In line 5 any \ characters are removed from $query. This is important to deal with complications arising if a command includes a single quote symbol, as it often will.

- If the resulting value of $query is not null, the query is then sent to the MySQL server (line 8) giving a 'resource' named $result. This is then processed by a user-defined function named processResult2 which generates the upper part of the display.
- Next the value of the table variable sent by the webform (i.e. the name of the table to be displayed) is trimmed and assigned to variable $table (line 14). If it is not null, the table name is sent to the MySQL server in two queries:
- SHOW COLUMNS FROM *tablename*
- and
- SELECT * FROM *tablename*
- These generate two resources $result1 and $result2 and these are passed to function showtable.

This just leaves functions processResult2 and showtable to be defined.

The definition of function processResult2 is given below. It is almost the same as function processResult defined in Sect. 15.2. The non-trivial changes (all additions) are shown in bold in the listing below.

```
function processResult2($query,$result){
if ($result=="") print "COMMAND FAILED<p>\n";
else if ($result==1) print "COMMAND SUCCEEDED<p>\n";
else { // must be SELECT, SHOW or DESCRIBE
  $numrows = mysql_num_rows($result);
  $numcols=mysql_num_fields($result);
  print "Number of rows: ".$numrows."<br>";
  print "Number of columns: ".$numcols."<p>\n";

  print "<table border=1>";
  if (strtolower(substr($query,0,8))=="describe"
    || strtolower(substr($query,0,4))=="show")
    print "<tr><td><b>Field</b></td><td><b>Type</b></td>"
    ."<td><b>Null</b></td><td><b>Key</b></td>"
        ."<td><b>Default</b></td><td><b>Extra</b></td></tr>\n";
  while ($row=mysql_fetch_array($result)){
    print "<tr>";
    for ($i=0;$i<$numcols;$i++) print "<td>".$row[$i]."</td>";
    print "</tr>";
  } //while
  print "</table>";
} //else
} // processResult2
```

The only change that needs explaining is the IF statement beginning

```
if (strtolower(substr($query,0,8))=="describe"
```

This checks whether the command begins with SHOW or DESCRIBE, as opposed to SELECT, taking into account the fact that the keyword may be written in any combination of upper and lower case letters, e.g. DEscrIBe. If it is, an initial header row with six entries such as Field and Type is displayed using the method described in Sect. 15.1 in connection with the command SHOW COLUMNS FROM mytable1.

Finally we come to function *showtable*. This takes the resource created by the SHOW COLUMNS FROM *tablename* command and uses it to generate a row of column headings, then takes the resource generated by the SELECT * FROM *tablename* command and uses it to generate the contents of table mytable1 itself. The function is very similar to the script listed near the end of Sect. 15.1.

```
function showtable($result1,$result2){
// Display table, including headings
print "<table border=1>\n";
print "<tr>\n";
while($row=mysql_fetch_array($result1)){
  print "<td><b>".$row[0]."</b></td>";
} //while
print "</tr>\n";
$numcols=mysql_num_fields($result2);
while ($row2=mysql_fetch_array($result2)) {
  print "<tr>\n";
  for ($i=0;$i<$numcols;$i++) print "<td>".$row2[$i]."</td>\n";
  print "</tr>\n";
} //while
print "</table>\n";
} //showtable
```

15.6 The PHP mysql_affected_rows Function

Executing any of the MySQL commands INSERT, UPDATE, REPLACE and DELETE returns only the value 1 (indicating success) or "" (indicating failure). In some situations this is not sufficient. For example

DELETE FROM mytable1 WHERE refnum>7000

will succeed even though no records are deleted (there are none with refnum > 7000 in our example).

If we wish to know whether any records were deleted, and if so how many, we can use the PHP function mysql_affected_rows. This takes a link identifier, such as $Link, as its only argument and returns the number of rows of the table changed by the DELETE command, e.g.

```
print "Rows affected: ".mysql_affected_rows($Link)."<p>";
```

If the DELETE command is invalid the value returned will be −1.

In general the mysql_affected_rows function returns the number of rows affected by the last MySQL INSERT, UPDATE, REPLACE or DELETE command.

15.7 The PHP mysql_insert_id Function

AUTO_INCREMENT fields were introduced in Sect. 13.4. This is a field which is automatically given a sequential number (generally starting at one and going up in steps of one) by MySQL whenever a new record is inserted into a table. This guarantees that each value will be different and means that the field can safely be used as a primary key.

A potential difficulty that can arise is that it may sometimes be desirable for PHP to know the value generated. For example it may be a customer reference number that has been generated and we wish to display a message telling the customer what his or her reference number is.

To deal with this we can use the PHP function mysql_insert_id. This function takes no arguments, so it is called by a statement such as

```
$n= mysql_insert_id();
```

It returns the value of the auto_increment field that was generated by the last query. If the previous query did not generate an AUTO_INCREMENT value the function returns the value 0. If no MySQL connection was established it returns the value FALSE.

15.8 Converting mysql_ Functions to mysqli_ Functions

The functions with names beginning mysql_ described in this chapter are currently in the process of being replaced by functions with names beginning with mysqli_. (The i supposedly stands for 'improved'.)

Depending on when you are using this book and which version of PHP is available to you, you may find that:

- the mysql_ functions are available but the mysqli_ ones are not
- both the mysql_ and the mysqli_ functions are available (in which case we recommend that you use the latter)
- the mysqli_ functions are available but the mysql_ ones no longer exist.

A little experiment may be needed to establish the position.

If you need or choose to switch to the mysqli_ functions the conversion is straightforward.

- All the function names beginning with mysql_ in this chapter can be replaced by the equivalent names beginning with mysqli_ with the three exceptions given below.

- Instead of mysql_connect with three arguments, you should use mysqli_connect with four arguments, the fourth being the name of the database to which you wish to connect, e.g.

```
$Link=mysqli_connect($sys_dblocalhost,$sys_dbusername,$sys_dbpassword,$DBName);
```

- Instead of mysql_db_query you should use mysqli_query which takes two arguments: a link and a database query. This function performs a query on the database specified by the corresponding mysqli_connect statement. An example is:

```
$result=mysqli_query($Link,$query);
```

- Calls to function mysql_num_fields should be replaced by calls to mysqli_field_count, which takes a link as its only argument. The function returns the number of columns retrieved by the most recent query on the connection represented by the *link* parameter. An example is:

```
$numfields=mysqli connect_field_count($Link);
```

Chapter Summary

This chapter describes how to use PHP to manage a MySQL database. It begins with a description of how to connect to a database from a PHP script and how to use PHP instructions to issue MySQL commands. For MySQL commands that return values other than simply true, indicating success, and false, indicating failure, it is shown how to process a special kind of variable known as a *resource* to extract the necessary information. A user-defined function is developed that can be used to display the results of any SELECT, SHOW or DESCRIBE command in tabular form. This is then used as the basis for a further function that will handle the output from any MySQL command.

The chapter goes on to show how by making use of PHP facilities such as variables it is often possible to avoid the use of complex MySQL commands. It then gives a detailed example of a PHP script to combine three MySQL tables and another example of a visual tool for processing MySQL commands. It is also shown how to find the version of MySQL you are using.

The chapter ends with a description of the PHP mysql_affected_rows and mysql_insert_id functions and an explanation of the difference between PHP functions with names prefixed with mysql_ and those prefixed with mysqli_.

Practical Exercise 15

(1) Using the table given in Sect. 15.1 (which was originally taken from Sect. 12.10) write a PHP script that will output the name, occupation and year of birth of each of the women in the table who have at least two children, arranged in ascending order of age

(2) Using the same table write a PHP script that will delete everyone born before 1982 and output the number of both men and women that have been removed.

Chapter 16
PHP in Action: Converting Data between Text Files and Database Tables

Chapter Aims
After reading this chapter you should be able to:

- understand issues relating to data cleaning
- use PHP to take data stored in a text file, clean it and convert it to a database table
- export data from a database table to a text file for archive purposes
- restore a database table from a backup held as a text file.

In this chapter we will illustrate how to take data stored on our website in a text file and convert it to form a table in our database. We will also show how to export data from a table to a text file on the website, e.g. for archive purposes. As well as providing further examples of PHP being used to issue MySQL commands, it will illustrate the use of the facilities of PHP, especially the string handling functions, to manipulate and 'clean' the data. Data cleaning is a troublesome necessity when working with real-world data, especially data that was not originally collected by an automatic process.

We will assume that you already know how to upload/download a text file to/from your website and also that you know how to specify that a text file is writeable. (This final part may need advice from your system administrator.)

M. Bramer, *Web Programming with PHP and MySQL*,
DOI 10.1007/978-3-319-22659-0_16

16.1 A Plays Dataset

In this first example a theatre company is planning a program of plays for the coming year. It creates a text file, each line of which gives the name of a play, the name of its writer, and the start and end dates of the production. We will assume this data is now on the website as text file *plays.txt*.

```
"Hamlet",William Shakespeare, Jan 12, Jan 23
"Waiting for Godot",Samuel Beckett,Feb 9,Feb 20
"Six Characters in Search of an Author",Luigi Pirandello,Mar 9,Mar 20
"Hedda Gabler",Henrik Ibsen Apr 6,Apr 17
"She Stoops to Conquer",Oliver Goldsmith, May 15
"Death of a Salesman",Arthur Miller,Jun 1,Jun 12
The Caretaker, Harold Pinter, Jun 29,Jul 10
A Streetcar Named Desire,Tennessee Williams,Jul 27,     Aug 7
The Threepenny Opera,Bertolt Brecht,Aug      24,Sep 4
Rosencrantz and Guildenstern are Dead,Tom Stoppard,Sept 21,Oct 2
Plenty,David Hare,Oct 19,Oct 30
Journey's End,R. C. Sherriff,Nov 16,Nov 27
```

Even in this small dataset, there are a surprising number of problems and/or errors. This is entirely typical of 'real world' data.

- The first six titles are enclosed in double quotes; the others are not. They all need to be removed.
- There is a comma missing which should separate the name Henrik Ibsen from the date Apr 6.
- There are unnecessary extra spaces inside the date Aug 24.
- There are unnecessary spaces after some of the commas.
- The starting date of 'She Stoops to Conquer', which should be May 4th, has been omitted.
- The date format, Jan 12, etc., is not very suitable for future processing, e.g. to check which is the next production after today's date.
- The name of the final play includes a quote character. This will cause a problem, as we will see.

With such a small dataset it is probably best for the company to correct all the problems on its hard disc and then upload a corrected version. However, even with quite small real-world datasets, even 50 or so records, this can be very hard to do 'by eye'. We will illustrate how a PHP script can be used to do at least most of the data cleaning automatically.

16.2 Data Cleaning for the Plays Dataset

We start by creating a new table *mytable2*, with five fields, the first of which is an auto_increment field named ind.

```
CREATE TABLE mytable2 (
ind INTEGER NOT NULL AUTO_INCREMENT,
playTitle VARCHAR(50),
playAuthor VARCHAR(50),
playStart CHAR(50),
playEnd CHAR(50),
PRIMARY KEY (ind)
)
```

We now read the file plays.txt and process it line by line. This is easy to do using the *file* function.

```
$inArray=file("plays.txt");
for ($i=0;$i<count($inArray);$i++){

// process $inArray[$i] and then output as a new record in the table

} // for $i
```

We would like to issue a series of MySQL commands, each one adding a new record to table mytable2, for example[1]:

INSERT INTO mytable2 VALUES('','Hamlet','William Shakespeare','Jan 12','Jan 23')

We need to create a string variable $outstring with the contents

'','Hamlet','William Shakespeare','Jan 12','Jan 23'

To do this we need to separate out the four fields in each of our records, enclose them in single quotes and join them by commas.

First we will assign $inArray[$i] to a variable $instring and then start the cleaning process by removing the double quote characters.

```
$instring=$inArray[$i];

$instring2=str_replace("\"","",$instring);

// If $instring started as
// "Hamlet",William Shakespeare, Jan 12, Jan 23
// $instring2 will now be
// Hamlet,William Shakespeare, Jan 12, Jan 23
```

We will now eliminate the unnecessary spaces. First separate $instring2 into four parts using the explode function and then trim each one, to remove any spaces at the beginning and/or end of the string.

---

[1]Note that the first item after the opening bracket following VALUES is an empty string. This is a placeholder for the value of the auto_increment field ind. When the INSERT operation takes place the value inserted will not be an empty string but the next integer in sequence.

```
$parts=explode(",",$instring2);
// this gives four parts $parts[0] to $parts[3]
for ($j=0;$j<4;$j++) $parts[$j]=trim($parts[$j]);
```

We now have the four parts separately. For the first line of the dataset $parts[0] to $parts[3] are now

Hamlet
William Shakespeare
Jan 12
Jan 23

We now want to combine these to form the string

'','Hamlet','William Shakespeare','Jan 12','Jan 23'

We can do this using the implode function, with values separated by a single quote, followed by a comma, followed by another single quote:

```
$outstring=implode("','",$parts);
```

This makes $outstring

Hamlet','William Shakespeare','Jan 12','Jan 23

We need to add the combination '',' at the beginning and a single quote at the end.

```
$outstring="'','".$outstring."'";
```

This makes $outstring

'','Hamlet','William Shakespeare','Jan 12','Jan 23'

We can now go on to construct a MySQL command by

```
$query="INSERT INTO mytable2 VALUES (".$outstring.")";
```

Combining these fragments of PHP with statements to update the current database we get the following:

```
1   <?php
2   include "sql.php";
3a  $Link=mysql_connect($sys_dblocalhost,$sys_dbusername,$sys_dbpassword)
3b    OR die(mysql_error());
4
5   $inArray=file("plays.txt");
6   for ($i=0;$i<count($inArray);$i++){
7     $instring=trim($inArray[$i]);
8     $instring2=str_replace("\"","",$instring);
9
10    $parts=explode(",",$instring2);
11    // this gives four parts $parts[0] to $parts[3]
12
13    for ($j=0;$j<4;$j++) $parts[$j]=trim($parts[$j]);
14    $outstring=implode("','",$parts);
15    $outstring="'','".$outstring."'";
16
17    $query="INSERT INTO mytable2 VALUES (".$outstring.")";
18    $result = mysql_db_query($DBName,$query,$Link);
19    print $query;
20    if ($result=="") print " ... INSERT failed<br>The command was: ".$query."<p>\n";
21    else print " ... INSERT SUCCEEDED<p>\n";
22
23  } // for $i
24  mysql_close($Link);
25  ?>
```

The trim function is used in line 7 to remove not only any leading or trailing spaces but also – and most importantly – the two end of line characters represented by \r\n which are (invisibly) at the end of each line of a text file. The trimming in line 13 is to remove any spaces before or after the commas in the original line of text. The script does not deal with the problem of the unhelpful date format (Jan 12, etc.). We will come back to that.

We will upload the script as a file named plays.php and execute it.

This produces INSERT SUCCEEDED messages for the first 11 INSERT INTO lines, but the 12th insertion fails with the message:

```
INSERT INTO mytable2 VALUES ('','Journey's End','R. C. Sherriff','Nov 16','Nov 27') ... INSERT
failed
```

The problem is the quote symbol in the title of the final play, embedded in the name 'Journey's End'. This additional quote causes a syntax error in the MySQL command which therefore fails.

Using PHP to examine the contents of mytable2 (as illustrated in Chap. 13) produces the following output.

ind	playTitle	playAuthor	playStart	playEnd
sal	Hamlet	William Shakespeare	Jan 12	Jan 23
2	Waiting for Godot	Samuel Becket	Feb 9	Feb 20
3	Six Characters in Search of an Author	Luigi Pirandello	Mar 9	Mar 20
4	Hedda Gabler	Henrik Ibsen Apr 6	Apr 17	
5	She Stoops to Conquer	Oliver Goldsmith	May 15	
6	Death of a Salesman	Arthur Miller	Jun 1	Jun 12
7	The Caretaker	Harold Pinter	Jun 29	Jul 10
8	A Streetcar Named Desire	Tennessee Williams	Jul 27	Aug 7
9	The Threepenny Opera	Bertolt Brecht	Aug 24	Sep 4
10	Rosencrantz and Guildenstern are Dead	Tom Stoppard	Sept 21	Oct 2
11	Plenty	David Hare	Oct 19	Oct 30

Although plays 4 and 5 were both accepted without a MySQL error being caused, the playEnd field for both is blank. We can see that the start time for Hedda Gabler has been merged with the author's name and one of the dates for 'She Stoops to Conquer' is missing.[2]

We could now accept this as the initial state of the mytable2 table and rely on using standard editing facilities (such as those which will be illustrated later in this chapter) to make the corrections. However we would like to have a script that automatically rejected invalid entries and corrected as many errors as possible automatically, especially as we may wish to use it again for similar data in the future. So we will delete the records already uploaded, revise our script and process everything again.

To delete all the records already on the table we insert after the '$Link=mysql_connect', etc. line the statement (Line 4 in the revised script below):

```
$result = mysql_db_query($DBName,"TRUNCATE mytable2",$Link);
```

Next we add a test to check whether the value of playEnd will be null. If so there must be an error in the data. (Lines 14, 15 and 24.)

We also need to deal with the problem of the quote symbol in the name of the final play. The best way to do this is probably to replace it by the two-character combination \' (i.e. backslash followed by quote). To do this we have added a second use of the str_replace function as line 9:

[2] One further point to note, which is not an error but a potential cause of confusion, is that there were six embedded spaces in the date Aug 24 but only one appears in the displayed table. All six spaces are present in the database table mytable2 itself, but displaying them in a webpage makes them subject to the general HTML principle that any number of spaces and newline characters are displayed as a single space.

```
<?php
include "sql.php";
$Link=mysql_connect($sys_dblocalhost,$sys_dbusername,$sys_dbpassword)
  OR die(mysql_error());
$result = mysql_db_query($DBName,"TRUNCATE mytable2",$Link);
$inArray=file("plays.txt");
for ($i=0;$i<count($inArray);$i++){
  $instring=trim($inArray[$i]);
  $instring2=str_replace("\"","",$instring);
  $instring2=str_replace("'","\'",$instring2);
  $parts=explode(",",$instring2);
  // this gives four parts $parts[0] to $parts[3]

  for ($j=0;$j<4;$j++) $parts[$j]=trim($parts[$j]);
  if ($parts[3]=="") print $instring." ... Too few fields<p>\n";
  else {
    $outstring=implode("','",$parts);
    $outstring="'".$outstring."'";

    $query="INSERT INTO mytable2 VALUES (".$outstring.")";
    $result = mysql_db_query($DBName,$query,$Link);
    print $query;
    if ($result=="") print " ... INSERT failed<br>The command was: ".$query."<p>\n";
    else print " ... INSERT SUCCEEDED<p>\n";
  } //else
} // for $i
mysql_close($Link);
?>
```

This time ten of the insertions succeed, but two of them fail, with error messages:

```
"Hedda Gabler",Henrik Ibsen Apr 6,Apr 17 ... Too few fields
"She Stoops to Conquer",Oliver Goldsmith, May 15 ... Too few fields
```

Using PHP to inspect the contents of mytable2 we now get:

ind	playTitle	playAuthor	playStart	playEnd
1	Hamlet	William Shakespeare	Jan 12	Jan 23
2	Waiting for Godot	Samuel Becket	Feb 9	Feb 20
3	Six Characters in Search of an Author	Luigi Pirandello	Mar 9	Mar 20
4	Death of a Salesman	Arthur Miller	Jun 1	Jun 12
5	The Caretaker	Harold Pinter	Jun 29	Jul 10
6	A Streetcar Named Desire	Tennessee Williams	Jul 27	Aug 7
7	The Threepenny Opera	Bertolt Brecht	Aug 2	Sep 4
8	Rosencrantz and Guildenstern are Dead	Tom Stoppard	Sept 21	Oct 2
9	Plenty	David Hare	Oct 19	Oct 30
10	Journey's End	R. C. Sherriff	Nov 16	Nov 27

This is definitely progress. The two invalid records have been rejected and the quote in the name Journey's End has been accepted. We now need to work on the issue of the dates playStart and playEnd.

A date such as 'Jan 12' is fine for human beings but is very unsuitable for automatic processing. A better way of storing the date would be as a six-character field in the format yymmdd. The dates in the table do not include the year, although the table was previously said to be for the forthcoming year. We cannot tell when you will be reading this text, dear Reader, but let us assume that the forthcoming year will be 2020. We would like to store the date Jan 12 as 200112 and Feb 9 as 200209. Note that both the month and the day number must be padded out to two digits with an initial space if necessary.

Both the playStart value and the playEnd value need to be dealt with in the same way, which suggests writing a function called, say, convertDate which can be used for both. The function will take one argument, a string such as 'Jan 12' and will return a string value such as '200112'.

We will insert the two statements

```
$parts[2]=convertDate($parts[2]);
$parts[3]=convertDate($parts[3]);
```

before Line 16 of the above script.

We now need to define function convertDate, which we will place at the end of the script just before the closing ?>line.

We will call the argument passed into the convertDate function by the variable name $oldDate. We use the explode function[3] to split $oldDate into two parts: everything before and everything after the first space. We then set $month to the first part and $day to the second, trimming both as we do so. This approach gets round the problem of multiple embedded spaces in values such as 'Aug   24'.

```
$thisdate=explode(" ",$oldDate,2);
$month=trim($thisdate[0]);
$day=trim($thisdate[1]);
```

We now need to convert a value such as 'Jan' for $month to the string '01'. This is straightforward using an array $monthnum with an associative index. We place the statements:

[3]This is an extended version of the explode function discussed previously. It has a third argument, in this case the number 2. The reason for this will be explained in Sect. 16.5 at the end of this chapter.

```
$monthnum=array("Jan"=>"01","Feb"=>"02","Mar"=>"03",
"Apr"=>"04","May"=>"05","Jun"=>"06",
"Jul"=>"07","Aug"=>"08","Sep"=>"09",
"Oct"=>"10","Nov"=>"11","Dec"=>"12");
```

at an early position in our function.

To complete the conversion we need to add just two more lines to those given previously. To construct the new form of the date we take three strings and join them together, using the dot operator for string concatenation, and then return the resulting string as the value of the function. The three component values are:

(a) The string "20", signifying year 2020
(b) A string corresponding to the numerical form of the month, e.g. '01', which is obtained from the character form of the month, such as 'Jan', using array $monthnum
(c) The value of $day, which is prefixed by a '0' character if $day is less than 10.[4]

```
$day<10 then $day='0'.$day;
$parts[2]="20".$monthnum[$month].$day;
```

The final form of function convertData is shown below.

```
function convertDate($oldDate){
$monthnum=array("Jan"=>"01","Feb"=>"02","Mar"=>"03",
"Apr"=>"04","May"=>"05","Jun"=>"06",
"Jul"=>"07","Aug"=>"08","Sep"=>"09",
"Oct"=>"10","Nov"=>"11","Dec"=>"12");

$thisdate=explode(" ",$oldDate,2);
$month=trim($thisdate[0]);
$day=trim($thisdate[1]);
if ($day<10) $day='0'.$day;
return "20".$monthnum[$month].$day;
} // convertDate
```

Making this and the other insertions into plays.php gives a new script *plays2.php*. Executing this uploads a revised version of table mytable2 with the same error messages for Hedda Gabler and She Stoops to Conquer being output as before.

Table mytable2 now looks like this.

[4]The handling of $day shows PHP's flexibility when using numerical and string data together. Variable $day has a string value, say '8' and yet it can be compared with the number 10 as if it were the number 8. As 8 is smaller than 10 we prefix a zero to $day, making the string '08'. (If instead we were to compare a $day value of '8' with the *string* '10', $day would be considered larger, which is definitely not what we want.)

ind	playTitle	playAuthor	playStart	playEnd
1	Hamlet	William Shakespeare	200112	200123
2	Waiting for Godot	Samuel Becket	200209	200220
3	Six Characters in Search of an Author	Luigi Pirandello	200309	200320
4	Death of a Salesman	Arthur Miller	200601	200612
5	The Caretaker	Harold Pinter	200629	200710
6	A Streetcar Named Desire	Tennessee Williams	200727	200807
7	The Threepenny Opera	Bertolt Brecht	200824	200904
8	Rosencrantz and Guildenstern are Dead	Tom Stoppard	2021	201002
9	Plenty	David Hare	201019	201030
10	Journey's End	R. C. Sherriff	201116	201127

It is easy to see that the playStart date 2021 is invalid. This is because the invalid month name Sept was converted by array $monthnum to an empty string.

We can leave development of the conversion script here. We have uploaded most of the required table and dealt with several problems, but there are two remaining jobs to do to complete the task of creating a satisfactory table of the forthcoming year's productions.

- We need to upload the data for Hedda Gabler and She Stoops to Conquer as two new records.
- We need to correct the invalid starting date for Rosencrantz and Guildenstern are Dead.

Constructing a script to enable us to make these changes will be the subject of Chap. 17.

16.3 Extracting Information from a Table: Finding the Next Production

Now we have a table (albeit a partial one) of the next year's (i.e. 2020s) play productions we will use it to find automatically the next production available from any given date.

For simplicity we will represent a date of interest in the form yymmdd (i.e. as a six-character string) and will make use of a function nextProduction that takes a date in "yymmdd" string form as its one argument, returns no value but displays details of the next production. We will test the function by applying it to four dates: December 18th 2019 (191218), June 6th 2020 (200606), November 27th 2020 (201127) and December 25th 2020 (201225).

The basic script is shown below. The definitions of functions nextProduction and another useful function decodeDate will replace the comment in line 11.

```
<?php
include "sql.php";
$Link=mysql_connect($sys_dblocalhost,$sys_dbusername,$sys_dbpassword)
  OR die(mysql_error());

nextProduction(191218);
nextProduction(200606);
nextProduction(201127);
nextProduction(201225);

mysql_close($Link);
// place functions here
?>
```

We now need to define function nextProduction. We will find the earliest value in field playEnd that is greater than or equal to the date provided. If one is found, we need to output the name of the play and its author, plus the starting and finishing dates. If there is no such value we will output a message saying that there are no further productions available.

If the value passed to nextProduction is 191218, as it is in one of our examples, we need to construct a MySQL command

SELECT * FROM mytable2 WHERE playEnd>=191218 ORDER BY playEnd LIMIT 1

and then execute it.

The only part of this command that changes from one of our specified dates to another is the date. We need to make that the value of variable $nextdate.

We now construct the MySQL command in variable $query using the PHP statement

```
$query="SELECT * FROM mytable2 WHERE playEnd>=".$nextdate
." ORDER BY playEnd LIMIT 1";
```

Ordering the records by the value of field playEnd and specifying LIMIT 1 will ensure that we always get the play that is ending soonest after or on the day specified. However there is a complication: how can we tell if our MySQL command did not find any records, i.e. if there are no further productions available? This latter situation must not be confused with the query failing. If no records are found, the value of $result will be a resource rather than an empty string indicating failure.

To deal with this we use the MySQL function mysql_num_rows which can be applied to the resource variable $result to find out how many rows were returned by the command. If the value is zero we know that no record was found, so there are no more productions available. (In all other cases precisely one value will be returned so the value of the function must be one. We do not need to test for this.)

This leads to the following definition of function nextProduction.

```
function nextProduction($nextdate){
global $Link,$DBName;
print "<u>".decodeDate($nextdate)."</u><br>\n";
$query="SELECT * FROM mytable2 WHERE playEnd>=".$nextdate
." ORDER BY playEnd LIMIT 1";
$result = mysql_db_query($DBName,$query,$Link);

if (mysql_num_rows($result)==0) print "No further productions available<p>\n";
else {
  $row=mysql_fetch_array($result);
  print "Our next production is ".$row[playTitle]." by ".$row[playAuthor]."<br>"
  ."The production starts on ".decodeDate($row[playStart])." and ends on
".decodeDate($row[playEnd])."<p>\n";
} //else
} // nextProduction
```

The above script uses a function that has not yet been defined named decodeDate. As the name suggests we are going to convert all three of the dates output (the date of interest and the start and end dates of the production) into human-friendly form, for example '191218' will be converted to '18 December 2019'.

The definition of function decodeDate is given below. First we extract the year, month and day components of the date using the string function *substr*. We use the month component, such as '04', with an array $monthname which has an associative index, to convert it into a string, in this case 'April'. Then we combine the various components, not forgetting to include the century (the string '20') and return that string as the value of the function.

```
function decodeDate($datenum){

$monthname=array("01"=>"January","02"=>"February","03"=>"March",
"04"=>"April", "05"=>"May","06"=>"June",
"07"=>"July","08"=>"August","09"=>"September",
"10"=>"October", "11"=>"November","12"=>"December");

// $datenum is date in yymmdd form, i.e a string of 6 digits
// start by extracting the three components
$year=substr($datenum,0,2);
$month=substr($datenum,2,2);
$day=substr($datenum,4,2);

return $day." ".$monthname[$month]." 20".$year;
} //decodeDate
```

If we insert these two function definitions into the original incomplete script and execute it we get the output given below.

18 December 2019
Our next production is Hamlet by William Shakespeare
The production starts on 12 January 2020 and ends on 23 January 2020

06 June 2020
Our next production is Death of a Salesman by Arthur Miller
The production starts on 01 June 2020 and ends on 12 June 2020

27 November 2020
Our next production is Journey's End by R. C. Sherriff
The production starts on 16 November 2020 and ends on 27 November 2020

25 December 2020
No further productions available

16.4 Backing up and Restoring a Table

In this section we will illustrate how to make a backup copy of the current state of table mytable2 as a text file on our website and how to restore the table from the backup should the need arise.

The idea is to convert each record in the table into a string such as

'','Hamlet','William Shakespeare','200112','200123'

with each field delimited by single quotes and with these fields separated by commas. (The first field is shown as just '' i.e. an empty string. It is a placeholder for the value in the auto_increment field ind.)

Each string is then written as a line of text to a file mytable2_backup.txt on our website. We will assume that you have sufficient privileges on your system to write text files as well as read them. (If you do not, ask your system administrator for advice.)

We will start with an incomplete script that reads the records from mytable2 and returns a resource variable $result from which records can be retrieved one-by-one in the form of an array, using a while loop.

```
<?php
include "sql.php";
$Link=mysql_connect($sys_dblocalhost,$sys_dbusername,$sys_dbpassword)
   OR die(mysql_error());
$query="SELECT * FROM mytable2 ORDER BY ind";
$result = mysql_db_query($DBName,$query,$Link);
mysql_close($Link);

$FP1=fopen("mytable2_backup.txt",'w'); // open text file for writing

while ($row=mysql_fetch_array($result)){
   // convert contents of $row and write record to text file
} //while

fclose($FP1); // close text file
print "Backup to file mytable2_backup.txt completed<p>\n";
?>
```

This leaves the core task of converting the field values to the form shown above, with fields delimited by quotes and separated by commas.

Before joining the various values together we first need to deal with any quote characters that there may be in the name of either the play or its author. As before we replace a quote by a backslash followed by a quote.

```
$row[1]=str_replace("\"","\\\"",$row[1]);
$row[2]=str_replace("\"","\\\"",$row[2]);
```

It is not necessary to place this in the script to backup the table but it will avoid complications later, when we come to writing a script to restore the contents of the table.

We can now join the fields together into a long string.

```
$nextline="\"".$row[1]."\",\"".$row[2]."\",\"".$row[3]."\",\"".$row[4]."\"";
```

Finally we append the end of line characters \r\n to the string and write it to the file.

```
fwrite($FP1,$nextline."\r\n");
```

This makes the final script:

```
<?php
include "sql.php";
$Link=mysql_connect($sys_dblocalhost,$sys_dbusername,$sys_dbpassword) OR die(mysql_error());
$query="SELECT * FROM mytable2 ORDER BY ind";
$result = mysql_db_query($DBName,$query,$Link);
mysql_close($Link);

$FP1=fopen("mytable2_backup.txt",'w');

while ($row=mysql_fetch_array($result)){
  $row[1]=str_replace("'","\'",$row[1]);
  $row[2]=str_replace("'","\'",$row[2]);
  $nextline="'".$row[1]."','".$row[2]."','".$row[3]."','".$row[4]."'";
  fwrite($FP1,$nextline."\r\n");
} //while

fclose($FP1);
print "Backup to file mytable2_backup.txt completed<p>\n";
?>
```

16.4.1 Restoring a Table

Once we have our backup text file the next question is how to restore it, i.e. replace the contents of mytable2 by it if for any reason the database table becomes corrupt.

For this we can use a simplified version of the script that we used to load the data from plays.txt into the table. We start by deleting the current contents of mytable2 using a TRUNCATE command. Then as we extract each line from the backup text file, we trim it and then place it into a MySQL INSERT INTO command. The reason for trimming each line is to remove the end of line characters represented by \r\n at the end of it. Omitting this step will mean that those characters are stored as the final part of all the values in the playEnd field in the database table, which is sure to lead to trouble at some stage when the data in the table is used.

Here is the complete script for the restore task.

```
<?php
include "sql.php";
$Link=mysql_connect($sys_dblocalhost,$sys_dbusername,$sys_dbpassword)
  OR die(mysql_error());

$query="TRUNCATE mytable2";
$result = mysql_db_query($DBName,$query,$Link);

$inArray=file("mytable2_backup.txt");
for ($i=0;$i<count($inArray);$i++){
  $nextstring=trim($inArray[$i]);

  $query="INSERT INTO mytable2 VALUES (".$nextstring.")";
  $result = mysql_db_query($DBName,$query,$Link);
  if ($result=="") print " ... INSERT failed<br>The command was: ".$query."<p>\n";
  else print " ... INSERT SUCCEEDED<p>\n";

} // for $i
mysql_close($Link);
?>
```

16.5 Using the *explode* Function When There Are Multiple Occurrences of the Separator

In Sect. 16.2 we promised an explanation of the use of an extended form of the explode function not seen before in this book to separate the month from the day in a string named $oldDate with a value such as 'Jan 12'.

We would expect the statement that would do this to be, e.g.

```
$thisdate=explode(' ',$oldDate);
```

This would be fine for the case of separating the values out from 'Jan 12', with $thisdate[0] and $thisdate[1] set to 'Jan' and '12' respectively.

Unfortunately when the value of $oldDate has multiple spaces (or in general multiple occurrences of the character(s) specified as the separator), the function does not work as might be expected and gives the probably unexpected result that $thisdate[1] is a null string.

It may be easier to understand what is going on if we use exclamation marks instead of spaces.

If we execute the PHP statement

```
$thisdate=explode("!","Jan!!!!!!12");
```

the explode function effectively considers the string "Jan!!!!!!12" to be made up of eight parts like this:

Jan	!	!	!	!	!	!	12

So array $thisdate has seven components

'Jan'	''	''	''	''	''	'12'

These are the part of "Jan!!!!!!12" before the first !, followed by the characters between the six ! characters, i.e. five null strings, followed by the characters after the last !, i.e. '12'.

Going back to the example of 'Jan   12', if we were certain that our values of $oldDate would always have six embedded spaces as this one has we could use $thisdate[6] to refer to the 'day part' of the string. However this is not the case.

The solution to our difficulty is to use an extended version of explode with an extra argument. The PHP statement

```
$thisdate=explode(' ',$oldDate,2);
```

means create an array $thisdate with just two elements. Everything before the first space will be assigned to $thisdate[0] and everything else will be assigned to $thisdate[1]. So $thisdate[1] will become '   12', i.e. five spaces followed by 12', from which the string '12' can be obtained by trimming.

Chapter Summary
This chapter describes how to use PHP to take data stored in a text file on a website, 'clean' it and convert it to a database table. It also shows how to export data from a database table to a text file on a website for archive purposes, and how to restore a database table from a backup held as a text file. This example also serves to illustrate the use of PHP facilities, especially the string handling functions to manipulate data.

Practical Exercise 16

(1) Change the final script given in Sect. 16.4 so that it can be used to backup table mytable1 given in Sect. 12.10 (and elsewhere). Your script should be written so that it will not need changing if additional fields are later added to the table.

(2) Using only the functions described in this chapter and in Chap. 5, define a function that will take a string representing a name, such as "John Henry Smith", "Michael R. J. W. Jones", "J. M. W. Turner", "R, C. Sherriff" or "Boz" and return the surname (assumed to be the final element).

Chapter 17
Using PHP to View and Edit Database Tables

Chapter Aims
After reading this chapter you should be able to:

- use PHP to find the tables in the current database and display the contents and/or structure of each one
- use PHP to create a visual table editing facility.

In this chapter we will look at methods of using PHP to view and edit database tables.

We start by developing a script to list the tables in the current database and to show the contents and/or the structure of each one. We then go on to develop a simple but effective visual editing facility for the table developed at the end of Sect. 16.2. With straightforward changes this script can be adapted for other tables with a primary key, although it is probably only worthwhile for quite small tables.

17.1 Analyzing the Current Database

We will develop a script to analyse the current database, which as always we will assume is named mydb1. We can obtain a list of tables using the MySQL command

```
SHOW TABLES
```


M. Bramer, *Web Programming with PHP and MySQL*,
DOI 10.1007/978-3-319-22659-0_17

The script below is a first attempt at this. As usual the file sql.php is included (line 2), as explained in Chap. 15. Next a link is made to the MySQL server (lines 3 and 3a). The link is closed in line 17. The necessary MySQL command is set up and executed in lines 5 and 6. The While loop between lines 8 and 15 generates the name of the tables in mydb1 one at a time. Each is listed followed by two links: Show Contents and Show Structure. The two links (lines 11 and 12) point to the same script with parameter *mode* set to either *showtable* or *showstructure* and parameter *table* set to the name of the table.

```
1   <?php
2   include "sql.php";
3   $Link=mysql_connect($sys_dblocalhost,$sys_dbusername,$sys_dbpassword)
3a    OR die(mysql_error());
4   print "<h3>Database ".$DBName.": List of Tables</h3>\n";
5   $query="SHOW TABLES";
6   $result = mysql_db_query($DBName,$query,$Link);
7   print "<table border=1>\n";
8   while ($row=mysql_fetch_array($result)){
9     print "<tr>\n";
10    print "<td>".$row[0]."</td>\n";
11    print "<td><a href=\"?mode=showtable&table=".$row[0]."\">Show Contents</a></td>\n";
12    print "<td><a href=\"?mode=showstructure&table=".$row[0]
13      ."\">Show Structure</a></td>\n";
14    print "</tr>\n";
15  } //while
16  print "</table>\n";
17  mysql_close($Link);
18  ?>
```

Running this script produces the following output.

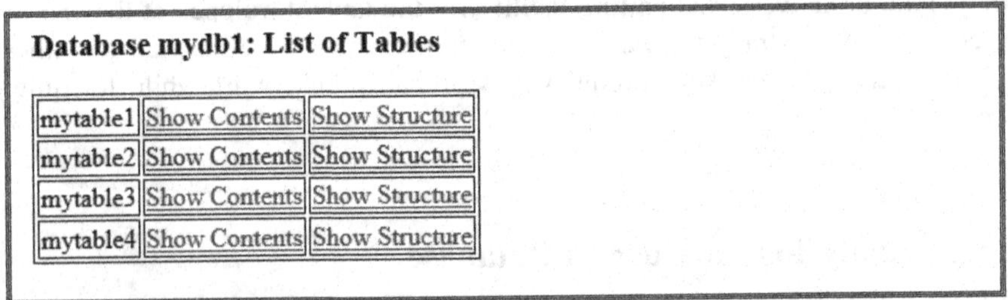
Database mydb1: List of Tables

mytable1	Show Contents	Show Structure
mytable2	Show Contents	Show Structure
mytable3	Show Contents	Show Structure
mytable4	Show Contents	Show Structure

We now need to adapt the script to receive the two parameter values and to use the value of mode to determine what action to take next. This gives us an outline script like this:

```
1  <?php
2  include "sql.php";
3  $Link=mysql_connect($sys_dblocalhost,$sys_dbusername,$sys_dbpassword)
3a   OR die(mysql_error());
4
5  $mode=$_GET['mode'];
6  $table=$_GET['table'];
7
8  if ($mode=="showtable"){
9  // script lines for showtable
10 }
11 else if ($mode=="showstructure"){
12 // script lines for showstructure
13 }
14 else { // display list of tables
15 print "<h3>Database ".$DBName.": List of Tables</h3>\n";
16 $query="SHOW TABLES";
17 $result = mysql_db_query($DBName,$query,$Link);
18 print "<table border=1>\n";
19 while ($row=mysql_fetch_array($result)){
20   print "<tr>\n";
21   print "<td>".$row[0]."</td>\n";
22   print "<td><a href=\"?mode=showtable&table=".$row[0]."\">Show Contents</a></td>\n";
23   print "<td><a href=\"?mode=showstructure&table=".$row[0]
24     ."\">Show Structure</a></td>\n";
25   print "</tr>\n";
26 } //while
27 print "</table>\n";
28 } // else
29 mysql_close($Link);
30 ?>
```

In lines 5 and 6 variables $mode and $table are set to the parameter values sent by the script (for the initial screen display these are both empty strings).

Next the value of $mode is tested in an IF … ELSE IF … ELSE structure (lines 8, 10, 11, 13, 14 and 28), with the main part of the previous script now made into the ELSE part of the script (lines 15–27).

All that remains is to replace the comments in lines 9 ('script lines for showtable') and 12 ('script lines for showstructure') by PHP statements.

There was a detailed description of how to display a table complete with column headings in Sect. 15.5. We will not repeat it here. It amounts to replacing the comment in line 9 by the lines

```
print "<h3>Contents of Table ".$table."</h3>\n";
$query1="SHOW COLUMNS FROM ".$table;
$result1 = mysql_db_query($DBName,$query1,$Link);
$query2="SELECT * FROM ".$table;
$result2 = mysql_db_query($DBName,$query2,$Link);
showtable($result1,$result2);
print "<p><a href=\"?\">Return to list of tables</a><p>\n";
```

and adding the definition of function showtable reproduced below before the closing PHP tag.

```
function showtable($result1,$result2){
// Display table, including headings
print "<table border=1>\n";
print "<tr>\n";
while($row=mysql_fetch_array($result1)){
  print "<td><b>".$row[0]."</b></td>";
} //while
print "</tr>\n";
$numcols=mysql_num_fields($result2);
while ($row2=mysql_fetch_array($result2)) {
  print "<tr>\n";
  for ($i=0;$i<$numcols;$i++) print "<td>".$row2[$i]."</td>\n";
  print "</tr>\n";
} //while
print "</table>\n";
} //showtable
```

With these changes clicking on the Show Contents link next to the name mytable2 produces the following output:

Contents of Table mytable2

ind	playTitle	playAuthor	playStart	playEnd
1	Hamlet	William Shakespeare	200112	200123
2	Waiting for Godot	Samuel Beckett	200209	200220
3	Six Characters in Search of an Author	Luigi Pirandello	200309	200320
4	Death of a Salesman	Arthur Miller	200601	200612
5	The Caretaker	Harold Pinter	200629	200710
6	A Streetcar Named Desire	Tennessee Williams	200727	200807
7	The Threepenny Opera	Bertolt Brecht	200824	200904
8	Rosencrantz and Guildenstern are Dead	Tom Stoppard	2021	201002
9	Plenty	David Hare	201019	201030
10	Journey's End	R. C. Sherriff	201116	201127

Return to list of tables

The last step is to replace the comment 'script lines for showstructure'. For this we use the MySQL command

SHOW CREATE *tablename*

which produces a listing of a CREATE TABLE command that could have been used to create the table in question. This can be done using the statements

```
print "<h3>Structure of Table ".$table."</h3>\n";
$query="SHOW CREATE TABLE ".$table;
$result = mysql_db_query($DBName,$query,$Link);
$row=mysql_fetch_array($result);
$struc=str_replace(PHP_EOL,"<br>",$row[1]);
print $struc."<p>";
print "<p><a href=\"?\">Return to list of tables</a><p>\n";
```

The value needed is the *second* element of array $row, i.e. $row[1]. The value of $row[0] is the table name itself. The statement

```
$struc=str_replace(PHP_EOL,"<br>",$row[1]);
```

is used to convert whatever is the appropriate character or combination of characters to denote 'newline' to an HTML <br> tag.

Clicking on the Show Structure link next to the name mytable2 now produces the following output:

```
Structure of Table mytable2

CREATE TABLE `mytable2` (
`ind` int(11) NOT NULL auto_increment,
`playTitle` varchar(50) default NULL,
`playAuthor` varchar(50) default NULL,
`playStart` varchar(10) default NULL,
`playEnd` varchar(10) default NULL,
PRIMARY KEY (`ind`)
) ENGINE=MyISAM AUTO_INCREMENT=11 DEFAULT CHARSET=latin1

Return to list of tables
```

Note that the SHOW CREATE TABLE command adds backtick characters around the table name and the field names that are not strictly necessary. It also outputs values for ENGINE and other parameters that were probably added by the MySQL system by default.

A complete listing of the script is given below for reference.

```
<?php
include "sql.php";
$Link=mysql_connect($sys_dblocalhost,$sys_dbusername,$sys_dbpassword)
  OR die(mysql_error());
$mode=$_GET['mode'];
$table=$_GET['table'];

if ($mode=="showtable"){
print "<h3>Contents of Table ".$table."</h3>\n";
$query1="SHOW COLUMNS FROM ".$table;
$result1 = mysql_db_query($DBName,$query1,$Link);
$query2="SELECT * FROM ".$table;
$result2 = mysql_db_query($DBName,$query2,$Link);
showtable($result1,$result2);
print "<p><a href=\"?\">Return to list of tables</a><p>\n";
}
else if ($mode=="showstructure"){
print "<h3>Structure of Table ".$table."</h3>\n";
$query="SHOW CREATE TABLE ".$table;
$result = mysql_db_query($DBName,$query,$Link);
$row=mysql_fetch_array($result);
$struc=str_replace(PHP_EOL,"<br>",$row[1]);
print $struc."<p>";
print "<p><a href=\"?\">Return to list of tables</a><p>\n";
}
else { // display list of tables
print "<h3>Database ".$DBName.": List of Tables</h3>\n";
$query="SHOW TABLES";
$result = mysql_db_query($DBName,$query,$Link);
print "<table border=1>\n";
while ($row=mysql_fetch_array($result)){
  print "<tr>\n";
  print "<td>".$row[0]."</td>\n";
  print "<td><a href=\"?mode=showtable&table=".$row[0]."\">Show Contents</a></td>\n";
  print "<td><a href=\"?mode=showstructure&table=".$row[0]."\">Show Structure</a></td>\n";
  print "</tr>\n";
} //while
print "</table>\n";
} //else
mysql_close($Link);
// ***************************************
function showtable($result1,$result2){
// Display table, including headings
print "<table border=1>\n";
print "<tr>\n";
while($row=mysql_fetch_array($result1)){
  print "<td><b>".$row[0]."</b></td>";
} //while
print "</tr>\n";
$numcols=mysql_num_fields($result2);
while ($row2=mysql_fetch_array($result2)) {
  print "<tr>\n";
  for ($i=0;$i<$numcols;$i++) print "<td>".$row2[$i]."</td>\n";
  print "</tr>\n";
} //while
print "</table>\n";
} //showtable
// ***************************************
?>
```

17.2 Building a Visual Table Editor

17.2.1 Developing an Editing Page

We start by reusing, with slight adjustments, the script developed in Chap. 15 for displaying the contents of a database table as a table in a web browser. We will start with this initial version of the script, which we will assume is stored in the file editor.php.

```
<?php
include "sql.php";
print "<b>Editor for table mytable2</b><p>\n";
$Link=mysql_connect($sys_dblocalhost,$sys_dbusername,$sys_dbpassword)
   OR die(mysql_error());
$query="SELECT * FROM mytable2";

$result = mysql_db_query($DBName,$query,$Link);
mysql_close($Link);

$numcols=mysql_num_fields($result);

print "<table border=1>\n";
while ($row=mysql_fetch_array($result)){
   print "<tr>\n";
   for ($i=0;$i<$numcols;$i++) print "<td>".$row[$i]."</td>\n";
   print "</tr>\n";
} //while
print "</table>\n";
?>
```

Running this script will display the contents of mytable2 (without column headings) as follows:

1	Hamlet	William Shakespeare	200112	200123
2	Waiting for Godot	Samuel Beckett	200209	200220
3	Six Characters in Search of an Author	Luigi Pirandello	200309	200320
4	Death of a Salesman	Arthur Miller	200601	200612
5	The Caretaker	Harold Pinter	200629	200710
6	A Streetcar Named Desire	Tennessee Williams	200727	200807
7	The Threepenny Opera	Bertold Brecht	200824	200904
8	Rosencrantz and Guildenstern are Dead	Tom Stoppard	2021	201002
9	Plenty	David Hare	201019	201030
10	Journey's End	R. C. Sherriff	201116	201127

We will next extend the script by adding two extra columns, which will contain an 'edit' link and a 'delete' link for each record.

We place these two lines after line 15 of the script. They both link to PHP page changetable.php with values specified in the URL for parameters *mode* (either 'edit' or 'delete') and *ref* (the value of the primary key).

```
print "<td><a href=changetable.php?mode=edit&ref=".$row[0].">Edit</a></td>\n";
print "<td><a href=changetable.php?mode=delete&ref=".$row[0].">Delete</a></td>\n";
```

We will also place an 'Add new record' link (with mode 'add') below the table, immediately before the closing PHP tag. This takes the form:

```
print " <a href=changetable.php?mode=add>Add new record</a>\n";
```

Running the script now gives the augmented table:

Editor for table mytable2

1	Hamlet	William Shakespeare	200112	200123	Edit	Delete
2	Waiting for Godot	Samuel Beckett	200209	200220	Edit	Delete
3	Six Characters in Search of an Author	Luigi Pirandello	200309	200320	Edit	Delete
4	Death of a Salesman	Arthur Miller	200601	200612	Edit	Delete
5	The Caretaker	Harold Pinter	200629	200710	Edit	Delete
6	A Streetcar Named Desire	Tennessee Williams	200727	200807	Edit	Delete
7	The Threepenny Opera	Bertolt Brecht	200824	200904	Edit	Delete
8	Rosencrantz and Guildenstern are Dead	Tom Stoppard	2021	201002	Edit	Delete
9	Plenty	David Hare	201019	201030	Edit	Delete
10	Journey's End	R. C. Sherriff	201116	201127	Edit	Delete

Add new record

There are three types of link shown here. For row 5

- clicking on Edit takes the web browser to *changetable.php?mode = edit&ref = 5*
- clicking on Delete takes the web browser to *changetable.php?mode = delete&ref = 5*
- Clicking on 'Add new record' takes the web browser to: *changetable.php?mode = add*

17.2.2 Developing the Destination Page

We now go on to develop changetable.php. As specified so far it needs to have three 'modes': edit, add and delete and we will soon discover that we need three more.

After taking the necessary action for each mode the script should provide a link to take the user back to editor.php in case more changes are needed.

In constructing our script there are some components that are sure to be needed.

- We will need to use MySQL to update the table, so we will include file sql.php as usual.
- We will need statements to assign the values of mode and ref passed in the URL to variables, which we will call by the obvious names $mode and $ref.
- We will need to print out a heading for the editing page and a further heading for each mode.
- We will need a series of if … else if statements to separate out the statements for each mode.

We have included all these in the outline script below.

```
<?php
include "sql.php";

$mode = $_GET['mode']; //in URL
$ref = $_GET['ref']; //in URL

print "<h3>Table Editor</h3>\n";

if ($mode=="delete"){
  print "<b>Delete record ".$ref."</b><p>";
  // statements for deleting record with number $ref go here
}
else if ($mode=="edit"){
  print "<b>Edit record ".$ref."</b><p>";
  // statements for editing record with number $ref go here
}
else if ($mode=="add"){
  print "<b>Add new record</b><p>";
  // statements for adding a new record go here
}
print "Click <a href=editor.php>here</a> to return to editing page<p>\n";
?>
```

Now if we point our web browser to editor.php and then click on the Delete link for row 5 we get the following:

Table Editor

Delete record 5

Click here to return to editing page

Similarly for the 'Edit ' and 'Add' links.

The hyperlink from 'here' takes us back to editor.php.

We will start with 'delete' mode as this is probably the easiest one to handle.

Although we could simply delete the record with primary key $ref, it is probably better to give the user the opportunity to change their mind and confirm the deletion, or otherwise, before it takes place.

We will change the display to this:

Table Editor

Delete record 5

Are you sure you want to delete this record?

yes no

Click here to return to editing page

Clicking on 'no' should return to the editor page editor.php. Clicking on 'yes' should take us back to the same page but with mode = delete2 this time and with ref as before. This is a fourth mode to add to our script. When the script detects this mode it should first carry out the deletion and then display

Table Editor

Deleting record 5

Record number 5 has been deleted

Click here to return to editing page

We first change the script so that when mode 'delete' is detected we give the user the choice between choosing 'no', which leaves the database unchanged and takes us back to editor.php, and 'yes', which takes us to the same page (i.e. changetable.php) with mode having the value delete2 and ref having the same value as before, so the link points to "?mode=delete2&ref=5". This gives us the following for mode 'delete'.

```
if ($mode=="delete"){
  print "<b>Delete record ".$ref."</b><p>";
  print "Are you sure you want to delete this record?<p>\n";
  print "<a href=?mode=delete2&ref=".$ref.">yes</a>    <a
href=editor.php>no</a><p>";
}
```

We now need to add a further section to our script to handle mode 'delete2'. Deleting a record is straightforward: we connect to the MySQL server and issue a DELETE command. Finally we test the value of variable $result in case for some reason the database cannot be updated. (Although the error message says 'It is not possible to make deletions at the present time' by far the most likely reason for such error messages to be displayed is a programming error that creates an invalid MySQL command.)

```
else if ($mode=="delete2"){
  print "<b>Deleting record ".$ref."</b><p>";
  $Link=mysql_connect($sys_dblocalhost,$sys_dbusername,$sys_dbpassword)
    OR die(mysql_error());
  $query="DELETE FROM mytable2 WHERE ind='".$ref."' LIMIT 1";
  $result = mysql_db_query($DBName,$query,$Link);
  mysql_close($Link);
  if ($result==1) print "Record with primary key ".$ref." has been deleted<p>\n";
  else print "It is not possible to make deletions at the present time - please try later<p>\n";
}
```

Let us assume that we decide not to delete record 5 but to edit it instead. With our script in its current form, clicking on the link to changetable.php?mode=edit&ref=5 gives us the skeleton output

Table Editor

Edit record 5

Click here to return to editing page

This needs to be augmented by a form which allows us to change the value of the various fields, such as this.

Table Editor

Edit record 5

Title of Play [The Caretaker]

Author(s) of Play [Harold Pinter]

Starting Date [20062!]

Finishing Date [200710]

[Reset] [Submit]

Click here to return to editing page

We will define our HTML form in such a way that after we make the desired changes and press Submit we jump to the same script again but this time with mode=edit2 and ref=5. The play title, author, etc. will also be passed to the script, but as form variables, not as part of the URL.

This gives us a fifth mode, edit2, for our script and we can safely expect that a sixth mode, add2, will be needed when we come on to adding a new record.

We can add to the previous outline script to deal with all six modes and to add in the code shown above for mode 'delete2' and changes made above for mode 'delete' to give the following.

```
<?php
include "sql.php";

$mode = $_GET['mode']; //in URL
$ref = $_GET['ref']; //in URL

print "<h3>Table Editor</h3>\n";

if ($mode=="delete"){
  print "<b>Delete record ".$ref."</b><p>";
  print "Are you sure you want to delete this record?<p>\n";
  print "<a href=?mode=delete2&ref=".$ref.">yes</a>    
  <a href=editor.php>no</a><p>";
}
else if ($mode=="delete2"){
  print "<b>Deleting record ".$ref."</b><p>";
  $Link=mysql_connect($sys_dblocalhost,$sys_dbusername,$sys_dbpassword)
    OR die(mysql_error());
  $query="DELETE FROM mytable2 WHERE ind='".$ref."' LIMIT 1";
  $result = mysql_db_query($DBName,$query,$Link);
  mysql_close($Link);
  if ($result==1) print "Record number ".$ref." has been deleted<p>\n";
  else print "It is not possible to make deletions at the present time - please try later<p>\n";
}
else if ($mode=="edit"){
  print "<b>Edit record ".$ref."</b><p>";
  // statements for editing record with number $ref go here
}
else if ($mode=="edit2"){
  print "<b>Editing record ".$ref."</b><p>";
  // statements for mode edit2 with record $ref go here
}
else if ($mode=="add"){
  print "<b>Add new record</b><p>";
  // statements for adding a new record go here
}
else if ($mode=="add2"){
  print "<b>Adding new record</b><p>";
  // statements for mode add2 go here
}
print "Click <a href=editor.php>here</a> to return to editing page<p>\n";
?>
```

We now need to fill in the missing instructions for modes edit, edit2, add and add2. We will start with edit.

The PHP needed to generate the Edit form for play number 5 shown above is in two parts:

- First, issue a MySQL command to retrieve the values currently in the table for that record.

- Second, display an edit form with those values as the default values for each field.

For the first part we issue a MySQL 'SELECT FROM' command.

```
$Link=mysql_connect($sys_dblocalhost,$sys_dbusername,$sys_dbpassword)
  OR die(mysql_error());
$query="SELECT * FROM mytable2 WHERE ind='".$ref."' LIMIT 1";
$result = mysql_db_query($DBName,$query,$Link);
mysql_close($Link);
$row=mysql_fetch_array($result);
```

This gives us all the values for the record with ind=5, as the elements of array $row. The array elements

$row[ind]	$row[playTitle]	$row[playAuthor]	$row[playStart]	$row[playEnd]

are now

5	'The Caretaker'	'Harold Pinter'	'200629'	'200710'

We will place this code in our script to replace the comment at line 25.

The form specification needs to include a text box for each of the last four fields, with its current value, such as $row[playTitle], used as the default value in the form's <input type=text> tag.

The PHP script to generate the edit form is complicated so we will build up to it piece by piece.

In the case of record 5 the edit form that needs to be generated is the following.

```
<form action="?mode=edit2&ref=5" method="POST" name="form1">
Title of Play <input name=playTitle type=text size=60 maxlength=60 value="The Caretaker"><p>
Author(s) of Play <input name=playAuthor type=text size=60 maxlength=60
  value="Harold Pinter"><p>
Starting Date <input name=playStart type=text size=6 maxlength=6 value="200629"><p>
Finishing Date <input name=playEnd type=text size=6 maxlength=6 value="200710"><p>
<input name="Reset" type="reset" value="Reset">     
<input name="Submit" type="submit" value="Submit"><p>
</form>
```

There are three points to note about this.

- The primary key field is treated differently from all the others. We definitely do not want the user to be able to change its value. On the other hand we do want the 'target page' that receives our form to know its value. We deal with this by leaving it out of the edit form and instead passing its current value to the target page in the <FORM> tag using the *ref* parameter.

- The four default field values are surrounded by double quote symbols, e.g. "The Caretaker". This is an HTML requirement when a default value includes an embedded space and it is probably wise always to include the quotes for text fields whatever the default value may turn out to be in a particular case. (Some other values such as Submit are also enclosed in double quote characters.)
- The 'action' parameter in the <form> tag specifies the URL of the target page, i.e. the page to which it jumps when the Submit button is pressed. A file name relative to the current page can be used, so to make the target page changetable.php?mode=edit2&ref=5 all we need to specify is ?mode=edit2&ref=5. The system deduces that we are referring to the current page, in this case changetable.php.

The five values shown in italic (5, The Caretaker, etc.) are those for this particular record and will need to be replaced by variables to make the form generally applicable for all records. However first each line needs to be made into a PHP print statement with the text enclosed in a Print statement. We will add the character combination \n (i.e. a newline) at the end of the string for each form object in the interests of making the 'source' of the web page readable.

If we take the line beginning Title of Play and make it into a print statement in the obvious – but wrong – way that will give us:

```
print "Title of Play <input name=playTitle type=text size=60 maxlength=60
value="The Caretaker"><p>\n";
```

The problem with this is the pair of double quote characters around The Caretaker. These are not permitted (in their current form) in a string enclosed in double quotes. They have to be 'escaped' by preceding each one by a backslash character. Doing that gives:

```
print "Title of Play <input name=playTitle type=text size=60 maxlength=60
value=\"The Caretaker\"><p>\n";
```

We next need to replace the constant The Caretaker by the value retrieved from the database table, which in general we can refer to by $row[playTitle]. This gives us the final version:

```
print "Title of Play <input name=playTitle type=text size=60 maxlength=60 value=\""
.$row[playTitle]."\"><p>\n";
```

Converting all the lines of the edit form into Print statements in this way gives us the following:

```
print "<form action=\"?mode=edit2&ref=".$ref."\" method=\"POST\" name=\"form1\">\n";
print "Title of Play <input name=playTitle type=text size=60 maxlength=60 "
  ."value=\"".$row[playTitle]."\"><p>\n";
print "Author(s) of Play <input name=playAuthor type=text size=60 maxlength=60 "
  ."value=\"".$row[playAuthor]."\"><p>\n";
print "Starting Date <input name=playStart type=text size=6 maxlength=6 "
  ."value=\"".$row[playStart]."\"><p>\n";
print "Finishing Date <input name=playEnd type=text size=6 maxlength=6 "
  ."value=\"".$row[playEnd]."\"><p>\n";
print "<input name=\"Reset\" type=\"reset\" "
  ."value=\"Reset\">     \n";
print "<input name=\"Submit\" type=\"submit\" value=\"Submit\"><p>\n";
print "</form>\n";
```

Normally we would just insert this latest piece of PHP script into the edit section of our evolving file changetable.php, just above the closing brace character } that was previously at line 26.

However in this case we will do something more complicated that may appear unnecessary. The point of it will become clear a little later on. We will take the PHP statements that define the 'edit' form and make them into a function genform which takes arguments $ref and $row and does not return a value.

We will also change the value edit2 in the <form> tag into a variable $nextmode and pass it into function genform as its third argument. (The point of this will also become apparent soon.) This makes the final definition of function genform the following. We will place it in our script immediately before the closing PHP tag, i.e. ?>.

```
function genform($ref,$row,$nextmode){
  print "<form action=\"?mode=".$nextmode."&ref=".$ref."\" "
    ."method=\"POST\" name=\"form1\">\n";
  print "Title of Play <input name=playTitle type=text size=60 maxlength=60 "
    ."value=\"".$row[playTitle]."\"><p>\n";
  print "Author(s) of Play <input name=playAuthor type=text size=60 maxlength=60 "
    ."value=\"".$row[playAuthor]."\"><p>\n";
  print "Starting Date <input name=playStart type=text size=6 maxlength=6 "
    ."value=\"".$row[playStart]."\"><p>\n";
  print "Finishing Date <input name=playEnd type=text size=6 maxlength=6 "
    ."value=\"".$row[playEnd]."\"><p>\n";
  print "<input name=\"Reset\" type=\"reset\" "
    ."value=\"Reset\">     \n";
  print "<input name=\"Submit\" type=\"submit\" value=\"Submit\"><p>\n";
  print "</form>\n";
  return;
} // genform
```

To use this function in the 'edit' section we only need to put a function call

```
genform($ref,$row,"edit2");
```

into our script immediately before the closing brace that used to be at line 26.

The reason for going to this trouble with function genform is that we can use it again with mode 'add'. In this case all we need to do is to replace the comment that used to be at line 33 by the single line

```
genform($ref,$row,"add2");
```

In this case it may be objected that for the 'add' section variable $row is just an undefined array. However this does no harm. Each of the default values $row[playTitle], etc. will be taken as an empty string, which is perfectly acceptable as a default value when adding a new record.

Our evolving script changetable.php has now grown to this:

```
1   <?php
2   include "sql.php";
3
4   $mode = $_GET['mode']; //in URL
5   $ref = $_GET['ref']; //in URL
6
7   print "<h3>Table Editor</h3>\n";
8
9   if ($mode=="delete"){
10     print "<b>Delete record ".$ref."</b><p>";
11     print "Are you sure you want to delete this record?<p>\n";
12a    print "<a href=?mode=delete2&ref=".$ref.">yes</a>    
12b    <a href=editor.php>no</a><p>";
13  }
14  else if ($mode=="delete2"){
15     print "<b>Deleting record ".$ref."</b><p>";
```

17.2.3 *Changing and Adding to a Table*

That just leaves us with two modes to deal with: edit2 and add2, to replace the comments that are currently at lines 34 and 42. They must both handle form values passed to the 'target page'. The difference between them is that to edit a record in a table we use the MYSQL command UPDATE, whereas to add a new record we use INSERT INTO.

For both modes we need to start by retrieving the four form variables passed to changetable.php. To do this we add these four lines to the code for modes 'edit2' and 'add2'.

For both modes we will also need to connect to the MySQL server, issue a MySQL command and then close the connection.

```
    $Link=mysql_connect($sys_dblocalhost,$sys_dbusername,$sys_dbpassword)
      OR die(mysql_error());
    $query="DELETE FROM mytable2 WHERE ind=".$ref." LIMIT 1";
    $result = mysql_db_query($DBName,$query,$Link);
    mysql_close($Link);
    if ($result==1) print "Record number ".$ref." has been deleted<p>\n";
    else print "It is not possible to make deletions at the present time - please try later<p>\n";
  }
  else if ($mode=="edit"){
    print "<b>Edit record ".$ref."</b><p>";
    $Link=mysql_connect($sys_dblocalhost,$sys_dbusername,$sys_dbpassword)
      OR die(mysql_error());
    $query="SELECT * FROM mytable2 WHERE ind='".$ref."' LIMIT 1";
    $result = mysql_db_query($DBName,$query,$Link);
    mysql_close($Link);
    $row=mysql_fetch_array($result);
    genform($ref,$row,"edit2");
  }
  else if ($mode=="edit2"){
    print "<b>Editing record ".$ref."</b><p>";
    // statements for mode edit2 with record $ref go here
  }
  else if ($mode=="add"){
    print "<b>Add new record</b><p>";
    genform($ref,$row,"add2");
  }
  else if ($mode=="add2"){
    print "<b>Adding new record</b><p>";
    // statements for mode add2 go here
  }
  print "Click <a href=editor.php>here</a> to return to editing page<p>\n";
  // ************************************
  function genform($ref,$row,$nextmode){
    print "<form action=\"?mode=edit2&ref=".$ref."\" "
      ."method=\"POST\" name=\"form1\">\n";
    print "Title of Play <input name=playTitle type=text size=60 maxlength=60 "
      ."value=\"".$row[playTitle]."\"><p>\n";
    print "Author(s) of Play <input name=playAuthor type=text size=60 maxlength=60 "
      ."value=\"".$row[playAuthor]."\"><p>\n";
    print "Starting Date <input name=playStart type=text size=6 maxlength=6 "
      ."value=\"".$row[playStart]."\"><p>\n";
    print "Finishing Date <input name=playEnd type=text size=6 maxlength=6 "
      ."value=\"".$row[playEnd]."\"><p>\n";
    print "<input name=\"Reset\" type=\"reset\" "
      ."value=\"Reset\">     \n";
    print "<input name=\"Submit\" type=\"submit\" value=\"Submit\"><p>\n";
    print "</form>\n";
    return;
  } // genform
  ?>
```

The difference between the two is the MySQL command used. For mode edit2 we need

```
$playTitle = $_POST['playTitle']; // from form
$playAuthor = $_POST['playAuthor']; // from form
$playStart = $_POST['playStart']; // from form
$playEnd = $_POST['playEnd']; // from form
```

For mode add2 we need

```
$Link=mysql_connect($sys_dblocalhost,$sys_dbusername,$sys_dbpassword)
  OR die(mysql_error());
// place line $query= etc. here
$result = mysql_db_query($DBName,$query,$Link);
mysql_close($Link);
if ($result==1) print "Record ".$ref." has been updated<p>\n"; // 'added' for mode add2
else print "Error: our database cannot be updated at the present time - please try again later<p>\n";
```

This completes the description of how to build an editor for table mytable2. It is appreciably more complex than most other examples in this book, but we hope you have found it instructive. You should be able to use it for editing your own tables with only quite minor changes, depending on which fields you use in your tables.

The final version of changetable.php is given below for completeness.

```
$query="UPDATE mytable2 SET playTitle='".$playTitle."',playAuthor='".$playAuthor
    ."',playStart='".$playStart."',playEnd='".$playEnd."' WHERE ind=".$ref;
```

```
$query="INSERT INTO mytable2  VALUES('','".$playTitle."','".$playAuthor."','"
  .$playStart."','".$playEnd."')";
```

```php
<?php
include "sql.php";

$mode = $_GET['mode']; //in URL
$ref = $_GET['ref']; //in URL

print "<h3>Table Editor</h3>\n";

if ($mode=="delete"){
  print "<b>Delete record ".$ref."</b><p>";
  print "Are you sure you want to delete this record?<p>\n";
  print "<a href=?mode=delete2&ref=".$ref.">yes</a>    
  <a href=editor.php>no</a><p>";
}
else if ($mode=="delete2"){
  print "<b>Deleting record ".$ref."</b><p>";
  $Link=mysql_connect($sys_dblocalhost,$sys_dbusername,$sys_dbpassword)
    OR die(mysql_error());
  $query="DELETE FROM mytable2 WHERE ind=".$ref." LIMIT 1";
  $result = mysql_db_query($DBName,$query,$Link);
  mysql_close($Link);
  if ($result==1) print "Record number ".$ref." has been deleted<p>\n";
  else print "It is not possible to make deletions at the present time - please try later<p>\n";
}
else if ($mode=="edit"){
  print "<b>Edit record ".$ref."</b><p>";
  $Link=mysql_connect($sys_dblocalhost,$sys_dbusername,$sys_dbpassword)
    OR die(mysql_error());
  $query="SELECT * FROM mytable2 WHERE ind=".$ref." LIMIT 1";
  $result = mysql_db_query($DBName,$query,$Link);
  mysql_close($Link);
  $row=mysql_fetch_array($result);
  genform($ref,$row,"edit2");
}
else if ($mode=="edit2"){
  print "<b>Editing record ".$ref."</b><p>";
  $playTitle = $_POST['playTitle']; // from form
  $playAuthor = $_POST['playAuthor']; // from form
  $playStart = $_POST['playStart']; // from form
  $playEnd = $_POST['playEnd']; // from form
  $Link=mysql_connect($sys_dblocalhost,$sys_dbusername,$sys_dbpassword)
    OR die(mysql_error());
  $query="UPDATE mytable2 SET playTitle='".$playTitle."',playAuthor='".$playAuthor
    ."',playStart='".$playStart."',playEnd='".$playEnd."' WHERE ind=".$ref;
  $result =  mysql_db_query($DBName,$query,$Link);
  mysql_close($Link);
  if ($result==1) print "Record ".$ref." has been updated<p>\n";
  else print "Error: our database cannot be updated at the present time - please try again
later<p>\n";
}
else if ($mode=="add"){
  print "<b>Add new record</b><p>";
  genform($ref,$row,"add2");
}
```

```
else if ($mode=="add2"){
  print "<b>Adding new record</b><p>";
  $playTitle = $_POST['playTitle']; // from form
  $playAuthor = $_POST['playAuthor']; // from form
  $playStart = $_POST['playStart']; // from form
  $playEnd = $_POST['playEnd']; // from form
  $Link=mysql_connect($sys_dblocalhost,$sys_dbusername,$sys_dbpassword)
    OR die(mysql_error());
  $query="INSERT INTO mytable2 VALUES('','".$playTitle."','".$playAuthor."','"
    .$playStart."','".$playEnd."')";
  $result = mysql_db_query($DBName,$query,$Link);
  mysql_close($Link);
  if ($result==1) print "Record ".$ref." has been added<p>\n";
  else print "Error: our database cannot be updated at the present time - please try again
later<p>\n";
}
print "Click <a href=editor.php>here</a> to return to editing page<p>\n";
// ************************************
function genform($ref,$row,$nextmode){
  print "<form action=\"?mode=".$nextmode."&ref=".$ref."\" "
    ."method=\"POST\" name=\"form1\">\n";
  print "Title of Play <input name=playTitle type=text size=60 maxlength=60 "
    ."value=\"".$row[playTitle]."\"><p>\n";
  print "Author(s) of Play <input name=playAuthor type=text size=60 maxlength=60 "
    ."value=\"".$row[playAuthor]."\"><p>\n";
  print "Starting Date <input name=playStart type=text size=6 maxlength=6 "
    ."value=\"".$row[playStart]."\"><p>\n";
  print "Finishing Date <input name=playEnd type=text size=6 maxlength=6 "
    ."value=\"".$row[playEnd]."\"><p>\n";
  print "<input name=\"Reset\" type=\"reset\" "
    ."value=\"Reset\">     \n";
  print "<input name=\"Submit\" type=\"submit\" value=\"Submit\"><p>\n";
  print "</form>\n";
  return;
} // genform
?>
```

Chapter Summary

This chapter shows how to use PHP to view and edit database tables. It starts by developing a script to list the tables in the current database and to show the contents and/or the structure of each one and goes on to develop a simple but effective visual table editing facility. This is illustrated using the table developed at the end of Sect. 16.2.

Practical Exercise 17

Augment the first script given in Sect. 17.1 so that the list of tables for database mydb1 that follows it also gives the number of fields and records for each table.

Chapter 18
PHP in Action: Maintaining a Membership List

Chapter Aims

After reading this chapter you should be able to:

- use PHP in conjunction with MySQL to maintain an organisation's membership records
- write a PHP script to register a user, log into a password protected website, create a password, issue a password reminder and manage a table of members
- write PHP statements to send an email from a PHP script.

In this chapter we will illustrate how to construct a simplified version of an application that is becoming increasingly common.

To set the scene we will imagine that the Erewhon Society, introduced in Chap. 1, has a trading subsidiary named Erewhon Trading Services (ETS) run by the Society's Vice-President Dr. Noone. ETS sells 'unconventional' products which are available to registered customers only. For legal reasons customers are referred to as belonging to the 'ETS Members' Club'.

18.1 Registration

A new customer (member) opens a web page with a form that they can use to register with ETS to receive discounts on its excellent products. This is designed to be simple to do. They just have to complete their forename, surname and email address and then choose a password. The system checks that the fields are not blank, that the email address has not already been used and that the password is at least six

M. Bramer, *Web Programming with PHP and MySQL*,
DOI 10.1007/978-3-319-22659-0_18

characters long. If everything is valid the system enters the details into a database table named *members1*. In future when the member logs in to the ETS site they will be greeted by name and given a list of items they can buy.

There is also a facility for the company's representative to log in and inspect the contents of the table.

We start by creating a table members1 with a suitable set of fields. We use PHP to issue the MySQL command

```
CREATE TABLE members1 (
    ind integer NOT NULL auto_increment,
    forename varchar(30) NOT NULL,
    surname varchar(30) NOT NULL,
    email varchar(30) NOT NULL,
    password varchar(20) NOT NULL,
    dateJoined char(6) NOT NULL,
    dateLast char(6) default NULL,
    numLogs integer default 0,
    PRIMARY KEY (ind)
)
```

- The ind field is an index number which starts at 1 and is automatically incremented by 1 for each new member.
- The fields forename, surname, email, password and dateJoined are all self-explanatory.
- The dateLast and numLogs fields are used to hold the date of the last login and the total number of logins respectively.

When a new member registers they will enter the values of the fields forename, surname, email and password. If the registration is valid the system will automatically add the value of dateJoined and issue a MySQL INSERT INTO command for table members1. The insertion process will automatically add the value of the primary key field ind, which is an auto_increment field. The final two fields will be left blank, but will be updated automatically each time the member logs in subsequently. For convenience we will store all dates in the six-character form YYMMDD, e.g. 191225 for Christmas Day 2019.

A basic registration form might look like this.

Erewhon Trading Services

Member Registration Form

You must complete all the fields

Forename

Surname

Your Email Address

Choose a Password (must be at least 6 characters)

Submit

We will assume there is an HTML file *start.htm* which will display this. The HTML to do so looks like this.

```
<html>
<head></head>
<body>
<h3>Erewhon Trading Services</h3>
<h3>Member Registration Form</h3>
You must complete all the fields<br>
<form action="registration.php" method="POST" name="form1">
Forename <input name=forename type=text size=30 maxlength=30><p>
Surname  <input name=surname type=text size=30 maxlength=30><p>
Your Email Address <input name=email type=text size=30 maxlength=30><p>
Choose a Password <input name=password type=text size=20 maxlength=20>
(must be at least 6 characters)  <p>
<input name="Submit" type="submit" value="Submit">
</form>
</body>
</html>
```

There are two points to note about this form.

- The four fields in the form have been given the names of the corresponding fields in table members1, i.e. forename, surname, email and password. This is just for convenience.
- The action field in the <form> tag refers to a PHP page *registration.php*, which has not yet been written. This is the page to which the values of the four fields will be sent when the user presses Submit.

After the first few members have joined, the members1 table might look like this (it is possible that a few of the members have used false names).

ind	forename	surname	email	password	dateJoined	dateLast	numLogs
1	Charles	Dickens	charles@xyzcomp.co.uk	abc123xyz	180930		0
2	Holly	Martins	holly@limecorp.co.at	defgh987	181124		0
3	Mary	Shelley	marys24@xyzabc.org.es	mysecret99	181124		0
4	jane	austen	jane@janecorp.org.uk	pqr27$jk	190625		0
5	Abraham	Stoker	abraham27@mycorp.com.it	secret789	190823		0
6	georgina	eliot	georginaeliot@abcde.org	mypass1	200718		0
7	Virginia	Foxx	vf@mycorp.com.uk	mypass1	200718		0
8	george	orwell	ericb@pqrcomp.org	bigbrother84	200314		0

The structure of the PHP script registration.php needs to be similar to this:

1. Include file sql.php, as we intend to issue MySQL commands.
2. Assign values sent from start.htm to suitable variables.
3. Trim all the field values to remove any leading and trailing spaces. Also convert any letters in the email field to lower case (to make it easier to compare email values later).
4. Test whether any of the values are blank. Also check whether the password is at least six characters long. Finally check whether the email address is already in the table.
5. If all the entries are valid {
    - generate value for dateJoined in YYMMDD form
    - enter new member into table members1
    - print a welcome message
    - display a link to return to start.htm to log in[1]

   }
   else {
    - print one or more error messages
    - display a link to return to start.htm to try again

   }

A miniature script dealing with points 1 and 2 plus printing out a title and providing a link back to start.htm would be:

```
<?php
include "sql.php";
print "<h3>Your Registration</h3>\n";

$forename = $_POST['forename']; // from form
$surname = $_POST['surname']; // from form
$email = $_POST['email']; // from form
$password = $_POST['password']; // from form

print "Click <a href=start.htm>here</a> to return to login/registration page<p>\n";
?>
```

[1] This facility will be added to start.htm in the next section.

As usual, it is not compulsory to assign the value sent by the form for field forename, say, to variable $forename rather than a variable with some other name, but it is often convenient to do so.

Point 3 can easily be dealt with using the string functions trim, to remove any leading and trailing spaces, and strtolower to convert any upper case letters in the password to lower case. We place the following statements before the final Print statement in the above box.

```
$forename=trim($forename);
$surname=trim($surname);
$email=trim(strtolower($email));
$password=trim($password);
```

To deal with point 4 we start by setting variable $OK to the value yes. Then we go through the four fields from start.htm one-by-one checking whether any of them is blank. If it is we print an error message and set the value of $OK to no.

If the value of $password is not blank we make a further test to check that its length is at least six characters, using the strlen function.

If $email is not blank we need to test whether the value chosen has already been used (i.e. the person entering their details has previously registered or has used someone else's email address by mistake). We will leave this part as a comment in the following PHP script fragment, which again is placed before the final Print statement in the first PHP box above.

```
$OK="yes";
if ($forename=="") {
  print "Forename field must not be blank<br>\n";
  $OK="no";
}
if ($surname=="") {
  print "Surname field must not be blank<br>\n";
  $OK="no";
}
if ($email=="") {
  print "Email field must not be blank<br>\n";
  $OK="no";
}
else {
  // test whether email has already been used
}
if ($password=="") {
  print "Password field must not be blank<br>\n";
  $OK="no";
}
else if (strlen($password)<6) {
  print "Your password must be at least six characters<br>\n";
  $OK="no";
}
```

We now need to replace the comment

// test whether email has already been used

We can test this by issuing a suitable PHP command. If the email address were abc@xyz.com the command would be

```
SELECT email FROM members1 WHERE email='abc@xyz.com' LIMIT 1
```

In the general form of this command given below the constant email address needs to be replaced by the variable $email.

Issuing a valid command of this form from a PHP script will return a variable $result with the value 1, whether or not any match with the contents of the table has been found. To find out how many matching rows of the table were found we can use the MySQL function mysql_num_rows($result). This will be zero if no match was found. Otherwise it implies that the email address is already in the table, i.e. there is a user input error. The PHP code for this test is as follows.

```
$Link=mysql_connect($sys_dblocalhost,$sys_dbusername,$sys_dbpassword)
  OR die(mysql_error());
$query="SELECT email FROM members1 WHERE email='".$email."' LIMIT 1";
$result = mysql_db_query($DBName,$query,$Link);
mysql_close($Link);
if (mysql_num_rows($result)>0) {
  print "There is already a user registered with your email address!<br>\n";
  $OK="no";
}
```

If after all the tests on the four input values the value of $OK is still yes we go on to step 5.

The most important parts of this are:

- generate value for dateJoined in YYMMDD form
- enter new member into table members1

Generating the value of dateJoined in YYMMDD format is simple using the date function.

```
$dateJoined=date("ymd");
```

We can enter the new member into table members1 by generating an INSERT INTO command with a single quote character before and after each field value. We will then test the value of $result to check whether the INSERT command succeeded. This gives the following fragment of script.

```
$Link=mysql_connect($sys_dblocalhost,$sys_dbusername,$sys_dbpassword)
  OR die(mysql_error());
$query="INSERT INTO members1 (forename,surname,email,password,dateJoined)"
  ." VALUES ('".$forename."','".$surname."','".$email."','".$password."','".$dateJoined."')";
$result = mysql_db_query($DBName,$query,$Link);
mysql_close($Link);
if ($result==1) print "Your registration has been accepted - welcome to our club!<p>\n";
else print "It is not possible to register you at the present time - please try later<p>\n";
```

Putting all the fragments of code above into a complete PHP script registration.php, this is what we get.

```
<?php
include "sql.php";
print "<h3>Your Registration</h3>\n";

$forename = $_POST['forename']; // from form
$surname = $_POST['surname']; // from form
$email = $_POST['email']; // from form
$password = $_POST['password']; // from form

$forename=trim($forename);
$surname=trim($surname);
$email=trim(strtolower($email));
$password=trim($password);

$OK="yes";
if ($forename=="") {
  print "Forename field must not be blank<br>\n";
  $OK="no";
}
if ($surname=="") {
  print "Surname field must not be blank<br>\n";
  $OK="no";
}
if ($email=="") {
  print "Email field must not be blank<br>\n";
  $OK="no";
}
else {
  $Link=mysql_connect($sys_dblocalhost,$sys_dbusername,$sys_dbpassword)
    OR die(mysql_error());
  $query="SELECT email FROM members1 WHERE email='".$email."' LIMIT 1";
  $result = mysql_db_query($DBName,$query,$Link);
  mysql_close($Link);
  if (mysql_num_rows($result)>0) {
    print "There is already a user registered with your email address!<br>\n";
    $OK="no";
  }
}
if ($password=="") {
  print "Password field must not be blank<br>\n";
  $OK="no";
}
else if (strlen($password)<6) {
  print "Your password must be at least six characters<br>\n";
  $OK="no";
}
if ($OK=="yes"){
  $dateJoined=date("ymd");
  $Link=mysql_connect($sys_dblocalhost,$sys_dbusername,$sys_dbpassword)
```

```
    OR die(mysql_error());
  $query="INSERT INTO members1 (forename,surname,email,password,dateJoined)"
    ." VALUES ('".$forename."','".$surname."','".$email."','".$password."','".$dateJoined."')";
  $result = mysql_db_query($DBName,$query,$Link);
  mysql_close($Link);
  if ($result==1) print "Your registration has been accepted - welcome to our club!<p>\n";
  else print "It is not possible to register you at the present time - please try later<p>\n";
} //if

print "Click <a href=start.htm>here</a> to return to login/registration page<p>\n";
?>
```

18.2 Logging in

Having successfully developed a registration system we will now go back and embellish the start.htm page shown earlier to include a login facility and a 'forgotten your password?' facility. The new version is in three parts separated by horizontal rules.

Erewhon Trading Services

Member Login Form

Your email address

Your password

Login

Forgotten your Password?

Enter your email address below and press the 'Send me my Password' button.

Send me my Password

Member Registration Form

You must complete all the fields

Forename

Surname

Your Email Address

Choose a Password (must be at least 6 characters)

Submit

The third part is the Member Registration Form as before. The new first part is the login form. The member simply enters their email address and password and presses 'Login'. The new second part is a 'Forgotten your Password?' facility. This time the member enters their email address and presses 'Send me my Password'.

The HTML for this is:

```
<html>
<head></head>
<body>
<h2>Erewhon Trading Services</h2>
<h3>Member Login Form</h3>
<form name="form3" method="post" action="login.php">
  <p>
   <input name="email" type="text" size="30" maxlength="30">
   Your email address</p>
  <p>
   <input name="password" type="text" size="12" maxlength="20">
   Your password</p>
   <input name="mode" type="hidden" value="log">
  <p>
   <input type="submit" name="Submit" value="Login">
  </p>
</form>
<hr>
<h3>Forgotten your Password?</h3>
<p>Enter your email address below and press the 'Send me my Password' button.</p>
<form name="form2" method="post" action="login.php">
  <p>
   <input name="email" type="text" size="30" maxlength="30">
  </p>
  <p>
   <input name="mode" type="hidden" value="pwd">
  </p>
  <p>
   <input type="submit" name="Submit" value="Send me my Password">
  </p>
</form>
<hr>
<h3>Member Registration Form</h3>
You must complete all the fields<p>
<FORM ACTION="registration.php" METHOD="POST" name="form1">
Forename <input name=forename type=text size=30 maxlength=30><p>
Surname  <input name=surname type=text size=30 maxlength=30><p>
Your Email Address <input name=email type=text size=30 maxlength=30><p>
Choose a Password <input name=password type=text size=20 maxlength=20> (must be at least 6
characters)
  <p>
   <input name="Submit" type="submit" value="Submit">
</form>
</body>
</html>
```

There are three forms. The third (the Member Registration Form) is as before. The first and second forms both have an action field of "login.php". These are distinguished by the first form having a hidden field with name "mode" and value "log". The second form also has a hidden field with name "mode", this time having value "pwd".

The outline structure of the login.php script is as follows.

```
<h2>Erewhon Trading Services</h2>
<?php
include "sql.php";
$mode=$_POST['mode'];
if ($mode=="log"){
  //process login
}
else if ($mode=="pwd"){
  // process send password request
}
?>
```

The PHP script needed to replace the comment 'process login' is given below.

```
1   $email=trim(strtolower($_POST['email'])); // from form
2   $password=trim($_POST['password']); // from form
3   if ($email!="" && $password!="") {
4a    $Link=mysql_connect($sys_dblocalhost,$sys_dbusername,$sys_dbpassword)
4b      OR die(mysql_error());
5     $query="SELECT * FROM members1 WHERE email='".$email
6       ."' AND password='".$password."' LIMIT 1";
7     $result = mysql_db_query($DBName,$query,$Link);
8     if (mysql_num_rows($result)>0){
9       $row=mysql_fetch_array($result);
10      print "<h3>Welcome ".$row[forename]." ".$row[surname]."</h3><p>\n";
11      if ($row[dateLast]=="") print "This is the first time you have logged in.<p>\n";
12      else print "You last logged in on ".$row[dateLast]."<p>";
13      print "Our range of products is listed below<p>\n";
14      $query="UPDATE members1 SET dateLast='".date("ymd")
15        ."',numLogs=numLogs+1 WHERE ind=".$row[ind];
16      $result = mysql_db_query($DBName,$query,$Link);
17    }
18    else{
19      print "We cannot find your email and/or password in our database.<p>\n";
20        print "Click <a href=start.htm>here</a> to go back and try again<p>\n";
21    }
22    mysql_close($Link);
23  } // if ($email!="" && $password!="")
24  else { //email or password is blank
25    print "Both your email address and your password must not be blank.<p>\n";
26    print "Click <a href=start.htm>here</a> to go back and try again<p>\n";
27  }
```

A script of this length may seem inscrutable but when it is broken down it should soon become apparent that writing PHP code to access MySQL database tables is very formulaic, with just a small number of basic ideas that are repeated each time.

It comprises the following steps.

1. Lines 1–2. Assign the email and password values sent from the form to variables. Before doing so we trim the value of email and convert it to lower case letters for purposes of matching against the stored value later. We also trim the value of password.

2. Lines 3 and 23–27. Check the email and password values are not null. If either of them is null, print an error message (lines 24–27). If both are non-null go on to lines 4 to 22.
3. Lines 4a, 4b and 22. Connect to the MySQL server and (later) close the connection.
4. Lines 5–6. Set up string $query to contain a MySQL SELECT command.
5. Line 7. Issue the command stored in $query.
6. Line 8 and 17–21. Test whether the SELECT command found any matching records. If it did, go on to lines 9–16. If not print an error message.
7. Line 9. Retrieve the values in the first row that was matched by the SELECT command and store them as array $row. (There can only be one row, so there is no need for a WHILE statement.)
8. Line 10. Print a message of welcome to the member.
9. Lines 11–12. Print a message that depends on whether or not the member has previously logged in.
10. Line 13. Print a message saying that the company's products will be listed below (we have omitted the listing to save space).
11. Lines 14–16. Issue a MySQL UPDATE command to enter today's date in the table and to increase the number of logins by one.

The function value date("ymd") in line 14 gives the current date in YYMMDD format.

It is worth noting how the number of logins is increased by one (lines 14–15). The UPDATE command issued takes the form

UPDATE members1 SET dateLast='YYMMDD',numLogs=numLogs+1 WHERE ind=index

The value to the right of numLogs= does not need any surrounding quotes as it is the value of the numLogs field (not the string constant 'numLogs') that is to be used and increased by one.

We next need to replace the comment 'process send password request' in the outline structure of the login.php script.

The PHP code for this is very similar to that for the login part of the script. The most interesting new part is the sending of the password by email, but at present we will just put a comment in line 16 instead of the code for that.

```
1  $email=trim(strtolower($_POST['email'])); // from form
2  if ($email==""){
3    print "Your email address must not be blank.<p>\n";
4    print "Click <a href=start.htm>here</a> to go back and try again<p>\n";
5  }
6  else { //email not blank
7a   $Link=mysql_connect($sys_dblocalhost,$sys_dbusername,$sys_dbpassword)
7b     OR die(mysql_error());
8    $query="SELECT forename,surname,password FROM members1 "
9      ."WHERE email='".$email."' LIMIT 1";
10   $result = mysql_db_query($DBName,$query,$Link);
11   mysql_close($Link);
12   if (mysql_num_row($result)>0){
13     $row=mysql_fetch_array($result);
14     print "Welcome ".$row[forename]." ".$row[surname]."<p>\n";
15     print "Your password has been sent to you by email.<br>\n";
16     // insert sending of email here
17   }
18   else {
19     print "We cannot find your email address in our database.<p>\n";
20     print "Click <a href=start.htm>here</a> to go back and try again<p>\n";
21   }
22 } // else email not blank
```

This script comprises the following steps.

1. Line 1. Assign the email value sent from the form to a variable. Before doing so we trim its value and convert it to lower case letters for purposes of matching against the stored value.
2. Lines 2–6 and 22. Check the email value is not null. If it is, print an error message (lines 3–4). If it is non-blank go on to lines 7 to 21.
3. Lines 7–8. Set up string $query to contain a MySQL SELECT command.
4. Lines 9–11. Connect to the MySQL server, issue the command stored in $query and close the connection.
5. Line 12 and 17–21. Test whether the SELECT command found any matching records. If it did, go on to lines 13–16. If not print an error message.
6. Line 13. Retrieve the values in the first row that was matched by the SELECT command and store them as array $row. (There can only be one row, so there is no need for a WHILE statement.)
7. Line 14–15. Print a message of welcome to the member and a message saying the password has been sent to the member by email.
8. Line 16. The code to generate an email goes here.

This just leaves the question of how to replace the comment 'insert sending of email here' in line 16. Sending email from a PHP script deserves a section of its own.

18.3 Sending Email from a PHP Script

PHP has a very useful facility for sending an email from inside a script. This simply involves calling the function *mail* with four strings as parameters, representing, from left to right:

- The Recipient (the To field)
- The Subject
- The Message
- Headers such as the From field and any copy (CC) or blind copy (BCC) fields.

The parameters can be string constants, e.g. "john.smith@smithcorp.com". However it is likely to happen quite often that the fields are extracted from a database and/or constructed by joining string constants and variables together and it is probably less error-prone to assign the values to four variables, say, $mailTo, $subject, $body and $headers and then to call the mail function by:

```
mail($mailTo,$subject,$body,$headers);
```

A typical (very simple) email might be:

```
$mailTo="john.smith@smithcorp.com";
$subject="Your message to me";
$headers="From: fred@fredcorp.org";
$body="Tuesday is OK for lunch";
mail($mailTo,$subject,$body,$headers);
```

If there is more than one recipient they can be separated by commas, e.g.

```
$mailTo="john.smith@smithcorp.com,mary.evans@evans-international.org.uk";
```

The $body value is likely to comprise more than one line. To get a line break character use the combination \r\n. To get a new paragraph with a blank line between it and the previous paragraph use \r\n\r\n. For example

```
$body="Dear John\r\n\r\nThanks for your message.\r\n\r\n"
."Tuesday is OK for lunch. I suggest we start about 1 p.m.\r\n\r\nFred";
```

(The string has been split into two parts joined by a dot to make it more readable on the printed page.)

Sending this message by

```
mail($mailTo,$subject,$body,$headers);
```

will then cause the following message to arrive in John Smith's inbox.

```
Dear John

Thanks for your message.

Tuesday is OK for lunch. I suggest we start about 1 p.m.

Fred
```

The headers field can include other information, including (open) copies and blind copies. For example:

```
$headers="From:fred@fredcorp.org\r\nCc: mary.smith@smithcorp.com\r\nBcc: john@xyzmail.org";
```

The Cc and Bcc fields are for (open) copies and blind copies, respectively. If there is more than one email address in either field they are separated by commas. Both Cc and Bcc can be spelt in any mixture of upper and lower case letters (CC, cc, BCC etc.). The fields must be separated by \r\n.

The mail function can be used on its own, e.g.

```
mail($mailTo,$subject,$body,$headers);
```

However it not only sends an email but returns a logical value true or false depending on whether or not the instruction succeeds. If we want to test whether or not the instruction succeeded we can do this in several ways, including these:

```
if (mail($mailTo,$subject,$body,$headers)) xxxxxxxx
```

```
if (mail($mailTo,$subject,$body,$headers)==1) xxxxxxxx
```

```
$res=mail($mailTo,$subject,$body,$headers);
if ($res==1) xxxxxxxx
```

We can now go back to give the code needed to replace the comment 'insert sending of email here' in line 16 of the script developed at the end of Sect. 18.2.

We can do it by:

```
$mailTo=$email;
$subject="Erewhon Trading Services: Your Password";
$headers="From: admin@erewhon.org";
$body="Erewhon Trading Company\r\n\r\nDear ".$row[forename]." ".$row[surname]
  ."\r\n\r\nYour password is ".$row[password]."\r\n\r\nA.Noone\r\nFor ETS";
mail($mailTo,$subject,$body,$headers);
```

(This does not include any test for whether or not the sending of the mail succeeded, but for simplicity we will ignore that complication here.)

Now if member Charles Dickens enters his email address in the 'Forgotten your Password?' form and presses the 'Send me my Password' button an email message is sent to him, apparently from admin@erewhon.org, and saying:

```
Erewhon Trading Services

Dear Charles Dickens

Your password is abc123xyz

A.Noone
For ETS
```

18.4 Generating Passwords

After Erewhon Trading Services new website had been live for a few months, its Sales Manager, Dr. Nemo, became very suspicious. Many of the members' names looked like works of fiction. Perhaps the email addresses were fictitious too? The names are not particularly important but the email addresses are, as in the future the company will want to use them for advertising mailshots. So Dr. Nemo decided on a change of policy: from now on members would not choose their own passwords - the registration system would generate them automatically and email them to members. Then there would be a very strong incentive for new members to enter valid addresses.

Modifying the registration web page to remove the password box is easy. We will concentrate on the registration.php file discussed earlier in this chapter.

If we start from that and remove all the lines referring to a password except the '$query=' statement (lines 40–41) we get the following. We have added comments at lines 37 and 45 to indicate where we need to add new code to generate the member's password and then to send it by email. We have also added print statements at lines 46–48 to welcome the new member and tell them that their password will be sent to them by email.

This gives the following as the first draft of a revised version of registration.php. The newly added parts are in **bold**.

```
1   <?php
2   include "sql.php";
3   print "<h3>Your Registration</h3>\n";
4
5   $forename = $_POST['forename']; // from form
6   $surname = $_POST['surname']; // from form
7   $email = $_POST['email']; // from form
8
9   $forename=trim($forename);
10  $surname=trim($surname);
11  $email=trim(strtolower($email));
12
13  $OK="yes";
14  if ($forename=="") {
15    print "Forename field must not be blank<br>\n";
16    $OK="no";
```

```
17   }
18   if ($surname=="") {
19     print "Surname field must not be blank<br>\n";
20     $OK="no";
21   }
22   if ($email=="") {
23     print "Email field must not be blank<br>\n";
24     $OK="no";
25   }
26   else {
27a    $Link=mysql_connect($sys_dblocalhost,$sys_dbusername,$sys_dbpassword)
27b      OR die(mysql_error());
28     $query="SELECT email FROM members1 WHERE email='".$email."' LIMIT 1";
29     $result = mysql_db_query($DBName,$query,$Link);
30     mysql_close($Link);
31     if (mysql_num_rows($result)>0) {
32       print "There is already a user registered with your email address!<br>\n";
33       $OK="no";
34     }
35   }
36   if ($OK=="yes"){
37     // Generate password as $password
38     $dateJoined=date("ymd");
39a    $Link=mysql_connect($sys_dblocalhost,$sys_dbusername,$sys_dbpassword)
39b      OR die(mysql_error());
40     $query="INSERT INTO members1 (forename,surname,email,password,dateJoined)"
41       ." VALUES ('".$forename."','".$surname."','".$email."','".$password."','".$dateJoined."')";
42     $result = mysql_db_query($DBName,$query,$Link);
43     mysql_close($Link);
44     if ($result==1) {
45       // Send email giving password
46       print "New member: ".$forename." ".$surname."<p>\n";
47       print "Your registration has been accepted - welcome to our club!<p>\n";
48       print "Your password has been sent to you by email<p>\n";
49     }
50     else print "It is not possible to register you at the present time - please try later<p>\n";
51   } //if
52   print "Click <a href=start.htm>here</a> to return to login/registration page<p>\n";
53   ?>
```

To replace the comment in line 37 we can make use of the PHP function 'rand' and a very useful user-defined function 'genRandomString'.

The function call

```
$x=genRandomString(4);
```

generates a sequence of four lower case letters and assigns it to variable $x. It is defined below. This function definition needs to be added to the PHP script and the most convenient place for that is probably just before the closing PHP tag. The user-defined function genRandomString uses the PHP system function *rand* which generates an integer in a specified range.

```
function genRandomString($numchars) {
  // generates a random string of $numchars lower case letters
  $characters = "abcdefghijklmnopqrstuvwxyz";
  $string ="";
  for ($i = 0; $i <$numchars; $i++) {
    $string.=$characters[rand(0,25)];
  }
  return $string;
} //genRandomString
```

The PHP statement

```
$password=genRandomString(4).rand(1001,9999);
```

will generate an eight character password, starting with four lower case letters and ending with four digits. Using the rand function with a range of values from 1001 to 9999 ensures that the value returned must always have four digits.

All that remains is to replace the comment at line 45 by the above statement followed by statements to send the password to the new member by email.

We can do this using the PHP mail function introduced in Sect. 18.3.

```
$mailTo=$email;
$subject="Erewhon Trading Services";
$headers="From: admin@erewhon.com";
$body="Erewhon Trading Services\r\n\r\nWe are pleased to welcome you "
  .$forename." ".$surname." as a new member.\r\n"
  ."Your password is ".$password."\r\n\r\nDr. A.Nemo, Sales Manager";
mail($mailTo,$subject,$body,$headers);
```

It would be better to make the final line

```
$res= mail($mailTo,$subject,$body,$headers);
```

and then test the value of $res to determine whether or not the sending of an email succeeded. If $res has the value 1 the email was successfully sent. Otherwise it was not sent and we would need to consider what to do next. However we will not pursue this further here.

If the email was successfully sent the new member will receive an email similar to this:

Erewhon Trading Services

We are pleased to welcome you Olivia Bryce as a new member.
Your password is pzwy3827

Dr. A.Nemo, Sales Manager

18.5 Managing the Members Table

We will now illustrate how ETS can access information about its members. We will create a web page control.php which initially displays

Erewhon Trading Services

Enter system password

Submit

Entering an invalid password and pressing Submit gives an error message.

Erewhon Trading Services

You are not authorised to access this page

Entering the correct password, which we will assume is erewhon1857, gives the welcome page

Erewhon Trading Services

Welcome system administrator!

(More here)

This last page will of course need to be embellished further.

A mixture of HTML and PHP to produce this effect would be as follows.

```
1  <html>
2  <head></head>
3  <body>
4  <h2>Erewhon Trading Services</h2>
5  <?php
6  $mode=$_GET['mode'];
7  if ($mode!="login"){
8  ?>
9    <form action="?mode=login" method="post" name="form1"><p>
10     <input name="pwd" type="text" size="20" maxlength="20">
11     Enter system password<p>
12     <input type="submit" name="Submit" value="Submit">
13   </form>
14 <?php
15 } else {
16   $pwd=$_POST['pwd'];
17   if (trim($pwd)=="erewhon1857") {
18     print "<b>Welcome system administrator!</b><p>\n";
19     print "(More here)";
20   }
21   else print "<b>You are not authorised to access this page</b>\n";
22 }
23 ?>
24 </body>
25 </html>
```

Here there are two PHP scripts (lines 5–8 and 14–23) with lines of HTML around them. It would instead be possible to put everything inside PHP tags <?php and ?> and then to place all the HTML inside PHP print statements, but there would be no benefit gained by doing that.

The action parameter in the <form> tag says action="?mode=login". This means that pressing Submit will send the value of pwd to the same page, with the parameter 'mode' set to login. It is as if the user clicks on a link to control.php?mode=login, with the important difference that the value of pwd is also transmitted.

When no 'mode' parameter has been included in the URL (i.e. the user just went to the page control.php) the login form is displayed. When mode=login is specified, the password is checked.

We will now concentrate on the code needed to replace line 19 which at present just prints the words '(More here)'.

Clearly there are many possibilities for the information that could be given to the system administrator, for example a listing of the complete contents of table members1. However we have seen this several times before. Instead we will concentrate on printing out some basic statistics:

- How many members are there?
- How many have not yet logged in?
- How many have joined in the last year?
- How many have joined in the last three months?

To do this we will use the MySQL function COUNT.

In a SELECT command COUNT(*) gives us the number of rows in a specified table. We can find the number of members using the command

SELECT COUNT(*) FROM members1
The COUNT(*) function can also be used with a WHERE clause, e.g.
SELECT COUNT(*) FROM members1 WHERE numLogs=0

However we will not use that approach here, as we wish to illustrate another way of using COUNT, which was discussed in Sect. 13.1.6. This is in conjunction with the MySQL IF function. To find the number of table entries for which numLogs is zero (i.e the number of members who have not yet logged in) we can use the command

SELECT COUNT(IF(numLogs=0,1, NULL)) FROM members1

This needs some explanation. If the condition 'numLogs=0' is satisfied the IF function returns the value 1. If it is not satisfied, a NULL value is returned. The COUNT function counts the number of 1 values and not the nulls, so the effect is to count the number of times that numLogs is zero.

We can combine the two SELECT COUNT commands as

SELECT COUNT(*), COUNT(IF(numLogs=0,1, NULL)) FROM members1

Before illustrating how to find the number of members that have joined in the last year or the last three months, it will help if we decide on today's date. Let us temporarily agree that it is April 30th 2020.

In our six digit YYMMDD format that is 200430. We can assign the date in that format to variable $today with the PHP function call

$today=date("ymd");

One year ago it was 190430. So in order to test whether a member joined in the last year we need to test whether the value of dateJoined is greater than '190430'. We can do this by the MySQL command

COUNT(IF(dateJoined>190430,1, NULL))

To test for those who joined in the last three months we need to test whether dateJoined is greater than '200130'. We can combine a test for this with the other three tests to give a SELECT command with the four tests separated by commas.

```
SELECT COUNT(*),
    COUNT(IF(numLogs=0,1, NULL)),
    COUNT(IF(dateJoined>190430,1, NULL)),
    COUNT(IF(dateJoined>200130,1, NULL))
FROM members1
```

Note this command is laid out on five lines simply in the interests of clarity. It can all be run together as a single line if preferred. In general if a string value appears on the right-hand side of a test it should be included in string quotes. However there is no need for quotes around the two dates above, as they are both numerical values. This argument still applies even though the dateJoined field was specified as CHAR(6). However it would also be valid to use string quotes, e.g. dateJoined>'190430'.

Executing the above SELECT command from a PHP script will produce a single row of output with four values, such as

267	59	46	22

The four values can be extracted from this and output in the usual way.

The problem with incorporating the SELECT command into a PHP script is of course that we cannot rely on it only being used on April 30th 2020! It has to be usable on any date and this introduces some complications. We will start by converting everything into PHP form except for the value 200130 which we will leave untouched (at present).

If the current date is held in our six-digit form in variable $today then the same month and day one year ago will be $today-10000. So a first (but incomplete) attempt at converting the SELECT command would be:

```
$today=date("ymd");
$query="SELECT COUNT(*),COUNT(IF(numLogs=0,1, NULL)),"
."COUNT(IF(dateJoined>$today-10000,1, NULL)),"
."COUNT(IF(dateJoined>200130,1, NULL)) "
."FROM members1";
```

The SELECT command held in $query is then issued as a MySQL command.

The difficult part is to find the value in six-digit date format that is three months less than $today. If the month is from April to December the answer is simply $today-300, e.g. 200430-300 is 200130. But what if the month is from January to March? It will help to examine some specific cases to derive a general rule.

- Three months before March (month 3) is December (month 12) the previous year.
- Three months before February (month 2) is November (month 11) the previous year.
- Three months before January (month 1) is October (month 10) the previous year.

From this we can see that the rule is

- If current month>3, to get three months earlier subtract 3 from month
- Otherwise, to get three months earlier add 9 to month and subtract 1 from the year.

So we need to start by extracting the month part from the six-digit date using the PHP substr function and then test the value of month. We then create a new variable $threeMonthsAgo with the value of $today reduced by (the numerical equivalent of) three months. We can do this by

```
$today=date("ymd");

$month=substr($today,2,2);
if ($month>3) {
  $threeMonthsAgo=$today-300;  // Subtract three months
}
else {
  $threeMonthsAgo=$today+900; // Add nine months
  $threeMonthsAgo=$threeMonthsAgo-10000; // Subtract one year
}
```

We can now complete the conversion of the SELECT command:

```
$query="SELECT COUNT(*),COUNT(IF(numLogs=0,1, NULL)),"
  ."COUNT(IF(dateJoined>".$today."-10000,1, NULL)),"
  ."COUNT(IF(dateJoined>".$threeMonthsAgo.",1, NULL)) "
  ."FROM members1";
```

Adding the lines necessary to issue the MySQL command and then extract the four values from the single row returned, gives the following as the complete replacement for the previous print "(More here)" statement.

```
$today=date("ymd");
$month=substr($today,2,2);
if ($month>3){
  $threeMonthsAgo=$today-300;
}
else {
  $threeMonthsAgo=$today+900; // Add nine months
  $threeMonthsAgo=$threeMonthsAgo-10000; // Subtract one year
}
$query="SELECT COUNT(*),COUNT(IF(numLogs=0,1, NULL)),"
  ."COUNT(IF(dateJoined>".$today."-10000,1, NULL)),"
  ."COUNT(IF(dateJoined>".$threeMonthsAgo.",1, NULL)) "
  ."FROM members1";
include("sql.php");
$Link=mysql_connect($sys_dblocalhost,$sys_dbusername,$sys_dbpassword)
  OR die(mysql_error());
$result = mysql_db_query($DBName,$query,$Link);
mysql_close($Link);
$row=mysql_fetch_array($result);
print "Number of members: ".$row[0]."<br>\n";
print "Number who have not yet logged in: ".$row[1]."<br>\n";
print "Members who have joined in the last year: ".$row[2]."<br>\n";
print "Members who have joined in the last three months: ".$row[3]."<p>\n";
```

With this much improved script the output given to the system administrator changes to this.

Erewhon Trading Services

Welcome system administrator!

Number of members: 267
Number who have not yet logged in: 59
Members who have joined in the last year: 46
Members who have joined in the last three months: 22

There are clearly many additional facilities that could be provided for the system administrator to use, but we will leave the affairs of Erewhon Trading Services here and bring this final chapter to a close.

Chapter Summary
This chapter gives a detailed example of the PHP and MySQL programming needed to maintain an organisation's membership list. Topics covered include user registration, logging into a password protected website, creating passwords, issuing password reminders, sending email from a PHP script and managing a table of members.

Practical Exercise 18
Write a PHP script that the ETS system administrator can use to send a promotional email to all members who joined in the last year but have not yet logged in.

Chapter 19
Appendices

19.1 PHP System Functions

19.1.1 Abbreviations Used in Specifications of Function Arguments

angleDeg: an angle measured in degrees
angleRad: an angle measured in radians
array: an array
int: an integer
num: a floating point number
posint: a positive or zero integer
str: a string
value: some value (used with function array only)
var: a variable

file: address of a file, relative to the current directory
dir: address of a directory, relative to the current directory
file/dir: address of either a file or a directory, relative to the current directory

(Note: absolute addresses such as /public_html/buildings/main.php are also permitted, but using these is not recommended.)

19.1.2 Terms Used in Specifications of Function Arguments

database name – see Chap. 15
filepointer (resource) – see Chap. 7
format specifier – see Chap. 6
link identifier (resource) – see Chap. 15
mode (for fopen) – see Chap. 7

M. Bramer, *Web Programming with PHP and MySQL*,
DOI 10.1007/978-3-319-22659-0_19

MySQL query – see Chap. 15
password – see Chap. 15
protection mode – see Chap. 7
result (resource) – see Chap. 15
servername – see Chap. 15
session variable – see Chap. 10
username – see Chap. 15

19.1.3 System Functions Applied to Numbers

Value Returned	Function	Meaning	Example
number	abs(num)	'Absolute value' of a number	abs(−8.4) and abs(8.4) are both 8.4
integer	ceil(num)	'Ceiling' of a number: the smallest integer greater than or equal to its value.	ceil(−6.4) is −6 ceil(9) is 9 ceil(8.2) is 9
number	exp(num)	Exponent function e to the power of the argument	exp(1) is 2.71828182846 exp(2.3) is 9.97418245481
integer	floor(num)	'Floor' of a number: the largest integer less than or equal to its value.	floor(−6.4) is −7 floor(9) is 9 floor(8.2) is 8
number	log(num)	Logarithm to base e (natural logarithm)	log(3.5) is 1.2527629685 log(1) is 0
number	log10(num)	Logarithm to base10	log10(10) is 1 log10(5.1) is 0.707570176098
number	max(num1,num2,…)	Returns the largest of the arguments. (Must be two or more arguments)	max(−6,8.3,27.4) is 27.4
number	min(num1,num2,…)	Returns the smallest of the arguments. (Must be two or more arguments)	min(−4.3,12.7,−8.9,0) is −8.9
number	pi()	Return value of pi to13 decimal places, i.e. 3.1415926535898 (Argument list must be empty)	
number	pow(num,num)	The first argument raised to the power of the second argument	pow(6,2) is 36 pow(8.3,2.4) is 160.615488049

(continued)

integer	rand(int,int)	Generates a pseudo-random integer between the first and the second arguments inclusive. (The second argument must be greater than the first)	rand(1,12) generates an integer from 1 to 12 inclusive
number	round(num)	The number is rounded to the nearest integer (if it is half-way between two integers, e.g. 8.5, it is rounded up)	round(4.4) is 4 round(4.5) is 5 round(4.6) is 5 round(–4.4) is –4 round(–4.5) is –4 round(–4.6) is –5
number	round(num, posint)	The number is rounded to the specified number of decimal places (if it is half-way between two values, it is rounded up). If the second argument is zero it means round to integer.	round(4.123456,3) is 4.123 round(4.12345,4) is 4.1235 round(–4.12345,4) is –4.1234
number	sqrt(num)	Square root of a non-negative number	sqrt(0.64) is 0.8

19.1.4 *Trigonometric Functions*

Value Returned	Function	Meaning
number	sin(angleRad)	Sine of the argument
number	cos(angleRad)	Cosine of the argument
number	tan(angleRad)	Tangent of the argument
angleRad	asin(num)	Inverse sine (arc sine) of the argument
angleRad	acos(num)	Inverse cosine (arc cosine) of the argument
angleRad	atan(num)	Inverse tangent (arc tangent) of the argument
number	sinh(angleRad)	Hyperbolic sine of the argument
number	cosh(angleRad)	Hyperbolic cosine of the argument
number	tanh(angleRad)	Hyperbolic tangent of the argument
angleRad	asinh(num)	Inverse hyperbolic sine of the argument
angleRad	acosh(num)	Inverse hyperbolic cosine of the argument
angleRad	atanh(num)	Inverse hyperbolic tangent of the argument
angleRad	deg2rad(angleDeg)	Convert a number of degrees to the equivalent in radians
angleDeg	rad2deg(angleRad)	Convert a number of radians to the equivalent in degrees

19.1.5 System Functions Applied to Arrays

Value Returned	Function	Meaning	Example
number	max(array)	Returns the largest of the array elements	If $arr contains the values 34.2, –8.2, 27.3, 0, 55.91 in that order, max($arr) is 55.91
number	min(array)	Returns the smallest of the array elements	If $arr contains the values 34.2, –8.2, 27.3, 0, 55.91 in that order, min($arr) is –8.2

19.1.6 System Functions Applied to Strings

Value Returned	Function	Meaning	Example
string	date(str)	Return a string giving some date and time information.	date("Y") returns the current year as a four-character string. See Chap. 5 for details.
string	ltrim(str)	'Left trim' a string, i.e. remove any spaces, tab characters, line feeds and carriage returns from the beginning	ltrim(" XYZ ") returns "XYZ "
string	rtrim(str)	'Right trim' a string, i.e. remove any spaces, tab characters, line feeds and carriage returns from the end	rtrim(" XYZ ") returns " XYZ"
string	str_replace(str1,str2, str3)	'String replace'. Replace every occurrence of str1 in str3 by str2.	str_replace("man","woman", "man, woman and child") returns "woman, wowoman and child"
integer	strlen(str)	Returns the number of characters in str (or zero for an empty string)	strlen("abc") returns 3
integer	strpos(str1,str2)	Returns the position of the first occurrence of str2 in str1*	strpos("xabcabdabe","ab") returns 1
string	strrev(str)	Returns a string with the characters from str in reverse order	strrev("hello") returns "olleh"
integer	strrpos(str1,str2)	Returns the position of the last occurrence of str2 in str1*	strrpos("xabcabdabe","ab") returns 7
string	strtolower(str)	Convert any upper case letters in str to lower case	strtolower("ABC99") returns "abc99"

(continued)

string	strtoupper(str)	Convert any lower case letters in str to upper case	strtoupper("abc99") returns "ABC99"
string	substr(str, int1,int2)	Substring. Returns the part of str that begins at the character numbered int1 and continues for a total of int2 characters	substr("elephant", 3, 4) returns "phan"
string	trim(str)	Trim a string, i.e. remove any spaces, tab characters, line feeds and carriage returns from the beginning and end	trim(" abc ") returns "abc"
string	ucfirst(str)	Returns a string identical to str except that if the first character is a lower case letter it is converted to upper case	ucfirst("john") returns "John"
string	ucwords(str)	Returns a string identical to str with the first character of each word capitalized. (A word is any string of characters that comes immediately after a space, tab, newline or carriage return.)	ucwords("john smith, 37") returns "John Smith, 37"
string	wordwrap(str1,int, str2)	Wraps string str to a column of int characters wide with lines separated by the break characters str2	wordwrap("The time has come the walrus said", 12," ") returns "The time has come the walrus said"

* Note: The characters in a string are numbered from left to right starting with zero, not one.

19.1.7 System Functions Applied to Variables

Value Returned	Function	Meaning	Example
logical	isset(var)	FALSE if the variable is uninitialized, otherwise TRUE	If $x has the value 8.3 $res=isset($x) returns TRUE

19.1.8 System Functions for Use with Arrays

Value Returned	Function	Meaning	Example
array	array(val1,val2,....)	Returns an array with the values of the arguments as the values of the array elements	$xyz=array(26,"dog",TRUE); creates an array $xyz with elements 0, 1 and 2 having the values 26, "dog" and TRUE, respectively

(continued)

logical*	arsort(array)	The same as asort. but values are sorted into descending order	arsort($myarray);
logical*	asort(array)	Similar to sort, but retains the key values.	asort($myarray); See Chap. 4
integer	count(array)	Number of elements in the array	$n=count($myarray);
array	explode(str1,str2)	Divides up str2 into parts separated by substring str1 and converts them into the elements of an array	explode("**","john**smith**37") returns an array with three elements: "john", "smith" and "37"
array	explode(str1,str2,int)	Divides up str2 into parts separated by substring str1 and converts them into the elements of an array. If int is positive, the returned array will contain a maximum of int elements with the last element containing the rest of str2. If int is negative, all components except the last -int are returned. If int is zero, it is treated as 1	explode("**","john**sm ith**37",2) returns an array with two elements: "john" and "smith**37"
string	implode(str,array)	Combines the elements of the array into a string separated by substring str	If the array $parts has three elements: "john", "smith" and "37" the function call implode(",",$parts) returns the string "john,smith,37"
logical*	krsort(array)	The same as ksort. but values are sorted into descending order	
logical*	ksort(array)	Similar to sort, but the sorting is in the order of the key values.	See Chap. 4
logical*	rsort(array)	The same as sort. but values are sorted into descending order	

(continued)

logical*	sort(array)	Sorts an array into ascending order of its values.	If array $alpha contains element 26, –4 and 7, the function will sort the elements of $alpha into the order –4,7,26.

*Returns the value TRUE if the sort succeeds or FALSE otherwise - but generally used as a 'stand-alone' function.

19.1.9 Formatted Print Functions

Value Returned	Function	Meaning	Example
integer*	printf(format specifier, var1, var2, …)	Prints a string in formatted form.	See Chap. 6
string	sprintf(format specifier, var1, var2, …)	As printf, but returns a string in formatted form.	See Chap. 6

* Returns an integer - the number of values output - but generally used 'standalone'.

19.1.10 System Functions for Use with Text Files

Value returned	Function	Meaning	Example
logical*	chdir(dir)	Change to new current directory (returns TRUE for success or FALSE for failure)	
logical*	chmod(file/dir,protection mode)	Change protection mode of specified file or directory (returns TRUE for success or FALSE for failure)	chmod($myfile,0666); (For protection modes see Chap. 7.)
string	dirname(file/dir)	Return path of file or directory	
logical	is_dir(file/dir)	Exists and is a directory	
logical	is_file(file/dir)	Exists and is a file	
logical	is_readable(file/dir)	File or directory exists and is readable	
logical	is_writable(file/dir)	File or directory exists and is writeable	
logical	is_writeable(file/dir)	File or directory exists and is writeable	
logical*	fclose(filepointer)	Closes file (returns TRUE for success or FALSE for failure)	fclose($fp1);

(continued)

array	file(file)	Convert text file to array	$arr1=file("../file1.txt");
logical	file_exists(file/dir)	File or directory exists	
integer	filesize(file)	Returns size of file in bytes (i.e. characters) of storage	$num=filesize("file1.txt");
resource (file pointer)	fopen(file,mode)	Opens a text file in a specified mode	$fp1=fopen("myfile.txt", "w"); (For modes see Chap. 7.)
integer*	fprintf(filepointer,format specifier, var1, var2, …)	Prints a string in formatted form. (Returns the number of bytes written.)	
string	fread(filepointer,int)	Read specified number of characters from a text file or up to the end of file, whichever is less	
integer*	fwrite(filepointer,str)	Write to specified text file (Returns number of bytes written or FALSE on error)	
string	getcwd()	Returns the absolute address of the working directory	
logical*	mkdir(dir,protection mode)	Create directory with specified name and path with specified protection mode (returns TRUE for success or FALSE for failure)	mkdir("mydir",0666);
array	pathinfo(file/dir)	Return associative array of components	
logical*	rename(file/dir, file/dir)	Rename file or a directory (including its contents). This can involve moving the file or directory to a different parent directory (returns TRUE for success or FALSE for failure)	
logical*	rmdir(dir)	Delete directory with specified name and path (returns TRUE for success or FALSE for failure)	
array	scandir(dir)	Return indexed array of directory contents (top-level only)	

* Function generally used in 'standalone' mode
file: address of a file, relative to the current directory
dir: address of a directory, relative to the current directory
file/dir: address of either a file or a directory, relative to the current directory
Note: absolute addresses such as /public_html/buildings/main.php are also permitted, but using these is not recommended.

19.1.11 Logical Functions

Value returned	Function	Meaning	Example
logical	is_numeric(str)	Value of str is numeric	$x=is_numeric("26.78");
logical	is_int(num)	Value of num is an integer	$z=is_num(34.2); Be careful when using this to test values entered in web forms - see Chap. 9

19.1.12 Functions Used with Sessions (see Chap. 10 for more details)

Value returned	Function	Meaning	Example
logical*	session_start()	Start a session. Returns true if it succeeds, else false.	session_start();
logical*	unset(session variable)	Unset a session variable. Returns true if it succeeds, else false.	unset($_ SESSION['var1']);
logical*	session_destroy()	Destroy a session. Returns true if it succeeds, else false.	session_destroy();

* Returns true for success or false for failure, but function is generally used in 'standalone' mode

19.1.13 Functions Used with Uploaded Files (see Chap. 10 for more details)

Value returned	Function	Meaning	Example
string	mime_content_type(file)	Returns the 'content type' of a file.	$s=mime_content_type ("xyz.pdf"); See Chap. 10 for details
logical*	move_uploaded_file(str1, str2)	Moves an uploaded file str1 to a new location str2. Returns true if it succeeds, else false.	move_uploaded_file("xyz.pdf", "docs/abc.pdf");

* Returns true for success or false for failure, but function is generally used in 'standalone' mode

19.1.14 Other System Functions

void**	die(str)	Terminate script immediately and display str as an error message	die('connection to server failed'); (Often used in conjunction with the mysql_connect function. See Chap. 15.)
logical*	mail(str1,str2,str3,str4)	Sends an email. (For the meanings of the four parameters see Sect. 18.3)	mail($mailTo,$subject,$body, $headers);
logical*	phpinfo()	Outputs detailed information about the configuration of PHP, including the version number	phpinfo();

* Returns true for success or false for failure, but function is generally used in 'standalone' mode
** Can only be used in 'standalone' mode

19.1.15 System Functions Used for Manipulating a MySQL Database

Value returned	Function	Meaning	Example
integer	mysql_affected_rows(link identifier)	Returns the number of rows affected by the last MySQL INSERT, UPDATE, REPLACE or DELETE command	$num=mysql_affected_rows ($Link);
logical*	mysql_close(link identifier)	Closes a previously opened database connection	mysql_close($Link);
resource (link identifier), if it succeeds, or false, if it fails	mysql_connect(servername, username,password)	Opens a connection to the MySQL Server (See Chap. 15.)	$Link=mysql_connect ($sys_dblocalhost, $sys_dbusername, $sys_dbpassword)

(continued)

Returns FALSE on error, otherwise TRUE for INSERT, UPDATE, DELETE queries and a 'result resource' for others	mysql_db_query (database name, MySQL query, link identifier)	Executes a query on a specified database.	$result=mysql_db_query ($DBName,$query,$Link);
string	mysql_error()	Returns the text of the error message from the last MySQL function executed	die(mysql_error());
array or FALSE (if no more rows)	mysql_fetch_array (result resource)	Returns an array of strings that corresponds to the fetched row, with both associative and numerical indices	$row=mysql_fetch_array ($result);
array or FALSE (if no more rows)	mysql_fetch_assoc (result resource)	Returns an associative array of strings that corresponds to the fetched row	$row=mysql_fetch_assoc ($result);
array or FALSE (if no more rows)	mysql_fetch_row (result resource)	Returns an indexed array of strings that corresponds to the fetched row	$row=mysql_fetch_row ($result);
integer or FALSE	mysql_insert_id()	Returns value of the auto_increment field that was generated by the last query. If the previous query did not generate an AUTO_ INCREMENT value it returns the value 0. If no MySQL connection was established it returns the value FALSE.	$n=mysql_insert_id();
int	mysql_num_fields (result resource)	Retrieves the number of fields returned in a result resource from a MySQL query	$num=mysql_num_fields ($result);
int	mysql_num_rows (result resource)	Retrieves the number of rows from a result set. (Only valid for statements like SELECT or SHOW that return an actual result set.)	$num=mysql_num_rows ($result);

* Returns true for success or false for failure, but function is generally used in 'standalone' mode

19.1.16 'Improved' System Functions Used for Manipulating a MySQL Database (See Sect. 15.8.)

resource (link identifier), if it succeeds, or false, if it fails	mysqli_ connect(servername, username, password, database name)	Opens a connection to the MySQL Server (See Sect. 15.8.)	$Link=mysqli_connect ($sys_dblocalhost, $sys_dbusername, $sys_dbpassword, $DBName);
Returns FALSE on error, otherwise TRUE for INSERT, UPDATE, DELETE queries and a 'result resource' for others	mysqli_query(link identifier, MySQL query)	Executes a query on the database specified in the associated mysqli_connect command (See Sect. 15.8.)	$result=mysqli_query ($Link, $query);
int	mysqli_field_count (link identifier)	Returns the number of columns for the most recent query on the connection represented by the 'link' parameter (See Sect. 15.8.)	$num=mysqli_field_ count ($Link);

19.2 PHP System Operators

19.2.1 Binary Arithmetic Operators Applied to Numerical Expressions

Operator	Example	Meaning
+	expr1+expr2	expr1 plus expr2
–	expr1 – expr2	expr1 minus expr2
*	expr1 * expr2	expr1 times expr2
/	expr1 / expr2	expr1 divided by expr2
%	expr1 % expr2	The remainder when expr1 is divided by expr2. (% is called the 'modulus operator'.)

19.2.2 *Unary Arithmetic Operators Applied to Numbers*

Operator	Example	Meaning
+	+$x +96.3	The value of the argument
–	–$y –8.4	The negative of the value of the argument

19.2.3 *System Operators Applied to Strings*

Operator	Example	Meaning
. [dot]	$x."dog"	The string formed by joining the string $x and the string "dog". This is called string concatenation.

19.2.4 *Relational Operators*

Operator	Example	Meaning
==	exp1==exp2	The two expressions are equal
!=	exp1!=exp2	The two expressions are not equal
>	exp1>exp2	exp1 is greater than exp2
>=	exp1>=exp2	exp1 is greater than or equal to exp2
<	exp1<exp2	exp1 is less than exp2
<=	exp1<=exp2	exp1 is less than or equal to exp2

19.2.5 *Logical Operators*

<table>
<tr><th>Operator</th><th>Name</th><th>Example</th><th>Meaning</th></tr>
<tr><td>&&</td><td>Logical And</td><td>val1 && val2</td><td>TRUE if val1 and val2 are both TRUE, otherwise FALSE</td></tr>
<tr><td>||</td><td>Logical Or</td><td>val1 || val2</td><td>TRUE if either val1 or val2 is TRUE (or both), otherwise FALSE</td></tr>
<tr><td>XOR</td><td>Logical XOR (exclusive OR)</td><td>val1 XOR val2</td><td>TRUE if either val1 or val2 is TRUE, but not both, otherwise it is FALSE</td></tr>
<tr><td>!</td><td>Logical Not</td><td>!val1</td><td>TRUE if val1 is FALSE, otherwise FALSE</td></tr>
</table>

19.2.6 Operators Giving a Simplified Notation for Assignment

	Is an abbreviation for this assignment statement
$x++;	$x=$x+1;
$x−−;	$x=$x−1;
$x+= $y;	$x=$x+$y;
$x−= $y;	$x=$x−$y;
$x*= $y;	$x=$x*$y;
$x/= $y;	$x=$x/$y;
$x%= $y;	$x=$x%$y;

Here $y can be replaced by any arithmetic expression.

19.2.7 Operators Giving a Simplified Notation for Joining Strings

	Is an abbreviation for this assignment statement
$x.=$y;	$x=$x.$y;

19.3 Summary of MySQL Commands

Here is a summary of all the MySQL commands used in this book. In all cases *tablename* can optionally be preceded by the name of a database followed by a dot.

ALTER TABLE *tablename*	ADD *fieldname field-specification* AFTER *fieldname* May optionally be followed by PRIMARY KEY	Add a field to a table after a specified column
ALTER TABLE *tablename*	ADD *fieldname field-specification* FIRST May optionally be followed by PRIMARY KEY	Add a field to a table as the first column
ALTER TABLE *tablename*	ADD *fieldname field-specification* May optionally be followed by PRIMARY KEY	Add a field to a table as the last column

(continued)

ALTER TABLE *tablename*	ADD PRIMARY KEY (*fieldname*)	To set a primary key for a table, when none already set. May also be a sequence of field names separated by commas.
ALTER TABLE *tablename*	ALTER *fieldname* DROP DEFAULT	Cancel the default value of a field
ALTER TABLE *tablename*	ALTER *fieldname* SET DEFAULT *value*	Set the default value of a field
ALTER TABLE *tablename*	AUTO_INCREMENT = *unsigned integer*	Changes the starting value of an auto_increment field (or the next value to be used if some records have already been created)
ALTER TABLE *tablename*	CHANGE *oldfieldname newfieldname field-specification*	Change a field name and/or specification in a table
ALTER TABLE *tablename*	DROP *fieldname1* ,DROP *fieldname2* ,DROP *fieldname3* *etc.* [DROP may optionally be followed by COLUMN each time]	Delete one or more fields from a table
ALTER TABLE *tablename*	DROP PRIMARY KEY	To remove an existing primary key from a table
ALTER TABLE *tablename*	MODIFY *fieldname field-specification*	Change a field specification in a table
ALTER TABLE *tablename*	RENAME TO *newtablename*	Change the name of a table
CREATE DATABASE *databasename*		Create an empty database with the given name
CREATE TABLE *tablename* (*specification*)		This is discussed in detail in Chap. 14
CREATE TABLE *tablename*	LIKE *oldtablename*	Create new table with same structure and field specifications as an existing one
DELETE FROM *tablename*	WHERE *condition* [optionally followed by LIMIT *number*]	Delete one or more records from a table. See Sect. 12.8 for more information about conditions

(continued)

DESCRIBE *tablename*		Equivalent to SHOW FIELDS FROM *tablename*
DROP DATABASE *databasename*		Delete a database
DROP TABLE *tablename*		Delete a table
INSERT INTO *tablename*	*(fieldnames separated by commas)* VALUES (*field values, separated by commas)*	Create a new record. The field values must be in the same order as the field names.
INSERT INTO *table2*	SELECT * FROM *table1*	Copy contents of table1 into table2
RENAME TABLE *tablename*	TO *newtablename*	Rename a table
REPLACE INTO *tablename*	(same as for INSERT INTO)	Same as INSERT INTO except that if an existing row has the same primary key value as a new row to be inserted, the existing row is deleted
SELECT * FROM *table1*	INNER JOIN *table2* ON *table1.field1=table2.field2* Can be followed by an optional ORDER BY clause. INNER JOIN can be replaced by LEFT OUTER JOIN or RIGHT OUTER JOIN	Combine tables (see Sect. 13.3)
SELECT * FROM *tablename*	WHERE condition ORDER BY fieldnames separated by commas [optional ASC or DESC after each one] LIMIT number Instead of a fieldname in the ORDER BY clause there can be the word FIELD followed by a fieldname and a list of values for the field, all separated by commas and enclosed in parentheses. See Sect. 13.1.1. Instead of any fieldname in the WHERE clause there can be a function (such as concat, greatest, least, min, max and avg) applied to one or more fieldnames. The WHERE, ORDER BY and LIMIT clauses are all optional. The LIMIT clause can also be LIMIT offset,number	Returns the values of all fields in some or all of the records in the table, possibly in a specified order and with a limit to the number returned
SELECT *fields separated by commas* FROM *tablename*	(As for SELECT * FROM *tablename)*	(As for SELECT * FROM *tablename)*

(continued)

SELECT COUNT(*) FROM *tablename*		Returns the number of records in the table
SELECT COUNT (*fieldname*) FROM *tablename*		Returns the number of records in the table where the field has a non-null value
SELECT COUNT (IF (*condition ,truevalue,falsevalue*)) FROM *tablename*		Returns the number of records in the table where a specified condition is met (see Sect. 13.1.6)
SELECT DISTINCT *fieldname* FROM *tablename*	May also be a sequence of field names, separated by commas.	Finds only the distinct values taken by a field or a combination of fields
SHOW COLUMNS FROM *tablename*		Equivalent to SHOW FIELDS FROM *tablename*
SHOW CREATE TABLE *tablename*		Gives a listing of a CREATE TABLE command that could have been used to create the table
SHOW DATABASES		Display a list of all the databases available to the user
SHOW FIELDS FROM *databasename.tablename*		Display information about the fields in the specified table in the specified database
SHOW FIELDS FROM *tablename*		Display information about the fields in the specified table in the current database
SHOW TABLES		Display a list of the tables in the currently selected database
SHOW TABLES IN *database*		Display a list of the tables in the specified database
SHOW VARIABLES		Display the values of a large number of system variables
SHOW VARIABLES	LIKE "version"	Display the version of MySQL that you are using

(continued)

TRUNCATE *tablename*		Empty a table, but retain structure (field names, field types etc.)
UPDATE *tablename*	SET *field=value* WHERE *condition* [optionally followed by LIMIT *number*] Can also be a succession of *field=value* pairs, separated by commas. *value* can also be a SELECT command enclosed in parentheses (see Sect. 13.2)	Change the value of one or more fields in one or more records in the specified table. If the WHERE clause and the LIMIT clause are omitted all the records in the table are changed.
USE *databasename*		Make *databasename* the current database

19.4 MySQL Operators and Functions

Expressions can be used at a number of places in MySQL statements, such as in the ORDER BY clause of SELECT commands, in the WHERE clause of a SELECT, DELETE or UPDATE command, or in the SET clause of an UPDATE command. There are many functions and operators available in MySQL and they can be used in all these kinds of expression. Here are examples of some of the most valuable uses.

19.4.1 Simple Conditions in WHERE Clauses

Each simple condition is of the form *field operator value*. These operators are called *comparison operators*. They return a result that is either true or false. The main ones are given in this table.

=	is equal to
!=	does not equal
<>	does not equal
<	is less than
<=	is less than or equal to
>	is greater than
>=	is greater than or equal to

Conditions can also make use of *arithmetic operators* including + – * and /.

Functions can also be used in conditions, including GREATEST and LEAST. These take the values of two or more numerical fields and return the largest and the smallest values, respectively.

Arithmetic operators and functions can appear on either side of the comparison operator. For example if i1, i2, i3, i4 and i5 are all integer fields, possible conditions include

WHERE i1 + i2 < i3–i4*i5
WHERE GREATEST(i1,i2,i3) > 99
WHERE LEAST(i2,i5) > LEAST(i1,i3,i4).

A further operator that can be used with either numerical or character fields is BETWEEN. Unlike the other operators this one takes two values after the operator, joined by AND. For example:

SELECT * FROM mytable1 WHERE yearBorn BETWEEN 1982 AND 2000

19.4.2 Complex Conditions in WHERE Clauses

Complex conditions can be constructed from simple conditions using the logical operators AND, OR and NOT. Parentheses can also be used to avoid ambiguity and to construct more complex conditions. For example:

SELECT * FROM mytable1 WHERE sex='F' AND (yearBorn>1980 OR numchild!=99) AND NOT (occupation='doctor' OR occupation='engineer')

19.4.3 Other Functions in SELECT Commands

Other functions available include the CONCAT function, which takes two or more character fields or string constants such as '...' and ' ' (space) and joins them together. For example

SELECT CONCAT(Forename,' ',Surname), sex FROM mytable1 WHERE numchild>1

A field used in a SELECT command can be replaced by a function applied to the values of the field. Functions MAX, MIN and ARG give the largest, smallest and average values of a field, respectively. For example:

SELECT MIN(yearBorn),MAX(yearBorn),MIN(Surname),MAX(Surname), MIN(numchild), MAX(numchild), AVG(numchild) FROM mytable1

19.4.4 UPDATE Commands

Functions can also be used with the SET clause in an UPDATE command, for example:

UPDATE mytable1 SET extra=CONCAT(Forename,' ',Surname)

19.5 Summary of Case-Sensitivity Rules: PHP and MySQL

19.5.1 PHP

	Case-Sensitive?
PHP Keywords IF, PRINT, ELSE etc.	No
Relational and logical operators (XOR etc.)	No
E-notation for numbers 12.3E7 etc.	No
Variable and array names*	Yes
String constants	Yes
System Function Names**	No
User-defined Function Names**	No
Logical constants (TRUE, FALSE)	No
System arrays: $_GET, $_POST, $_REQUEST, $_SESSION and $_FILES	Yes
System constants M_PI, PHP_EOL	Yes

*Starts with $ then a sequence of letters, underscores and digits. The character after $ must not be a digit.
** The same as variable names but with no initial $ sign

19.5.2 MySQL

Database and table names	Depends on the operating system used by the server that holds the database. We recommend you to assume that *both* are case sensitive and act accordingly.
Field Names	No
Field Values	Yes
MySQL keywords (such as INSERT INTO and UPDATE)	No

19.5.3 Other

Variables in an extended URL (e.g. register.php?x=yes)	Yes

19.6 Principal HTML Tags

This list gives a brief description of the principal HTML tags used in this book. It is not intended as a comprehensive list.

<!DOCTYPE>	The 'doctype declaration'. Should be the first line of an HTML page, above the <html> tag.
<html> </html>	Tags to mark start and end of an HTML page (after the doctype declaration). Between them there should be a head followed by a body.
<head> </head>	Start and end of the head of an HTML page.
<body> </body>	Start and end of the body of an HTML page.
Tags used inside the head of an HTML page	
<title> </title>	Start and end of a title (an optional part of the head of an HTML page).
<meta>	May be used in the head of an HTML page to provide metadata about the page.
<link>	May be used in the head of an HTML page to link to a style sheet.
Tags used inside the body of an HTML page	
<h1> </h1>	Start and end a level 1 heading.
<h2> </h2>	Start and end a level 2 heading.
<h3> </h3>	Start and end a level 3 heading.
	Start and end bold font.
	Start and end italic.
-	Start and end underlining.
<font> </font>	Start and end font specification.
<p> </p>	Start and end a paragraph.
 	Line break.
<hr>	Horizontal rule.
<img>	Used to place an image in an HTML page.
<ol> </ol>	Start and end an ordered list (i.e. one with numbered items)
<ul> </ul>	Start and end an unordered list (i.e. one with items prefixed by 'bullets')
<li> </li>	Start and end an item in an ordered or unordered list
<a href> </a>	Placed before and after the desination of a link in an HTML page. (Strictly an <a> tag with an href attribute.)
<form> </form>	Start and end of a form (forms are the topic of Chap. 9)
<table> </table>	Start and end of a table definition
<tr> </tr>	Start and end of a row definition within a table
<td> </td>	Start and end of a cell (column) definition within a row of a table

19.7 Specimen Solutions to Practical Exercises

19.7.1 Practical Exercise 2

(1) $happy-BIRTHDAY is invalid. Variable names must not include hyphens.
$27_Today is invalid. Variable names must not have a digit immediately after the $ sign.
john is invalid. Variable names must begin with a $ sign.
$abc!_*xyz is invalid. Variable names must not include special characters such as ! and *.

(2) (a) I live at 26 Queen\'s Road
(b) Nothing. The 'unescaped' single quote in O'Brien will cause the script to terminate with an error message.
(c) This is a backslash\
(d) I live at 26 Queen\'s Road
(e) My name is John O'Brien
(f) This is a backslash\
(g) He said "Hello" to me
(h) the value of the variable is 296.4
(i) the value of the variable is
[$xyzpounds is an uninitialised variable]
(j) a strange string abc$xyz 296.4 here is a backslash\

(3) Some possibilities are −4.87316E2, −4.87316e2, −4873.16E−1 and −4873.16e−1.

(4) None of the names beginning with a $sign are valid. Of the remainder, only happy-BIRTHDAY is invalid as function names (like variable names) must not include hyphens.

19.7.2 Practical Exercise 3

(1) 0.4
(2) The arithmetic expression $x+$y needs to be enclosed in parentheses.
(3) TRUE
Note: the logical expression includes an XOR operator, so when it is evaluated it needs to be enclosed by an outer pair of parentheses (see Sect. 3.2.8). This applies whether the value is found using an assignment such as this

```
$res=($x && $y XOR ($x||$y));
print "The value is ".$res;
```

or a Print statement such as this:

```
print "The value is ";
print ($x && $y XOR ($x||$y));
```

(4)

```
for ($i=2;$i<=40;$i+=2) print $i." squared is ".$i*$i."<br>";
```

(5) (a)

```
$i=0;
$found="no";
while ($i<count($numbers) && $found=="no"){
  if ($numbers[$i]==$val) $found="yes"; else $i++;
}

if ($found=="yes") print "Value ".$val." is at position ".$i."<br>";
else print "Value ".$val." is not in the array<br>";
```

(b)

```
$i=0;
$found="no";
do {
  if ($numbers[$i]==$val) $found="yes"; else $i++;
} while ($i<count($numbers) && $found=="no");

if ($found=="yes") print "Value ".$val." is at position ".$i."<br>";
else print "Value ".$val." is not in the array<br>";
```

(6)

```
if ($month=="February") print "28 or 29 days";
else if (($month=="April") || ($month=="June") || ($month=="September")
  || ($month=="November")) print "30 days";
else print "31 days";
```

19.7.3 Practical Exercise 4

(1)

```
for ($i=0;$i<count($marks);$i++){
  $sum=0;
  for ($j=0;$j<=2;$j++){
    $sum+=$marks[$i]{$j};
  }
  print "Total mark for student ".$i." is ".$sum."<br>";
}
```

(2) We can test the effect of using sort by the script

```
$monthnames = array (
'01' => 'January',
'02' => 'February',
'03' => 'March',
'04' => 'April',
'05' => 'May',
'06' => 'June',
'07' => 'July',
'08' => 'August',
'09' => 'September',
'10' => 'October',
'11' => 'November',
'12' => 'December');

sort($monthnames);
foreach($monthnames as $k=>$v) print $k."=>".$v."<br>";
```

which gives the output

```
0=>April
1=>August
2=>December
3=>February
4=>January
5=>July
6=>June
7=>March
8=>May
9=>November
10=>October
11=>September
```

The month names have been sorted into alphabetical order, which is not likely to be helpful.

If instead we use the script

```
$monthnames = array (
'01' => 'January',
'02' => 'February',
'03' => 'March',
'04' => 'April',
'05' => 'May',
'06' => 'June',
'07' => 'July',
'08' => 'August',
'09' => 'September',
'10' => 'October',
'11' => 'November',
'12' => 'December');

ksort($monthnames);
foreach($monthnames as $k=>$v) print $k."=>".$v."<br>";
```

The output is

```
01=>January
02=>February
03=>March
04=>April
05=>May
06=>June
07=>July
08=>August
09=>September
10=>October
11=>November
12=>December
```

The array has been sorted in order of the 'keys', which are the index values 01, 02 etc., and thus retains its original ordering.

(3) The script below

```
$s="malcolm,johnson,male,1997,associate,2012,married,2,melbourne";

$arr=explode(",",$s);
for ($i=1;$i<count($arr);$i++){
  $new[$i-1]=$arr[$i];
}
$newval=implode("**",$new);
print "The original string was ".$s."<br>";
print "The new string is ".$newval."<br>";
```

produces the output

```
The original string was malcolm,johnson,male,1997,associate,2012,married,2,melbourne
The new string is johnson**male**1997**associate**2012**married**2**melbourne
```

19.7.4 Practical Exercise 5

(1)

```
$newstring=str_replace("a","**",$oldstring);
```

(2)

```
$newname=ucfirst(ltrim(strtolower($name)));
```

(3)

```
$arr=explode("**",$date);
$arr[1]="December";
$newdate=implode("**",$arr);
```

(4)

```
print date("d/m/Y");
```

19.7.5 Practical Exercise 6

A possible solution is:

```
printf("format1:   %.2f   <br>format2:   %.6e   <br>format3:   %'*12f   <br>end   of
test<br>",$x,$x,$x);
```

Assuming that $x has value 62.917, the output will be:

```
format1: 62.92
format2: 6.291700e+1
format3: ***62.917000
end of test
```

19.7.6 Practical Exercise 7

```
<?php
$arr=scandir($path); // must not end with /
for ($i=2;$i<count($arr);$i++){
  $next=$path."/".$arr[$i];
  if (is_dir($next)) print "<b>".$next."</b>";
  else print $next;
  if (is_readable($next)) print " R";
  if (is_writeable($next)) print " W";
  print "<br>";
} // for
?>
```

19.7.7 Practical Exercise 8

(1)

```
function hypo($a,$b){
return sqrt($a*$a+$b*$b);
} // hypo
```

(2)

```
function printArray($arr){
for ($i=0;$i<count($arr);$i++){
  for ($j=0;$j<count($arr[$i]);$j++) print $arr[$i][$j]." ";
  print "<br>";
} // for i
} // printArray
```

(3)

```
function printArray2($arr){
print "<table border=1>";
for ($i=0;$i<count($arr);$i++){
  print "<tr>";
  for ($j=0;$j<count($arr[$i]);$j++) print "<td>".$arr[$i][$j]."</td>";
  print "</tr>";
} // for i
print "</table>";
} // printArray2
```

(4) The HTML <img> tag is described in Sect.5.4.

```
function displayImage($imgfile,$width=150,$height=200){
print "<img src=\"".$imgfile."\" width=".$width." height=".$height.">\n";
} //displayImage
```

(5)

```
function setArray(&$arr,$val=0){
for ($i=0;$i<count($arr);$i++){
  for ($j=0;$j<count($arr[$i]);$j++) $arr[$i][$j]=$val;
} // for i
} // setArray
```

19.7.8 Practical Exercise 9

(1) Webform in Sect. 9.2.

```
<?php
include "wfutils.php";
?>
<p><strong>Enter your details below</strong></p>
<form name="form1" method="post" action="mydir/destin1.php">
Forename <?php wftext("forename",20,50,"");?> *
 Surname <?php wftext("surname",20,50,"");?>
 * </p><p>Address <?php wftextarea("address",2,24,"");?>
 *</p><p>Age Group
<?php
$pairs=array("under        20"=>"group1","20        to        40"=>"group2","40        to
60"=>"group3","60+"=>"group4");
wfbuttons("agegroup",$pairs,"","   ");
?>
<p> Nationality <?php wfselectlist("nationality","countries.txt");?>
<p>I agree to the terms and conditions
<?php wfcheckbox("tsandcs","terms","no");?>
</p><p>
<?php wfsubmitreset();?>
</form>
</p><p>Press the Submit button to send us your form<p>
```

Webform in Sect. 9.4.

```
<?php
include "wfutils.php";
?>
<b>Enter your details below</b><p>
<form   name="form2"   method="post"   action="destin1.php"   enctype="multipart/form-
data">
Student Number
<?php wftext("snumber",6,6,"");?>
 *<p>
Password
<?php wfpassword("spassword",20,20,"");?>
 * </p>
<?php wfhidden("projectRef","COMP102/3");?>
Upload your project report (maximum 1MB)<br>
<?php wfhidden("MAX_FILE_SIZE","1048576");?>
<input type="file" name="report"> * </p>
<p></p>
<input type="submit" name="Submit" value="Submit">
</form>
```

The file countries.txt contains

```
British*GB
French*FR
United States*US
Chinese*CN
```

(2) The extensions need to be changed to php.

19.7.9 Practical Exercise 10

```
<?php
$snumber=trim($_POST['snumber']);
$spassword=trim($_POST['spassword']);
$projectRef=$_POST['projectRef'];

if ($snumber=="" || $spassword=="") print "Error - student number or password is blank";
else if ($_FILES['report']['name']=="") print "Error - no file uploaded";
else if ($_FILES['report']['type']!="application/pdf") print "Error - uploaded file is not a PDF";
else {
  $filename=$projectRef."_".$snumber.".pdf";
  if (move_uploaded_file($_FILES['report']['tmp_name'], "projects/".$filename))
    print "The file has been uploaded with the name ".$filename;
  else print "Sorry, there was an error uploading your file";
} // else
?>
```

19.7.10 Practical Exercise 11

A suitable script is given below.

The number of occurrences of each incorrect password are accumulated in associative array $errors. (All passwords are forced into lower case first.) The array is sorted using the ksort function before the invalid passwords and the frequency of each one are output.

```
<?php
$arr=file("login.txt");

for ($i=0;$i<count($arr);$i++){
  $next=trim($arr[$i]);
  $parts=explode(",",$next);
  if ($parts[3]=="failed"){
    $wrongpass=strtolower($parts[2]);
    $errors[$wrongpass]++;
  } //if
} //for

print "<b>Breakdown of Invalid Accesses</b><p>";
ksort($errors);
foreach($errors as $k=>$v)
  print $k." (".$v.")<br>";
?>
```

Running this script gives a tabulation such as the following.

```
Breakdown of Invalid Accesses

erewhon (23)
nemo (12)
password (35)
password1 (27)
secret (14)
xyz (7)
```

19.7.11 Practical Exercise 12

(1) The invalid ones are acd-def (hyphens are not permitted in unquoted names) father's_name (apostrophes are not permitted in unquoted names)
(2) REPLACE INTO mytable1 (refnum,Forename,Surname,sex,occupation, cityBorn,yearBorn)VALUES (1927,'Bryony','McTavish','F','doctor','New York', 1988)
(3) (a) DELETE FROM mytable1 WHERE Surname='Johnson'
    (b) ALTER TABLE mytable1 ADD variance INTEGER AFTER yearBorn followed by
    UPDATE mytable1 SET variance=yearBorn-1960

19.7.12 Practical Exercise 13

(1) (a) SELECT * FROM mytable1 ORDER BY yearBorn LIMIT 1
    (b) SELECT DISTINCT cityBorn FROM mytable1 WHERE sex='F'

(c) ALTER TABLE mytable1 DROP PRIMARY KEY followed by
ALTER TABLE mytable1 ADD PRIMARY KEY (cityBorn,yearBorn)

(2) There is no guarantee that the combination of cityBorn and yearBorn will be unique.

(3) SELECT DISTINCT AnimalType FROM mytable4 INNER JOIN mytable5 ON mytable4.Name=mytable5.Name2 WHERE Canfly='yes' ORDER BY Name (The results are of course bird and insect, in that order.)

19.7.13 Practical Exercise 14

Possible solutions are as follows

```
CREATE TABLE mytable1 (
refnum int(4) NOT NULL default '0',
Forename varchar(30) NOT NULL default '',
Surname varchar(30) NOT NULL default '',
sex enum('M','F') default NULL,
occupation varchar(30) default NULL,
cityBorn varchar(30) NOT NULL default '',
yearBorn year(4) NOT NULL default '0000',
numchild int(11) default NULL,
PRIMARY KEY (refnum)
)

CREATE TABLE mytable4 (
ind int(11) NOT NULL auto_increment,
Name varchar(20) default NULL,
Legs int(11) default NULL,
Wings int(11) default NULL,
Canfly enum('yes','no') default NULL,
PRIMARY KEY (ind)
)

CREATE TABLE mytable5 (
Name2 varchar(20) default NULL,
AnimalType varchar(20) default NULL
)
```

19.7.14 Practical Exercise 15

(1) A suitable script is given below.

```
<?php
include "sql.php";

$Link=mysql_connect($sys_dblocalhost,$sys_dbusername,$sys_dbpassword)
  OR die(mysql_error());
$query="SELECT Forename,Surname,occupation,yearBorn FROM mytable1 "
."WHERE sex='F' AND numchild>=2 ORDER BY yearBorn DESC";

$result = mysql_db_query($DBName,$query,$Link);
mysql_close($Link);

if ($result=="") print "SELECT failed<br>The command was: ".$query."<p>\n";
else {
  // SELECT succeeded
  while ($row=mysql_fetch_array($result)){
    print $row[Forename]." ".$row[Surname]
      ." ".$row[occupation]." ".$row[yearBorn]."<br>";
  } //while
} //else
?>
```

The output from running this script is as follows.

```
Ann Williams doctor 1997
Mary Johnson technician 1989
Frances Bryce translator 1980
Jane Wilson unemployed 1972
```

(2) This is a suitable script.

```
<?php
include "sql.php";

$Link=mysql_connect($sys_dblocalhost,$sys_dbusername,$sys_dbpassword)
  OR die(mysql_error());
$query="DELETE FROM mytable1 WHERE sex='F' AND yearBorn<1982";
$result = mysql_db_query($DBName,$query,$Link);
print "Number of women deleted: ".mysql_affected_rows($Link)."<p>";

$query="DELETE FROM mytable1 WHERE sex='M' AND yearBorn<1982";
$result = mysql_db_query($DBName,$query,$Link);
print "Number of men deleted: ".mysql_affected_rows($Link)."<p>";
mysql_close($Link);
?>
```

The output from running it is given below.

```
Number of women deleted: 3

Number of men deleted: 1
```

19.7.15 *Practical Exercise 16*

(1) A possible solution is given below.

```
1 <?php
2 include "sql.php";
3 $Link=mysql_connect($sys_dblocalhost,$sys_dbusername,$sys_dbpassword)
4   OR die(mysql_error());
5 $query="SELECT * FROM mytable1 ORDER BY refnum";
6 $result = mysql_db_query($DBName,$query,$Link);
7 mysql_close($Link);
8 $FP1=fopen("mytable1_backup.txt",'w');
9 while ($row=mysql_fetch_row($result)){
10   $nextline="";
11   for ($i=0;$i<count($row);$i++){
12     if ($i>0) $nextline.=",";
13     $nextline.="'".$row[$i]."'";
14   }
15   fwrite($FP1,$nextline."\r\n");
16 } //while
17 fclose($FP1);
18 print "Backup to file mytable1_backup.txt completed<p>\n";
19 ?>
```

Variable $nextline is (partly) generated by a 'for' loop in lines 12-14 for the elements of array $row. (If additional fields are added to the table later this will not need to be changed.) Each element of array $row is enclosed in quotes (line 13) and all but the first is preceded by a comma (line 12).

Note that line 9 is
while ($row=mysql_fetch_row($result)){
not
while ($row=mysql_fetch_array($result)){

This is important for line 11
for ($i=0;$i<count($row);$i++){
to work correctly. Function mysql_fetch_array generates both an associative and a numerical index and for this reason the value of count($row) will be 16 not the expected 8.
With this script the content of file mytable1_backup.txt will be the following.

```
'634','James','Robinson','M','none','Geneva','2007','0'
'1851','Martin','Johnson','M','butcher','London','1970','99'
'1927','Bryan','Brown','M','engineer','Toronto','1987','2'
'2461','Ann','Williams','F','doctor','Paris','1997','2'
'2547','Mary','Johnson','F','technician','Paris','1989','3'
'2947','Jane','Wilson','F','unemployed','Dresden','1972','10'
'3842','Frances','Bryce','F','translator','Northampton','1980','2'
'4821','Sarah','Green','F','engineer','Paris','1981','1'
```

Numbers such as 634 have all been enclosed in quotes but that does no harm.

(2) One way of doing this is to reverse the name string using the *strrev* function described in Sect. 5.3.5, then use the *explode* function to extract the component before the first space and finally use *strrev* again to return the reverse of it as the value of the function. This gives the following function definition.

```
function findSurname($name){
$namerev=strrev($name);
$arr=explode(" ",$namerev);
return strrev($arr[0]);
}// findSurname
```

19.7.16 Practical Exercise 17

One solution is to add the following lines before line 14.

```
$query2="SELECT * FROM ".$row[0];
$result2=mysql_db_query($DBName,$query2,$Link);
print "<td>".mysql_num_fields($result2)." fields</td>";
print "<td>".mysql_num_rows($result2)." records</td>";
```

19.7.17 Practical Exercise 18

A possible script is given below.

```
<?php
include("sql.php");
$today=date("ymd");

$Link=mysql_connect($sys_dblocalhost,$sys_dbusername,$sys_dbpassword)
  OR die(mysql_error());
$query="SELECT forename,surname,email FROM members1 "
  ."WHERE dateJoined>".$today."-10000 AND numLogs=0";
$result = mysql_db_query($DBName,$query,$Link);
mysql_close($Link);

$subject="Erewhon Trading Services: Special Offer for New Members";
$headers="From: admin@erewhon.org";

while ($row=mysql_fetch_array($result)){
    $mailTo=$row[email];
    $body="Erewhon Trading Company\r\n\r\nDear ".$row[forename]." ".$row[surname]
      ."\r\n\r\nWe have a special promotional offer for new members. "
      ."Just quote discount code nemo1984 with your next order!"
      ."\r\n\r\nA.Noone\r\nFor ETS";
    mail($mailTo,$subject,$body,$headers);
} //while
print "Messages sent!";
?>
```

19.8 Glossary

Words in **bold** are cross-references to other entries in the glossary.

Absolute Address Of A File	The full address of a file on a server, beginning with / signifying the root directory.
Appending To A File	Writing a new record to the end of an existing file
Argument List	A list of all the **arguments** of a function separated by commas and enclosed in parentheses
Argument Of A Function	One of the values passed to a function in an **argument list** (enclosed in parentheses) which determines the value it returns and/or how it behaves
Arithmetic Expression	An expression that evaluates to a number (see Sect. 3.2.1)
Arithmetic Operator	An arithmetic operator is similar to a function, but generally takes the form of a symbol such as + or *. They are either written between two numerical constants or arithmetic expressions (a binary operator) or written in front of a numerical constant or arithmetic expression (a unary operator).
Array	A collection of data values that share a common name
Array Element	A member of an **array**
Array Index	An integer value that indicates the position of an **array element** in an **array** (counting from left to right, starting at zero)
Assignment Statement	A PHP statement that gives a value to a **variable**

(continued)

Associative Array	An **array** comprising a collection of (key, value) pairs
Auto_Increment Field	A field that is automatically given a sequential number by **MySQL** whenever a new **record** is inserted into a **database table**
Backtick	A 'slanting quote' character (`). Used in MySQL to surround names that include embedded spaces, hyphens etc.
Binary Operator	See **arithmetic operator**
Built-In Function	Another name for **system function**
Checkbox	An object on a **webform**
Closing PHP Tag	The combination? > used to end a set of PHP statements
Column Definition	In **MySQL**, a definition of the **data type** and some other information about each **field**
Concatenate Strings	Join two or more strings together
Concatenation Operator	The operator . [dot] used to join two or more strings or string constants
Conditional Expression	An expression used in a number of types of PHP statement that evaluates to a logical value, either TRUE or FALSE
Constant	A fixed data value such as 45.3, TRUE or "dog"
Current Database	In **MySQL** the database to which MySQL commands refer by default
Current Directory	The **directory** on a web server in which a file currently pointed to by a web browser is stored
Current Working Directory	Another term for **current directory**
Data Cleaning	The process of amending or removing data in a database that is incorrect, incomplete, wrongly formatted, or duplicated.
Data Type	In **MySQL**, one of the kinds of data available to the system (e.g. INTEGER, VARCHAR)
Database Table	A principal component of a **relational database**. Each table contains information about a related set of **entities.**
Destination Page	The page to which the web browser should point when the **Submit button** of a **webform** is pressed
Directory	A basic component of the hierarchical file storage on a web server. A directory can hold one or more files or other directories.
Disabled Field	A field on a **webform** which is 'greyed out' and cannot be changed by the user. When the **Submit button** is pressed no value is sent to the **destination page**.
Do…While Statement	A type of PHP statement, described in Chap. 3
Empty Statement	A PHP statement with no content, i.e. a semicolon (;) on its own.
E-Notation	See **exponent notation**
Entity	One of a set of objects of the same kind that are 'described' by the values in a **record** of a **database table**
Escape Sequence	A combination of characters used in a string constant that enables a value to be entered that otherwise could not be. In PHP escape sequences always begin with a backslash character \
Exponent Notation	A notation used to indicate that a number should be multiplied by a power of 10, e.g. 34.5E3 means 34.5 * 10^3, i.e. 34500

(continued)

Extended URL	A web address extended by one or more variable=value pairs, separated by & symbols and preceded by? (See Sect. 10.3)
Field	A column of a **database table**, containing information about a property of all the **records** in the table
Field Name	The name of a **field** in a **database table**
Field Type	The type of a **field** in a **database table** (e.g. INTEGER or DATE)
File Box	An object on a **webform**
File Field	An object on a **webform**
File Pointer	An object that 'points to' an open text file. It is created when the file is opened.
File Protection	The status of a file as being available for reading, writing or execution by different types of people (the third category is not applicable for PHP files)
Folder	Another term for **directory**
For Loop	Another name for a **For statement**
For Statement	A type of PHP statement, described in Chap. 3
Forcing Input Into Lower/Upper Case	Changing a string of characters so that all upper case letters are replaced by the equivalent lower case ones, or vice versa
Foreach Statement	A type of PHP statement, described in Chap. 4
Form Object	A general name for any kind of object on a **webform**
Format Specifier	A component of a **format string**, e.g. %.2f signifying 'output the number rounded to two decimal places'. (See Chap. 6.)
Format String	A **string** used as an **argument** to a printf, sprintf or fprintf function that specifies the format in which the **variables** forming the rest of the **argument list** will be output.
Function Call	As part of a PHP statement, a reference to the name of a function followed by its arguments in parentheses. This causes the function to be evaluated with those values as arguments.
Function Library	In PHP a personal collection of **user-defined functions** that are stored together in one or more **PHP files** and can be inserted into **scripts** using the include or require functions as required
Function Name	The name of a function. In PHP these are the same as **variable names** except that they must not begin with a $ sign.
Global Variable	A **variable** used in a **PHP script** outside a function definition. (See Chap. 8.)
Hidden Field	An object on a **webform**
Home Directory	The directory on a web server in which the home page of the website is stored.
Host Name	The name of the server on which **MySQL** is installed
HTML	An abbreviation for HyperText Markup Language. The language in which web pages are written for display in a web browser
HTML File	A file comprising lines of **HTML**
If Statement	A PHP statement that specifies what action to take if a specified condition is (and, in some cases, is not) met. See Chap. 3
Include Statement	A type of PHP statement, described in Chap. 3

(continued)

Include_Once Statement	A type of PHP statement, described in Chap. 3
Index Value	An integer value used to refer to the position of an element of an **indexed array**
Indexed Array	An **array** with a numerical **index value** or **key**
Inner Join	A type of **Join clause** available in **MySQL**
Internal Function	Another name for **system function**
Join Clause	A component of a MySQL command used to combine records from two or more tables
Key	See **associative array**
Left Outer Join	A type of **Join clause** available in **MySQL**
LIMIT Clause	A component of a **MySQL** command
Link Identifier	A **resource** that holds information about a connection from a **PHP script** to a **MySQL** server
Local Variable	A **variable** used in a function definition. It is completely separate from any **variable** of the same name used outside the definition. (See Chap. 8.)
Log File	A file used to record information about the usage of one or more webpages
Logical Constant	One of the constants TRUE and FALSE
Logical Expression	An expression that evaluates to a logical constant TRUE or FALSE (see Sect. 3.2.8)
Looping Variable	A **variable** used in a **for statement**, a **while** statement or a **do… while** statement
Making A Join	Combining **database tables** using a **Join clause**
Mathematical Constant M_PI	In PHP the constant M_PI which has the value 3.14159265358979323846 (i.e. pi to 20 places of decimals).
Mode (When Opening A File)	A specification of the uses to which the file may be put. In PHP possible modes include read, write and append.
MySQL	A database **query language**. A variant of the language SQL
MySQL Database	A popular type of **relational database**
MySQL Database Management System	A collection of programs that enable information to be stored in, modified in and extracted from a MySQL database.
Open A File	Make a file available for use
Opening PHP Tag	The combination <?php used to begin a set of PHP statements
ORDER BY Clause	A component of a **MySQL** command
Password Field	An object on a **webform**
Path of a File or Directory	The route to a file or directory either from the current directory (relative path) or from the root directory (absolute path). See also **absolute address of a file** and **relative address of a file**
PHP	A programming language used for generating webpages. The main topic of this book.
PHP File	A file with the extension php. It will generally comprise statements written in PHP, but may also comprise a mixture of PHP and HTML or even solely lines of HTML.
PHP Script	A set of PHP statements starting with an **opening PHP tag** and ending with a **closing PHP tag**

(continued)

PHP Scripting Block	A term often used to denote a short **PHP script**
phpMyAdmin	A software package designed to facilitate the management of a **MySQL** database using a web browser
Popup	Another term for **popup window**
Popup Window	A small webpage which appears on top of the currently displayed webpage
Primary Key	A **field** or combination of fields that uniquely identifies each **record** in a **database table**
Print Statement	A type of statement used in a PHP script. It passes a number of characters to the user's web browser, as opposed to directly displaying them on the user's screen
Protection Mode Of A File	A number such as 0776 from which may be extracted the status (readable, writeable, executable or some combination of the three) of a file for the owner who uploaded it to the server, the members of a group set up by the server administrator and the rest of the world
Query Language	A language in which commands that enable information to be stored in, modified in and extracted from a database can be written.
Radio Button	An object on a **webform**
Radio Group	A collection of **radio buttons**
Readonly Field	A field on a **webform** which cannot be changed by the user but will be sent to the **destination page** when the **Submit button** is pressed
Record	A row of a **database table**, containing information about one **entity**.
Recursive Definition	A type of definition in which an entity is defined in terms of a simpler version of itself (such as the definition of **arithmetic expression** in Sect. 3.2.1)
Relational Database	A type of database in which information is stored in a number of two-dimensional structures called **tables**.
Relative Address Of A File	The address of a file on a server, relative to the **current directory**
Require Statement	A type of PHP statement, described in Chap. 3
Require_Once Statement	A type of PHP statement, described in Chap. 3
Reset Button	An object on a **webform**
Resource	A special **variable** holding a reference to an external 'resource' such as a handler for an opened file or a database connection
Right Outer Join	A type of **Join clause** available in **MySQL**
Scalar Variable	Sometimes used to mean a **variable** that is not an **array**
Script	See **PHP script**
Scripting Block	See **PHP scripting block**
Select Box	An object on a **webform**
Sending Page	The page on which information sent in a **webform** to a **destination page** is located
Session Variable	**Variables** that are passed from one webpage to another in sequence
Standalone Function	A function that can be used on its own, rather than on the right-hand side of an **assignment statement**

(continued)

Statement Group	A sequence of PHP statements enclosed in brace characters. Used in **IF statements, While statements, Do…While Statements, For statements** and **Foreach statements**
Static Webpage	A webpage with a fixed content regardless of who is viewing it or when
String	Often used to mean a **string constant**
String Concatenation Operator	An operator written as a dot character. It is placed between two or more **strings** or **string variables** to indicate that they should be joined together.
String Constant	A fixed string of characters such as "hello world"
String Expression	An expression that evaluates to a **string constant** (see Sect. 3.2.5)
String Variable	A **variable** used to hold an ordered sequence of characters such as "hello world"
Sub-Directory	A **directory** contained inside another directory
Submit Button	An object on a **webform**
Switch Statement	A type of PHP statement, described in Chap. 3
System Associative Array	An **associative array** provided automatically by the PHP system, for example $_POST
System Function	A function provided by the implementers of PHP to perform commonly required tasks or tasks that it would not be possible for the PHP programmer to write using the statements in the language.
Text Box	An object on a **webform**
Text Field	An object on a **webform**
Textarea Box	An object on a **webform**
Textarea Field	An object on a **webform**
Tuple	Another term for **record**
Two-Dimensional Array	An **array** of arrays (effectively a two-dimensional table).
Unary Operator	See **arithmetic operator**
User-Defined Function	The same as a **system function** but defined by the user (i.e. the PHP programmer)
Variable	Part of the computer's memory that can be used to store a value.
Variable Name	The name of a **variable**. In PHP these begin with a $ sign.
Variables Passed By Reference	**Variables** can be passed into a **user-defined function** either by reference or by value. The distinction is discussed in Sect. 8.7
Variables Passed By Value	**Variables** can be passed into a **user-defined function** either by reference or by value. The distinction is discussed in Sect. 8.7
Webform	A form displayed on a web page into which the user can enter information
WHERE Clause	A component of a **MySQL** command
While Loop	Another name for a **While statement**
While Statement	A type of PHP statement, described in Chap. 3

Index

M. Bramer, *Web Programming with PHP and MySQL*,
DOI 10.1007/978-3-319-22659-0

Printed in the United States
By Bookmasters